THE PUBLIC-PRIVATE NATURE OF CHARITY LAW

Is charity law a 'private law' or a 'public law' subject? This book maps charity law's relationship to the public law–private law divide, arguing that charity law is best understood as a hybrid (public-private) legal tradition that is constantly seeking to maintain an equilibrium between the protection of the autonomy of property-owning individuals to direct and control their wealth, and the furtherance of competing public visions of the good. Of interest to scholars and charity lawyers alike, *The Public-Private Nature of Charity Law* applies its unique lens both to traditional topics such as the public benefit rule and charity law's rules of standing, and to more contemporary issues such as the co-optation of charitable resources by threatened welfare states and the emergence of social enterprise.

The Public-Private Nature of Charity Law

Kathryn Chan

•HART•
OXFORD • LONDON • NEW YORK • NEW DELHI • SYDNEY

HART PUBLISHING
Bloomsbury Publishing Plc
Kemp House, Chawley Park, Cumnor Hill, Oxford, OX2 9PH, UK

HART PUBLISHING, the Hart/Stag logo, BLOOMSBURY and the Diana logo are trademarks of Bloomsbury Publishing Plc

First published 2016
Paperback edition, 2019

A catalogue record for this book is available from the British Library.

Library of Congress Cataloging-in-Publication Data

Names: Chan, Kathryn, 1976– author.

Title: Thep ublic-private nature of charity law / Kathryn Chan.

Description: Oxford ; Portland, Oregon : Hart Publishing, an imprint of Bloomsbury Publishing Plc, 2016. | based on author's thesis (doctoral - University of Oxford, 2014) issued under title: Th e public-private nature of charity law in England and Canada. | Includes bibliographical references and index.

Identifiers: LCCN 2016024692 (print) | LCCN 2016025230 (ebook) | ISBN 9781782258483 (hardback) | ISBN 9781782258490 (Epub)

Subjects: LCSH: Charity laws and legislation—England. | Charity laws and legislation—Canada.

Classifica tion: LCC K797 .C48 2016 (print) | LCC K797 (ebook) | DDC 346/.0642—dc23

LC record available at https://lccn.loc.gov/2016024692

ISBN: HBK: 978-1-78225-848-3
PB: 978-1-50992-796-8
ePDF: 978-1-78225-850-6
ePub: 978-1-78225-849-0

Typeset by Compuscript Ltd, Shannon

To my father, who loves the law of charities

ACKNOWLEDGEMENTS

This book is based on my doctoral thesis, which was completed at the University of Oxford Faculty of Law. I owe a great debt of gratitude to all those who supported me during that journey, and through the subsequent preparation of this work.

A number of people and institutions deserve particular mention. Professor Mark Freedland was a wise and generous thesis supervisor, and continued to support me in the development of this work when I was no longer under his charge. Professors Paul Craig and Lionel Smith provided constructive and challenging comments at the examination stage. Wolfson College, Oxford, provided an institutional home, and a place of care for my children. The Social Sciences and Humanities Research Council of Canada and the Pierre Elliott Trudeau Foundation provided both financial and institutional support.

I am grateful to the early mentors who helped me to embark on this endeavour: my father, Blake Bromley, Shauna Van Praagh and Jane Glenn of McGill University, and the Honourable Nicholas Kasirer of the Quebec Court of Appeal. I thank Peter Oliver for providing early encouragement to attend Oxford, and for pointing me to some of the theoretical material upon which this thesis is based.

A number of friends and colleagues provided advice, encouragement and comments on various drafts of the work: Freya Kodar, Maneesha Deckha, Mary Synge, Jacob Weinrib, Howie Kislowicz, Kate Glover, Vanessa MacDonnell, Pooja Parmar, Jennifer Beard and Blake Bromley. Roark Lewis, Spencer Chang and Sarah Chaster provided valuable research assistance and editorial support.

I thank the faculty and staff at the University of Victoria Faculty of Law, particularly Dean Jeremy Webber, former Dean Donna Greschner, Associate Dean Elizabeth Adjin-Tettey, and Associate Dean Gillian Calder, for providing me with the space and support to finish this work in the early years of my appointment.

Lastly, and most importantly, I acknowledge the friends and family who sustained me during the length of this project, including my parents, Marion and Blake Bromley. I am deeply grateful to Gus, who made considerable sacrifices (and many dinners) in order for me to be able to complete this work. And I am grateful to, and for, Noah, Molly and Jerome, who made coming home each day a joyful event.

CONTENTS

LIST OF ABBREVIATIONS

BCBCA	British Columbia Business Corporations Act, SBC 2002, c 57
C3	British Columbia community contribution company
CA 1960	Charities Act 1960 (UK)
CA 2006	Charities Act 2006 (UK)
CA 2011	Charities Act 2011 (UK)
CAA (Ont)	Charities Accounting Act, RSO 1990, c C-10
Canadian Charter of Rights and Freedoms	Canadian Charter of Rights and Freedoms, Part I of the Constitution Act, 1982, being Schedule B to the Canada Act 1982 (UK) 1982, c 11
Charity Commission	Charity Commission for England and Wales
CIC	Community interest company (UK)
Companies (AICE) Act 2004	Companies (Audit, Investigations and Community Enterprise) Act 2004 (UK)
Constitution Act 1867	Constitution Act, 1867 (UK), 30 & 31 Vict c 3, as amended, reprinted in RSC 1985, App II, No 5
CRA	Canada Revenue Agency
CTA 1853	Charitable Trusts Act 1853 (16 & 17 Vict c 137)
CTA 1860	Charitable Trusts Act 1860 (23 & 24 Vict c 136)
CTAA 1855	Charitable Trusts Amendment Act 1855 (18 & 19 Vict c 124)
ECHR	European Convention on Human Rights and Fundamental Freedoms
Final Brougham Report (1837)	Report of the commissioners appointed in pursuance of an act of Parliament made and passed in the 5th and 6th years of King William IV, c 71, intituled, 'an act for appointing commissioners to continue the inquiries concerning charities in England and Wales, until the first day of March 1837'.
HMRC	Her Majesty's Revenue and Customs

Hodgson Review (2012)	*Trusted and Independent: Giving Charity back to Charities—a Review of the Charities Act 2006* (by Lord Hodgson of Astley Abbotts)
ITA	Income Tax Act, RSC 1985, c 1 (5th supp), as amended
Nathan Report	*Report of the Committee on the Law and Practice related to Charitable Trusts* (Cmd 8710, 1952) (chaired by Lord Nathan)
OLRC Report	Ontario Law Reform Commission, *Report on the Law of Charities* (Canada, 1996)
Private Action, Public Benefit	*Private Action, Public Benefit: A Review of Charities and the Wider Not-for-Profit Sector* (London: Strategy Unit Report, 2002)
SC on Public Charities (1835)	Report from the Select Committee appointed to examine and consider evidence in the several reports presented to the House from the commissioners appointed to inquire concerning charities in England and Wales, together with the minutes of evidence, HC (1835)
Statute of Elizabeth	Charitable Uses Act 1601 (UK)

TABLE OF CASES

United Kingdom

Canada

Australia

TABLE OF LEGISLATION

United Kingdom

United Kingdom Statutory Instruments

Canadian Statutes

Canadian Statutory Instruments

Other Statutory Instruments

1

The Law of Charities and the Public Law–Private Law Divide

I. Introduction

> In my judgment ... the world of charity is essentially private.[1]
>
> Charitable trusts are public, not private, trusts.[2]

The law of charities has not traditionally displayed a great deal of concern for how its own subject matter should be analysed or understood. Rooted in the practices of England's equitable and ecclesiastical courts, and anchored for centuries to the Preamble of an Elizabethan statute, the charity law tradition of the common law world is most commonly described through a narrative, and thus perceived through a lens, which emphasizes these features of its rich history. The historical lens, as any other, has certain optical effects. It accentuates the judicial provenance of much of the law of charities, and the casuistic quality of the decisions establishing which philanthropic impulses the courts will in perpetuity enforce. It highlights the isolated quality of the law of charities and the way in which it seems to perch, an abiding reminder of equity's historic separateness, somewhere outside the core disciplines of the private law. And it accentuates the extent to which the law of charities is 'common' to the common law world.

The historical lens, then, captures much that is true about the law of charities. However, it also has a number of limitations, the gravity of which has increased in recent years. The lens does not fully capture, for example, the extent to which charity law is now rooted in statutory instruments and controlled by statutory regulators, not only in England and Wales, but also in other parts of the common law world. It fails to convey the degree to which charities, and thus the laws pertaining to charities, are enmeshed in debates about the proper scope of the welfare state and the appropriate ambit of human rights instruments. The historical lens understates the degree of variation between the laws governing charities in different common law jurisdictions, and the effect that different institutional settings

[1] *R (Weaver) v London & Quadrant Housing Trust* [2009] EWCA Civ 587 [155] (Rix LJ dissenting).

[2] *Catholic Care (Diocese of Leeds) v The Charity Commission for England and Wales* [2010] EWHC 520 (Ch) [65].

have had on the core doctrines of the tradition. And it masks a traditional lack of theory about the purpose of charity law, and its place on our legal map.[3]

The project of this book is to address some of these limitations by bringing another 'lens' to bear on the modern law of charities in a number of common law jurisdictions. The chosen lens is that of the public law–private law divide, a central conceptual tool for the organization of legal information. The book examines various aspects of the law of charities in terms of their relationship with the contested categories of 'public law' and 'private law', doing so in the hope of achieving three related goals. The first of these may, in the tradition of Peter Birks, be identified as the *mapping* goal: it is to begin exposing where the law of charities 'sits' in a doctrinal world that can be viewed as conceptually divided into the public and the private. The second, and related, goal of the book is a *comparative* mapping goal: it is to identify the similarities and differences between certain laws governing charities in different jurisdictions, in order to illustrate the range of existing charity law 'maps' within the common law world, and the corresponding range of views about charities to which those maps give effect. Finally, the book has an *evaluative* goal, which is to contribute to the creation of a useful normative discourse about the function of charity law in modern society and the merit of specific charity law rules.

In pursuing these goals, the book makes four central claims. The first claim is that the charity law tradition that evolved in the English Chancery courts (the 'common law charities tradition') was historically a true 'hybrid' of private law and public law, in the sense that it accorded comparable importance to the autonomy interests of benevolent property owners, and to the public interest in properly and effectively administered charity property. The second claim is that the contemporary regimes of charity regulation that have evolved in England and Wales and other common law jurisdictions are also legal hybrids, but in changed and varied senses, which reflect the diverse public interests that have come to bear on the law of charities through the tradition's interaction with tax law, human rights law and modern government welfare policies. The third claim is that although each of these regimes is unique, it is nonetheless possible to identify a general dichotomy between 'civil' and 'tax-based' regimes of charity regulation, based on the public interests that each regulator is mandated to protect. My final

[3] On the under-theorization of charity law, see M Harding, 'What is the Point of Charity Law?' in K Barker and D Jensen (eds), *Private Law: Key Encounters with Public Law* (Cambridge, Cambridge University Press, 2013) 147. A number of recent works have begun to fill these gaps: see, eg, J Garton, *The Regulation of Organised Civil Society* (Oxford, Hart Publishing, 2009), M Turnour, 'Modernising Charity Law: Steps to an Alternative Architecture for Common Law Charity Jurisprudence' in M McGregor-Lowndes and K O'Halloran, *Modernising Charity Law: Recent Developments and Future Directions* (Cheltenham, Edward Elgar, 2010) and M Harding, *Charity Law and the Liberal State* (Cambridge, Cambridge University Press, 2014). There is also a rich literature on the distinctive charity law of the United States, which this book will only touch on. A good starting point is W Powell and R Steinberg (eds), *The Nonprofit Sector: A Research Handbook*, 2nd edn (New Haven, CT, Yale University Press, 2006).

claim is that the varied public interests exerting influence on the law of charities have combined to make charity law an increasingly *public-leaning* hybrid, which development is reflected in the contemporary emergence of 'social enterprise' vehicles that are both increasingly autonomous in character and subject to lighter-touch regulatory regimes.

The public law–private law lens that is applied throughout this book is substantially doctrinal, in the sense that it relies on 'language and concepts that are internal rather than external to law'.[4] Nevertheless, it seeks to expand charity law's self-understanding in ways that require elaboration.[5] Therefore, in what follows, this introduction will examine the concept of the public law–private law divide, its relationship to the law of charities, and the particular account of the divide that will be employed for purposes of this work. Finally, the introduction will outline and explain the structure of the remainder of the book.

II. The Public Law–Private Law Divide: The History of a Concept

The conceptual division of law into public and private, though a relatively recent phenomenon in the common law, has preoccupied jurists since the earliest days of the Western legal tradition. The history of the division has been extensively examined in the literature,[6] and my aim at this point is to provide only a very brief preliminary summary of that literature. For the Romans, the distinction between public law—that concerning the Roman state—and private law—that concerning the well-being of individuals—stood at the forefront of their system of legal classification,[7] although little doctrinal energy was spent delimiting the scope of each legal sphere.[8] With the collapse of the Roman Empire and the ascendancy of feudalism and Germanic law, the distinction lost for a time its practical and intellectual force, medieval society being governed by an assortment of laws deriving from a variety of relationships and sources of authority.[9] Following the revival

[4] Stephen A Smith, 'Taking Law Seriously' (2000) 50 *University of Toronto Law Journal* 241, 255.

[5] For a classic treatment of private law as a 'dynamic, self-understanding enterprise', see E Weinrib, *The Idea of Private Law* (Cambridge, MA, Harvard University Press, 1995). The term 'self-understanding' is also used by Smith: Smith (n 4) 249–50.

[6] See, eg, A Erh-Soon Tay and E Kamenka, 'Public Law-Private Law' in S Benn and G Gaus (eds), *Public and Private in Social Life* (London, Croom Helm, 1983) 67; JH Merryman, 'The Public Law-Private Law Distinction in European and American Law' (1969) 17 *Journal of Public Law* 3; F Pollock, 'The Contact of Public and Private Law' (1923) 1 *CLJ* 255; HF Jolowicz, *Roman Foundations of Modern Law* (Oxford, Clarendon Press, 1957).

[7] J. Inst. 1.1.4. See also D. I.I.I.2.

[8] Jolowicz (n 6) 49–53.

[9] Tay and Kamenka (n 6) 69–70; see also Jolowicz (n 6) 52, calling it a 'modern commonplace' that in medieval times, public and private law were indistinguishable.

of classical Roman legal learning in the twelfth century, however, the public law–private law distinction became foundational to the structure of European law, ultimately underpinning the organization of the continental codes, and the formal separation of civil courts and administrative tribunals in countries such as Germany and France.[10]

England and Wales was much slower than the Continent to develop a 'consciously articulated distinction' between public law and private law.[11] The historical English aversion to the notion of a separate category of public law, traceable back to the twelfth century,[12] was concretized by the Victorian jurist Albert Dicey, who argued in his *Introduction to the Law of the Constitution* that the 'universal subjection of all classes to one law administered by the ordinary courts' was a key element of the rule of law.[13] Despite the various criticisms to which it was subjected, Dicey's defence of formal equality before the law and his criticism of the French system of *droit administratif* is widely credited with having held back the development of a distinct, English public law tradition for almost a century.[14] Dicey's work was also 'remarkably influential' in various of the colonies to which England's common law tradition had spread.[15]

It was during the course of the twentieth century that unique 'public law' and 'private law' traditions developed within the common law world. The rise of a self-conscious 'public law' came first, emerging as a response to the rapid expansion of the welfare state, and concomitant concerns about the dangers of untrammelled bureaucratic power. Within the course of five or six decades, administrative law had gone from 'supposed nonexistence to professional acceptance and respectability' in the United Kingdom, and was developing quickly in other common law jurisdictions.[16] Together with constitutional law, administrative law was soon understood as one of two central pillars of a broader public law tradition. The self-conscious identification of a distinctive *private law* tradition followed (and likely followed from) these public law developments.[17] As public law became more

[10] Jolowicz (n 6) 49.

[11] P Cane, *Administrative Law*, 4th edn (Oxford, Oxford University Press, 2004) 12. See also *O'Reilly v Mackman* [1983] 2 AC 237 (HL) 277.

[12] See Tay and Kamenka (n 6) 73, describing how England's single system of royal courts 'eschewed any division' that might put the King into a special category of law.

[13] AV Dicey, *An Introduction to the Study of the Law of the Constitution*, 10th edn (London, Macmillan Press Ltd, 1959) 193.

[14] M Freedland, 'The Evolving Approach to the Public/Private Distinction in English Law' in Mark Freedland and Jean-Bernard Auby (eds), *The Public Law/Private Law Divide: une entente assez cordiale?* (Oxford, Hart Publishing, 2006) 96–97.

[15] In Canada, see *National Corn Growers Association v Canada (Import Tribunal)* [1990] 2 SCR 1324 [3]; H Arthurs, 'Rethinking Administrative Law: a Slightly Dicey Business' (1979) 17 *Osgoode Hall Law Journal* 1, 4–5. In Australia, see *Chu Kheng Lim v Minister for Immigration* (1992) 176 CLR 1 (HCA) 27.

[16] M Taggart, 'Prolegomenon to an Intellectual History of Administrative Law in the Twentieth Century: the Case of John Willis and Canadian Administrative Law' (2005) 43 *Osgoode Hall Law Journal* 223, 228.

[17] For a compelling account of the emergence of English private law, see D Priel, 'The Political Origins of English Private Law' (2013) 40 *Journal of Law and Society* 481.

dominant, a growing group of private law jurists began to argue that 'property, tort, contract, restitution (and perhaps also trusts) … constituted a conceptually distinct part of the law'.[18]

The development of distinctive 'public law' and 'private law' traditions in the Anglo-Commonwealth world has been paralleled by the development of a sizeable Anglo-Commonwealth literature debating the validity and the function of the public law–private law divide. This literature provides the starting point for this work's analysis of the law of charities, and we will have occasion to examine it more fully in what follows. By way of context, however, it is important to note that the body of literature upon which this book relies has been driven to a large extent by major statutory developments in the UK, which have had the effect of making the distinction between public law and private law an issue of dispositive concern. Principal among these developments has been the introduction, now 30 years past, of a separate procedure for judicial review matters in the UK, built around the concept of a 'public law claim'.[19] The enactment of the UK Human Rights Act 1998, which imposes liability for human rights infractions on a range of 'public authorities', has been equally influential.[20]

This historical context has significantly influenced the shape of recent Anglo-Commonwealth debates over the public law–private law divide. Two characteristics of these debates are particularly worthy of consideration. First, a significant proportion of the early academic commentary on the distinction between public law and private law was written from a 'public law' perspective, and focused either on the appropriateness of having a separate judicial review procedure or of subjecting particular decisions to judicial or human rights review.[21] This focus gave a distinctive hue to the debate,[22] and cast many of the later 'private law' perspectives on the nature of the divide as responses to these public law arguments.[23] Second, the public law-private law literature upon which this book relies, though broadly an Anglo-Commonwealth literature, is oriented towards the structure and concerns of UK law. Various explanations could be offered for this state of affairs,

[18] ibid 490.

[19] The history of these procedural changes is outlined in most English administrative law texts: see, eg, P Craig, *Administrative Law*, 7th edn (London, Sweet & Maxwell, 2012) 836.

[20] Scholarly interest in the public law–private law divide was also driven by the privatization agenda of the government of Margaret Thatcher and the rise of the 'new public management'. See generally Cane, (n 11) 1–7, 11–18; P Cane, 'Accountability and the Public/Private Distinction' in N Bamforth and P Leyland (eds), *Public Law in a Multi-Layered Constitution* (Oxford, Hart Publishing, 2003) 247, 256.

[21] C Harlow, '"Public" and "Private" Law: Definition without Distinction' (1980) 43 *MLR* 241, 250; GS Morris and S Fredman, 'The Costs of Exclusivity: Public and Private Re-examined' [1994] *PL* 69. See also Dawn Oliver, noting in 1999 that 'more attention is paid to defining public law than private law': D Oliver, *Common Values and the Public-Private Divide* (Cambridge, Cambridge University Press 1999) 15.

[22] For an argument that this focus 'distorted' the debate, see N Bamforth, 'The Public Law-Private Law Distinction: A Comparative and Philosophical Approach' in P Leyland and T Woods (eds), *Administrative Law Facing the Future: Old Constraints and New Horizons* (Oxford, Oxford University Press, 1997) 137.

[23] See, eg, G Samuel, 'Public and Private Law: a Private Lawyer's Response' (1983) 46 *MLR* 558.

but one major factor appears to be that the designations 'public law' and 'private law' have fewer dispositive consequences in other common law jurisdictions, and thus attract less judicial and scholarly attention. We shall examine this claim more closely in what follows. For present purposes, it suffices to note that the common law debate over the existence and the validity of the public law–private law divide is centred in the UK.[24] The book will therefore rely heavily on the work of English legal theorists in developing its claims about the relationship between charity law and the respective spheres of public law and private law.

III. Mapping the Law of Charities across the Public Law–Private Law Divide

A. Why Map At All?

As I indicated in the previous section, this book is, initially at least, concerned with mapping. It examines the common law charities tradition through the lens of the public law–private law divide in order to better understand how this tradition stands in relationship to the public law and private law spheres. It examines contemporary regimes of charity regulation through this same lens, and aims to also understand how these regimes relate to the common law and to each other. In these varied, relational senses, the book aims to 'situate' the law of charities on a fundamental doctrinal map.

I argue that this mapping project is one worth pursuing. It is worthwhile despite the common law's well-known aversion to sorting methodology,[25] and despite the notoriously unsystematic character of charity law.[26] Indeed, it may be worthwhile for precisely these reasons. The act of sorting information is valuable because it forces us to evaluate the significance of the information at hand.[27] And the act of sorting *law* is valuable because it tends towards clarity and predictability, two basic requirements of the rule of law.[28] 'A good map', as Stephen Smith observes, will help ensure that like cases are decided alike, and guard against the

[24] The leading Canadian public law texts contain virtually no discussion of the public law–private law divide. Canadian scholarship arguably has a stronger tradition of using the divide as a critical tool: see, eg, Susan B Boyd (ed), *Challenging the Public/Private Divide: Feminism, Law and Public Policy* (Toronto, University of Toronto Press, 1997).

[25] See generally SA Smith, 'A Map of the Common Law' (2004) 40 *Canadian Business Law Journal* 364, 367; N Kasirer, 'English Private Law, Outside-In' (2003) 3 *Oxford University Commonwealth Law Journal* 249, 253.

[26] *Oppenheim v Tobacco Securities Trust Co Ltd* [1951] AC 297 (HL) 307.

[27] Smith (n 25) 365. See also P Birks, *English Private Law* (Oxford, Oxford University Press, 2000) li ('Information which cannot be sorted is not knowledge').

[28] Smith (n 25) 366, 382.

dangers of arbitrariness.[29] These are compelling arguments for applying a sorting methodology to the law of charities, particularly in a jurisdiction like Canada, where administrative discretion has become the hallmark of the field. The project of mapping the law of charities is worthwhile, in sum, because it orients the field towards coherence and justice, and because even if the end result turns out to be unsatisfying, we will have learned something important through the mapping process itself.

Despite embracing a sorting methodology, however, I do not start from the position that charity law, or even the individual doctrines and procedures that constitute it, are straightforwardly amenable to a binary classificatory scheme. Such a position is neither intuitive nor consistent with the literature that exists, and would tend to produce an overly simple map.[30] I do not intend to argue, therefore, that the law of charities is exclusively a 'public law' or 'private law' discipline. Rather, I will suggest that charity law lies somewhere within the contested border region between public law and private law, and that it partakes in significant ways of each. This public–private *hybridity*, I claim, is an essential characteristic of the law of charities. By paying attention to this characteristic, we may improve both our understanding of the function of charity law in modern society and our ability to evaluate specific charity law rules.

In selecting hybridity as the key *motif* animating its doctrinal map of the law of charities, this book stakes out a distinctive position in broader debates over legal mapping.[31] It is a position that acknowledges law's complexity, but asserts the ability of legal maps to help us understand both the interrelationship between legal concepts and processes of legal change. The focus on hybridity also distinguishes the book from an existing body of doctrinal scholarship examining the relationship between public law and private law. In recent years, scholars have shown an increasing interest in identifying areas where public law and private law doctrines 'intersect', and debating the merits of their cross-fertilization. Some, like Matthew Conaglen, have conducted detailed analyses of the similarities and differences between specific legal rules.[32] A substantial number of commentators have addressed the impact of constitutional principles on substantive, private law doctrines,[33] while a smaller number have considered how 'private law' principles might flow the other way.[34]

[29] ibid; see also Kasirer (n 25) 262.

[30] On the dangers of overly simple maps, see S Waddams, *Dimensions of Private Law: Categories and Concepts in Anglo-American Legal Reasoning* (Cambridge, Cambridge University Press, 2003) 2.

[31] For an overview of these debates, see J Weinrib, 'What Can Kant Teach Us about Legal Classification?' (2010) 23 *Canadian Journal of Law and Jurisprudence* 203.

[32] M Conaglen, 'Public-private Intersection: Comparing Fiduciary Conflict Doctrine and Bias' [2008] *PL* 58.

[33] See, eg, the collection of essays in D Friedmann and D Barak-Erez (eds), *Human Rights in Private Law* (Oxford, Oxford University Press, 2001).

[34] See M Moran, 'The Mutually Constitutive Nature of Public and Private Law' in A Robertson and Hang Wu Tang (eds), *The Goals of Private Law* (Oxford, Hart Publishing, 2009).

While this body of literature has unquestionably enriched our understanding of the interrelationship between public law and private law, the language of 'intersection' and 'cross-fertilization' tends to reinforce the picture of a binary legal world in which legal doctrines, procedures and institutions have a single, or at least primary, site of belonging. Thus, within Conaglen's comparative analysis of fiduciary conflict doctrine and bias, the former doctrine is clearly identified as a private law doctrine, although one that may share certain characteristics with the public law of bias.[35] Similarly, in Mayo Moran's work, discrimination law is clearly understood to be a public law subject, although one that may draw on private law concepts of personhood to give it substance.[36] Public law and private law are 'mutually constitutive' within this picture, but specific legal doctrines remain situated within either one or the other sphere.

It may indeed be the case, as this body of work suggests, that most doctrines, procedures and institutions have a single or primary site of belonging within either the public law or private law sphere. This question, while important, is far beyond the scope of the present work. My more limited claim is that whatever the answer to this question, it is also possible to envisage public and private colliding *within* a singular legal doctrine, procedure or institution, such that that doctrine, procedure or institution could not safely be said to have a primary site of belonging in *either* the public law or private law sphere. The question that such a doctrine, procedure or institution would naturally raise is how the subject's identity is divided between its constituent private and public elements.[37] While the concepts of cross-fertilization and intersection might assist in this inquiry, the concept of hybridity would seem to provide the most appropriate analytical and evaluative tool.

The use of hybridity as an academic discourse has become current in only the last three or four decades.[38] Today, however, the concept of a hybrid—a 'thing composed of mixed or incongruous elements'[39]—plays an important role in a variety of disciplines, ranging from genetics to cultural studies to anthropology. Hybridity theory depends on the 'prior assumption of … fixed boundaries', but often seeks to problematize and destabilize these boundaries, and to explore the border zones that surround them.[40] In the context of cultural and literary studies, hybridity and the related concepts of métissage, creolization, and border identity are invoked primarily to explain 'new' hybrid forms—the 'increasingly mixed sites' of contemporary belonging and affiliation that exist in modern societies.[41]

[35] Conaglen (n 32).

[36] Moran (n 34) 31. As we shall see, however, Moran was one of the first to recognize the hybrid nature of the law of charitable trusts: see n 48 below.

[37] S Simon, 'Cultural and Textual Hybridity' (2001) 2 *Across Languages and Cultures* 217, 226.

[38] Pieterse traces the thematization of hybridity back to the 1980s: see N Pieterse, 'Hybridity, So What?: the Anti-Hybridity Backlash and the Riddles of Recognition' (2001) 18 *Theory, Culture & Society* 219, 222–23.

[39] Katherine Barber (ed), *Canadian Oxford Dictionary* (Oxford, Oxford University Press, 1998) 693 ('hybrid').

[40] Pieterse (n 38) 220, 226.

[41] Simon (n 37).

However, scholars also refer to 'existing or, so to speak, old hybridity', which involves 'different ways of looking at historical and existing cultural and institutional arrangements'.[42] According to Pieterse, this is 'a more radical and penetrating angle that suggests not only that things are no longer the way they used to be, but were never really the way they used to be, or used to be viewed'.[43]

The concept of hybridity, as developed in the field of cultural and literary studies, provides a useful conceptual tool for this book's mapping goals. By simultaneously acknowledging and destabilizing perceived boundaries, hybridity theory creates space for the mapping of a legal discipline, such as the law of charities, which does not have a primary site of belonging in either the public law or private law sphere. Hybridity theory also offers a promising source of language and imagery for this book's evaluative goal of contributing to a useful normative discourse about the place of charity law in modern society. Literary studies scholars sometimes describe hybrids as 'locuses of conflict' between differing values and ideas,[44] which can display 'the lack of total reciprocity between signifying systems'.[45] Hybrid *texts*, for their part, are described as being characterized by dissonances, disparate vocabulary and a lack of cohesion, which characteristics are attributable to differences in the prevalent assumptions of their composite linguistic cultures.[46] Literary studies scholars also describe hybridization as a *dynamic* phenomenon, and suggest that the subject components of the hybrid form may be alternately dominant and subsidiary.[47] We will see that many of these descriptors of hybrid literary phenomena are equally apt descriptors of the law of charities and its constituent doctrines, procedures and institutions.

B. Why This Mapping Tool?

The more difficult question, in many ways, is whether the public law–private law divide is the best foundation upon which to build a map of the law of charities. Previous scholarship has considered the relationship between charity law and the respective categories of public law and private law, and suggested that it is worthy of further study.[48] However, it is not the only possible sorting tool.

[42] Pieterse (n 38) 221.
[43] ibid.
[44] C Schaffner and B Adab, 'The Idea of the Hybrid Text in Translation: Contact as Conflict' (2001) 2 *Across Languages and Cultures* 167.
[45] Simon (n 37) 220–21.
[46] Simon (n 37) 217; B Niall, 'Interpreting the Objectively Strange and the Strangely Objective: Hybrid Texts in Social Discourse and in the Social Sciences' (2001) 2 *Across Languages and Cultures* 251; Schaffner and Adab (n 44) 175.
[47] Schaffner and Adab (n 44) 168–69; Alexis Nouss, 'The Butterfly and the Translator: Reflections on Hybrid Textuality' (2001) 2 *Across Languages and Cultures* 227.
[48] The first scholar to explore these relationships appears to have been Harold Hanbury, a leading authority on the English law of equity: see HG Hanbury, *Essays in Equity* (Oxford, Clarendon

Maurice Cullity, for example, has examined the ways in which the law of charities is a 'hybrid' of several distinct legal disciplines, including trust law, corporate law and tax law.[49] A more recent co-authored work categorizes the rules governing charities in several jurisdictions according to an identified set of 'core functions' of charity law.[50] All of these mapping schemes may enhance our understanding of the law of charities and improve the law's coherence and predictability. Nevertheless, there are several compelling arguments for organizing our thinking about the law of charities around the public law–private law divide.

The first reason why the public law–private law divide is an appropriate sorting tool for the law of charities is simply that the divide represents a fundamental 'organizational claim' of the law.[51] The relationship between a given classificatory scheme and the public law–private law divide will therefore often loom as a question, even if it is a question the classifier wishes to avoid. Peter Birks's ambitious project to map all of the core subjects of the common law according to a broadly Romanist model aptly illustrates this reality. As Birks was careful to point out in the preface to *English Private Law*, the object of that work was not to investigate the 'boundary disputes' between private law and public law, but rather to decipher the internal structure of each 'sub-unity' of the law, and articulate its principal components.[52] Even before the publication of a companion volume entitled *English Public Law*, however, the most basic division that Birks's taxonomy communicated was precisely that between public law and private law.[53] While charity law's location within section G (Property for Purposes) of chapter 4 (Property (General Principles)) of Birks's scheme is undoubtedly significant, therefore, the

Press, 1934) 93–101. The lens has been applied, to varying extents, by several authors since then: see, eg, M Freedland, 'Charity Law and the Public/Private Distinction' in C Mitchell and SR Moody (eds), *Foundations of Charity* (Oxford, Hart Publishing, 2000); M Moran, 'Rethinking Public Benefit: The Definition of Charity in the Era of the Charter' in J Phillips, B Chapman and D Stevens (eds), *Between State and Market: Essays on Charities Law and Policy in Canada* (Montreal, McGill-Queen's University Press, 2001); A Parachin, 'Regulating Philanthropy: Is Charity Public or Private?' (CBA National Charity Law Symposium, Toronto, 4 May 2012). I briefly considered the lens in an earlier work, suggesting at that time that there were reasons to resist the view that the common law of charities was public: K Chan, 'Taxing Charities/Imposer les Organismes de Bienfaisance: Harmonization and Dissonance in Canadian Charity Law' (2007) 55 *Canadian Tax Journal* 481, 541. In the American context, see E Brody, 'Respecting Foundation and Charity Autonomy: How Public is Private Philanthropy?' (2010) 85 *Chicago-Kent Law Review* 571. Moran was possibly the first to identify the charitable trust as a 'hybrid of public and private relationships': ibid 257. However, her piece did not analyse these relationships in detail.

[49] M Cullity, 'The Charitable Corporation: a 'Bastard' Legal Form Revisited' (2001) 17 *The Philanthropist* 17.

[50] M McGregor-Lowndes, K O'Halloran and K Simon, *Charity Law and Social Policy: National and International Perspectives on the Functions of the Law Relating to Charities* (Dordrecht, Springer, 2008). The identified core functions are protection, policing, mediation and adjustment, and support.

[51] Smith (n 4) 250–51.

[52] Birks (n 27) xxxvi.

[53] ibid xxxvi–xxxix, asserting that the whole law is 'either public law or private law'.

more fundamental implication of the *Private Law* and *Public Law* volumes is that the law of charities belongs to the private law sphere.[54]

A second and related reason for applying the public law-private law lens to the law of charities is that public law and private law provide 'two distinct sets of starting points' for thinking about legal regulation.[55] While private law is concerned with rendering intelligible the immediate connection between two litigating parties, public law casts its gaze over a wider group of persons that are indirectly connected through politically determined goals.[56] And while private law operates against a general backdrop of freedom, public law demands that the actions of its subjects be grounded in a legal rule:

> For private persons, the rule is that you may do anything you choose which the law does not prohibit … But for public bodies the rule is opposite, and so of another character altogether. It is that any action to be taken must be justified by positive law.[57]

One consequence of these distinct starting points is that the labels 'public' and 'private' have tremendous rhetorical force in charity regulation, as they do in other legal spheres. To say that charities are 'private' is generally to imply that neither government nor the broader community may normally interfere in their governance or in the expenditure of their resources without substantial justification. To label charities as 'public', on the other hand, is to suggest the opposite—namely, that the actions taken by charities to define their benefiting community and distribute the charitable resources they hold must normally be authorized and controlled by rules of law.

A third reason for using the public law–private law divide as a sorting tool for the law of charities is that binary public/private classifications are increasingly being used in legal regimes with which the law of charities intersects. The English[58] Civil Procedure Rules, for example, provide that an institution will be amenable to judicial review if it acts or fails to act 'in relation to the exercise of a public function'.[59] The Human Rights Act 1998, the Equality Act 2006, and the Companies Act 2006 are on a growing list of UK legislative instruments that impose obligations and liabilities on institutions that perform 'functions of a public nature'.[60]

[54] See ibid [4.485] and onwards. Charities also receive a very brief mention in the Private Law chapter on succession, and in the Public Law sections on offences against property and Standards of Review and Human Rights in English law: see [7.170] (wills); [7.144], [26.33].

[55] Freedland (n 14) 123.

[56] Weinrib (n 5) 8.

[57] *R v Somerset County Council, ex p Fewings* [1995] 1 All ER 513, 524 (Laws LJ). See also M Taggart, 'The Province of Administrative Law Determined?' in *The Province of Administrative Law* (Oxford, Hart Publishing, 1997) 5. In Canada, see *Reference re Provincial Judges* [1997] 3 SCR 3 [10].

[58] For ease of reference the term 'English' is used throughout to describe the law in England and Wales.

[59] CPR 54.1(2)(a)(ii).

[60] Human Rights Act 1998 (UK), s 6; Equality Act 2006 (UK), s 52; Companies Act 2006 (UK), s 54. For a more complete list, see H Woolf, J Jowell, A Le Sueur, C Donnelly and I Hare, *De Smith's Judicial Review*, 7th edn (London, Sweet & Maxwell, 2013) [3–072].

If the relationship between these instruments and the English charitable sector was at one time largely theoretical, this is clearly no longer the case. Claimants in England and Wales have relied on their provisions to argue that charities must give a fair hearing to those affected by their decisions, or protect their legitimate expectations, or respect their human rights.[61]

Public/private designations have historically been less prominent in the statutory lexicons of other jurisdictions, as I have already suggested, and have therefore played a smaller dispositive role in those jurisdictions. While the UK's reformed judicial review procedure is built around the concept of a 'public law claim', for example, the jurisdiction-defining concept in Australia's federal judicial review procedure is that of a 'decision of an administrative character', defined in terms of the source of the decision maker's powers.[62] However, even in jurisdictions where other terms are used to demarcate the limits of judicial review and human rights law, the public–private binary may find legal expression. The terms 'public' and 'private' operate in a variety of specialized regulatory regimes,[63] and in Canada the terms 'public law' and 'private law' play a crucial role in delineating the particular composition of the bijural legal tradition of the province of Quebec.[64] Notions of the public and the private may also exert an *indirect* influence: this has been the case with the application provision of the Canadian Charter of Rights and Freedoms, as we shall see in Chapter 6. While not all jurisdictions rely on public/private classifications to the extent of English law, therefore, there seem to be few if any jurisdictions in respect of whose positive law the public–private binary is entirely without influence.

A fourth and final reason why the public law–private law divide is an appropriate sorting tool for the law of charities is that the identity of charity law has *always* been significantly divided between its public and private elements. Indeed, looking back at the history of the law in this area, it can plausibly be claimed that the charitable trust was a public–private hybrid from its very inception, in the sense that it represented the adaptation of a private law institution in the service of a perceived public interest. As historical accounts of trust law point out, medieval landowners and their lawyers developed the legal predecessor of the trust in order to 'evade certain incidents associated with the transmission of land to their heirs under the rules of common law, and to have a wider power of disposition of land than these common-law rules permitted'.[65] The trust was designed as a facilitative institution

[61] *Scott v National Trust* [1998] 2 All ER 705 (Ch); *R (Baldwin) v Charity Commissioners for England and Wales* (2001) 33 HLR 48 (QB) [55]. See also J Garton, 'The Judicial Review of the Decisions of Charity Trustees' [2006] *Trust Law International* 160, 178–79.

[62] Administrative Decisions (Judicial Review) Act 1977 (Aus) s 3; see also Judiciary Act 1903 (Cth) s 39B(1), extending judicial review to decisions made by an 'officer of the Commonwealth'. In Canada, the situation is similar: see Federal Court Act, RSC 1970, c 10 (2nd Supp) s 2(1).

[63] See, eg, Privacy Act 1993 (NZ) s 96C; Trade-marks Act, RSC 1985, c T-13 s 9.

[64] *St-Hilaire v Canada* [2001] 4 FC 289 (CA) [40].

[65] MR Chesterman, *Charities, Trusts, and Social Welfare* (London, Weidenfeld and Nicolson, 1979) 3. See also LA Sheridan and GW Keeton, *Keeton & Sheridan's The Modern Law of Charities*, 4th edn (Chichester, Barry Rose, 1992).

for the transfer and usage of property, which would maximize a property owner's autonomy to determine how he or she would give that property away.[66] In this sense, the trust has always been anchored firmly to the law of property, one of the 'twin pillars' of private law.[67]

Since its early beginnings, however, the apparatus of the trust was also employed to facilitate gifts of property for pious causes, and eventually charitable objects.[68] In cases where the trust was so employed, the institution adapted itself to reflect the perceived public interest in such uses of property. As Gareth Jones notes, extensive privileges and protections were granted to charitable trusts in the sixteenth and seventeenth centuries, to ensure that philanthropic efforts were not 'frustrated by the formalism and rigidity of the common law'.[69] Charitable trusts were not bound by any statute of limitations until 1833, and were exempted from most aspects of the rule against perpetuities.[70] In cases where the perceived public interest in the charitable use of property was seen to be under threat, the Crown and the Chancellor would also step in to ensure the property's proper management, or to direct it to a more suitable charitable use. The courts described this jurisdiction over the administration of charity property in public law terms from early days. In the eighteenth-century case of *AG v Downing*, for example, Lord Wilmot rejected an argument that the court should not enforce a charitable trust because the trustees had predeceased the settlor, stressing that the court's role in administering and protecting charitable trusts was mandated by the Constitution itself:

> The individuals, named as trustees, are only the nominal instruments to execute that intention. And if they fail, either by death, or being under disability to act, or refusing to act, *the constitution has provided a trustee*. The King, as *parens patriæ*, has the superintending power over all charities, abstracted from the Statute of 43 Eliz and antecedent to it, 2 P Wms 119; and that paternal care and protection is delegated to this Court.[71]

In the leading nineteenth-century case of *Moggridge v Thackwell*, Lord Eldon again described the role of the courts and the Crown in administering property dedicated to charitable purposes in public law terms, calling it 'the doctrine of the constitution of the country'.[72]

It appears, then, that there are compelling arguments for seeking to bring the public law-private law lens to bear on the contemporary law of charities in

[66] S Gardner, *An Introduction to the Law of Trusts*, 2nd edn (Oxford, Oxford University Press, 2003) 29.

[67] Birks (n 27) xxxviii. This is indeed where it fits within Birks's scheme: see sections III(4)(D) and (G).

[68] Chesterman (n 65) 4.

[69] GH Jones, *History of the Law of Charity, 1532–1827* (Cambridge, Cambridge University Press, 1969) 59.

[70] H Picarda, *The Law and Practice Relating to Charities*, 4th edn (London, Bloomsbury Professional, 2010) 496.

[71] *A-G v Lady Downing* (1767) Wilmot 1, 97 ER 1 (Ch) 24.

[72] *Moggridge v Thackwell* (1803) 7 Ves 36, 32 ER 15 (Ch) 34. See also *Morice v Bishop of Durham* (1804) 9 Ves 399 (Ch) 539; on appeal (1805) 10 Ves 522.

common law jurisdictions. The centrality of the divide as an organizational claim of Western law, the important dispositive implications it carries, and the long-standing identification of charity law with both the public law and private law spheres all suggest that this is a project worth pursuing. At the same time, legitimate concerns might be raised about a proposal to analyse and compare complex regimes of charity regulation from the perspective of the public law–private law divide. An initial concern relates to the potentially vast scope of the project; the final part of this introduction seeks to address this concern by clarifying the book's limited ambit. A more serious concern, as I have already indicated, is that people 'mean different things' when they talk about the public law–private law divide.[73] The risk of divergent meanings increases when one starts to talk about multiple jurisdictions.[74] Before outlining the book's comparative hypothesis, therefore, this introduction will offer a working account, for the purposes of this book, of how the public law and private law spheres are constituted, and how they are distinguished.

IV. Understanding the Public Law–Private Law Divide

As the ever-expanding literature on the topic attests, the concept of the public law–private law divide has generated rather more controversy than consensus among the academy, the Bar and the Bench. Two debates dominate the modern literature. The first concerns the very existence of the public law–private law divide, and its value as a legal tool.[75] The second concerns the *nature* of the divide, and the basis or bases upon which a distinction between public law and private law can properly or usefully be drawn.[76] Competing accounts of the boundary between public law and private law continue to be put forward, as scholars aim to construct a theory of the divide that explains the modern law.

The present project is not focused on entering this theoretical debate, so much as engaging with its key lines of argument and applying them to the charity law domain. It is not my intention to articulate a 'new' theory of the public law–private law divide in this introduction, nor to make essentialist claims about the nature of either legal sphere to a greater extent than necessary. Rather, my objective is to review the main currents of the Anglo-Commonwealth literature on the public law–private law divide, and to extract from that literature a theory of the

[73] Cane (n 20) 275.

[74] *Re Norway's Application* [1990] 1 AC 723 (HL) 802–03, cited in Woolf and others (n 60) [3-001] ('the identification of public law matters differs from country to country, sometimes in minor respects and sometimes in major respects').

[75] Samuel (n 23); Harlow (n 21); Oliver (n 21).

[76] Bamforth (n 22) 140; W Lucy, 'What's Private about Private Law' in Andrew Robertson and Tang Hang Wu (ed), *The Goals of Private Law* (Oxford, Hart Publishing, 2009) 47.

divide that will provide useful insights into the law of charities. The exercise of extraction will evidently involve the making of a number of normative choices. However, I proceed on the basis that the public law–private law divide is what Brian Tamanaha would call a 'non-falsifiable' concept: it provides a vocabulary and a framework for understanding and organizing legal information, but is not, in itself, prone to proof or disproof. Such a non-falsifiable concept, as Tamanaha points out, is best understood in terms of its *usefulness*, and its use value is 'a function of the purposes for which it is constructed'.[77] After providing a brief overview of the contemporary Anglo-Commonwealth literature on the public law–private law divide, therefore, my aim will be to identify an account of the divide that is adequate to sustain the book's mapping and evaluative goals.

A. Competing Theories

If there is any point on which scholars of the public law–private law divide are unanimous, it is that there is some level of operational, descriptive distinction between public law and private law. The divide represents one of the law's fundamental 'organizational claims', as I have already indicated, such that a number of central common law phenomena are routinely explained in terms of their relationship with one domain, and their non-relationship with the other.[78] Thus, jurists commonly describe the core disciplines of constitutional law and administrative law as 'public law' disciplines, while property law, tort law and contract law are understood to fall within the 'private law' domain. Other legal subjects fit less easily with this nomenclature. Nevertheless, even those who criticize the public law–private law distinction most vociferously accept that it is in fact used to draw divisions within the law.[79] At the very least, the terms 'public law' and 'private law' may be said to describe the law's self-understanding of certain paradigmatic legal rules, which govern relations between individuals and the state, on the one hand, and relations between individuals, on the other.

If jurists are agreed on the existence of an operational public law–private law divide, however, they have also subjected it to trenchant criticism.[80] Many of these critiques reflect the ever-increasing difficulties of distinguishing public and private law in practice. The coherence of the idea of a *single*, descriptive public law–private law divide has been undermined by the growing number of legal regimes and

[77] B Tamanaha, 'A Non-Essentialist Version of Legal Pluralism' (2000) *Journal of Law and Society* 296, 300, citing B Bix, 'Conceptual Questions in Jurisprudence' (1995) 1 *Legal Theory* 465. See also C Stone, 'Corporate Vices and Corporate Virtues: Do Public/Private Distinctions Matter?' (1982) 130 *University of Pennsylvania Law Review* 1441, 1442 ('A concept has a valid place, as long as it can germinate good coherent insights').

[78] Lucy (n 75) 49.

[79] C Sampford, 'Law, Institutions and the Public/Private Divide' (1991) 20 *Federal Law Reports* 185, 187; Oliver (n 21) 1; Harlow (n 21).

[80] See again Sampford (n 79); Oliver (n 21); Harlow (n 21).

contexts in which terms such as 'public law', 'private law' and 'public function' play a dispositive role.[81] In addition, critics allege, the hybridization of our institutional and functional arrangements has compromised any capacity that the descriptive public law–private law divide once had to explain or categorize modern laws and institutions.[82] In a world where government entities are being corporatized, public utilities are being privatized, and government services are being contracted out, the descriptive limits of binary public–private classifications are becoming increasingly evident.

With the growing consensus about the limited *descriptive* capacity of a binary 'public law–private law' framework, the debate around the public law–private law divide has shifted significantly to the divide's *conceptual* function of evaluating, directing and nurturing operational rules.[83] This shift has raised another set of issues regarding the divide's normative basis: are the public law and private law spheres each concerned with protecting distinct values, and if so, which values does each sphere protect? Neither of these questions has elicited a clear consensus. Dawn Oliver, perhaps the most notable sceptic of the usefulness of the divide, claims that a common set of 'key values' underlies *all* legal rules and principles, whether these rules are conventionally classified as public law or private law.[84] The opposing viewpoint, most prominently articulated by Peter Cane, claims that there *is* a normative or values-based public law–private law divide, which can be maintained even in the boundary areas where the descriptive divide is of little use.[85] The task of legal regulation, on this account, is to strike a balance between the demands of competing public law and private law values in the context of particular social activities.[86]

For those that defend the existence of a normative public law–private law divide, the challenge remains of identifying the values associated with each pole. Scholars have responded to this challenge in a variety of ways, which generally reflect the particular 'side' of the divide from which they write. Private law theorists, many of whom have been concerned to defend private law from being understood in terms of external goods or ends, have premised 'internalist' accounts of the private law on 'the normative primacy of individual personality',[87] and associated the private law sphere with the values of autonomy, privacy, freedom and consent.[88] Public law theorists, who have been concerned to protect the identity of public law in the face

[81] See Taggart (n 57) 4; Oliver (n 21) 14.
[82] Cane (n 20) 248; Oliver (n 21) 12.
[83] For an early example of this focus, see Stone (n 77) 1442–43.
[84] D Oliver, 'The Underlying Values of Public and Private Law' in M Taggart (ed,) *The Province of Administrative Law* (Oxford, Hart Publishing, 1997) 217; Oliver (n 21) ch 3. The values that Oliver identifies are individual dignity, autonomy, respect, status and security.
[85] Cane (n 20) 274–75. Cane relies heavily on the work of Günther Teubner in developing his argument: see G Teubner, 'After Privatization? The Many Autonomies of Private Law' (1998) 51 *CLP* 393.
[86] ibid 275.
[87] See, eg, A Brudner, *The Unity of the Common Law* (Berkeley, CA, University of California Press, 1997) 13.
[88] Sampford (n 78) 190–91.

of deregulatory and privatizing trends, have variously associated the public law sphere with the values of openness, fairness, participation, impartiality, accountability and rationality.[89] Rather less common law scholarship is expressly directed to the question of how public law and private law values are divided from each other and how they interrelate. Ernest Weinrib's important account distinguishes private law from 'other legal orderings' on the basis of the distinct justificatory structures and normative bases of corrective and distributive justice.[90] However, there are competing accounts of the divide's overarching normative basis, one of which (to which we will return) frames the values-based dichotomy between public law and private law in terms of the law's relationship with the respective spheres of individual project pursuit and collective project pursuit.

Within the common law literature, then, the public law–private law divide remains a deeply contested concept. To the extent that the scholarship evidences any consensus over the divide's existence and nature, it seems to be limited to the 'platitude' that there is 'no single, comprehensive, and compelling distinction between "public" and "private".'[91] This seemingly modest consensus over what the divide is *not* has proved productive, however, for it has encouraged the identification and mapping of the divide's plural meanings and manifestations. Mark Freedland's work, for example, has highlighted that the public law–private law divide exists in multiple legal dimensions.[92] In one dimension, it might serve to characterize a project, function or institution in terms of whether it attracts the regulatory impulses of private law or public law. In another, it might serve as a tool for characterizing processes of adjudication and regulation. In yet another dimension, the public law–private law divide might be used to characterize substantive rules or doctrines in terms of their relationship to each pole.[93] A multidimensional public law–private law divide is admittedly a complex analytical tool. However, Freedland's work holds out the possibility that we might improve our understanding of an area of legal doctrine by breaking that doctrine down into its constituent elements, and analysing the relative strength of public law and private law thinking within each individual element.

Recent scholarship has also improved our understanding of the *plural* nature of the divide. William Lucy has made important contributions in this regard, identifying four general versions of the public–private distinction that have been formulated outside the legal system, but also have a life within it.[94] Two of these

[89] See Taggart (n 57) 3, and the sources cited therein.

[90] Weinrib (n 5), in particular s 1.7. See also the discussion in Lucy (n 75) 52–58, and E Weinrib, 'Legal Formalism' (1988) 97 *Yale Law Journal* 949.

[91] W Lucy, 'Private and Public: Some Banalities about a Platitude' in C MacAmhlaigh, C Michelon and N Walker (eds), *After Public Law* (Oxford, Oxford University Press, 2013) 217.

[92] Freedland (n 14) 108.

[93] ibid.

[94] Lucy (n 91) 63. Lucy acknowledges that his list of versions may not be exhaustive. The two that are not considered here—the distinction between public and private goods, and the distinction between the realm of law/politics and the realm of the family/household—may also resonate in the law of charities.

versions are particularly relevant to the present work on the law of charities. The first distinguishes between the realm of the state, on the one hand, and the realm beyond or free from the state, on the other.[95] This version of the public–private distinction has multiple, specific analogues in contemporary law, coming into play when courts seek to determine whether an act is properly covered by a human rights instrument or is subject to judicial review.[96] Even the state–non-state distinction is associated with multiple doctrinal tests of publicness, however, and jurists evince a level of disquiet with each. According to Lucy, this disquiet reflects our suspicion 'that not all that is meaningfully public is covered by these two approaches, and that not all they relegate to the non-public realm is meaningfully private'.[97]

The disquiet we feel about the first version of the distinction, Lucy asserts, can be explained by the strength and 'gravitational pull' of a second. This second way of distinguishing public from private, which dates back to Roman law, is to contrast 'matters of general concern' with 'matters of individual concern'.[98] A significant feature of this idea, Lucy notes, is that it may be used in a variety of ways: the contrast may plausibly be between *almost all* (public) and *some* (private), or between *many* (public) and *one or few* (private). An equally significant feature of the distinction is that it is not premised upon the existence of the state. On the contrary, the distinction between matters of general concern and matters of individual concern specifically envisages 'public concerns and interests that can be conceived independently of the state' and thus refutes the common assumption that 'anything of public or collective interest must *ipso facto* involve the state or be of state interest'.[99] These and other general versions of the public–private distinctions may be in play in our thinking about specific legal doctrines, Lucy concludes, and each version can destabilize the others.[100]

B. A Project-based Account for Mapping the Law of Charities

The rich and disputatious literature on the public law–private law divide provides a number of different lenses through which one might analyse and evaluate legal doctrine. All of these lenses serve a function, and it does not seem inherently problematic that several accounts of the divide could coexist.[101] From the perspective of the law of charities, however, certain narratives about the distinction between public and private have special resonance. I will adopt and elaborate upon aspects

[95] ibid 74.
[96] ibid 76.
[97] ibid 77.
[98] ibid 67.
[99] ibid 70. Lucy states that this version of the distinction has particular resonance in judicial deliberations over the charitable nature of a trust.
[100] ibid 80.
[101] Lucy (n 76) 74.

of these narratives in what follows, beginning with the claim that there is a values-based dichotomy between public law and private law, the most useful account of which for purposes of analysing the law of charities is an account framed in terms of the law's relationship with the respective spheres of individual project pursuit and collective project pursuit.

The claim that the public law and private law spheres should be understood in terms of the value they respectively accord to collective project pursuit and individual project pursuit was originally made by Nigel Simmonds, in the context of an article aimed at defending private law from public law's distributive and aggregative perspectives.[102] In the article, Simmonds describes the distinction between public law and private law as 'the expression of a deep tension within our political aspirations':

> On the one hand is the value we place upon individual project pursuit: the freedom of the individual to formulate and execute his or her own plans and projects without regard to the value or disvalue placed upon the content of those plans and projects by others. On the other hand is our recognition of the contingency of social formations and the impossibility of wholly abdicating responsibility for the overall character of our own society. Such recognition leads us to the value of collective project pursuit: our collective freedom and responsibility to determine, through appropriate mechanisms, the broad structural features of our own society.[103]

Private law is the law of individual project pursuit, according to Simmonds, while public law protects the projects of the collectivity and regulates the powers exercised on its behalf.[104]

Simmonds's work on the tension between individual and collective project pursuit has been picked up and supported by William Lucy, who has sought to articulate the nature of the spaces where each of these forms of project pursuit dominates in a liberal democracy.[105] There is a certain realm, Lucy asserts, within which liberalism places great value on the ability of individuals to author their own lives, 'independently of the directives of the community'.[106] Lucy does not define this realm, but asserts that it includes our choices about where we work, whether we have a family, what we consume, and the nature of our emotional and sexual lives.[107] Liberalism is committed to protecting the conditions of individual autonomy within this realm of 'private project pursuit', without regard to whether the individual choices made are good or bad.[108]

[102] NE Simmonds, 'The Possibility of Private Law' in J Tasioulas (ed), *Law, Values and Social Practices* (Aldershot, Dartmouth, 1997) 130.

[103] ibid 144.

[104] ibid 145.

[105] William Lucy, *Philosophy of Private Law* (Oxford, Oxford University Press, 2007); Lucy (n 76).

[106] Lucy (n 76) 59.

[107] ibid 59.

[108] ibid. It is not clear why Lucy prefers the terms 'private project pursuit' and 'public project pursuit' to the terms 'individual project pursuit' and 'collective project pursuit'.

While liberalism is committed to protecting autonomy in the realm of our 'private' projects, however, there is another realm within which liberalism places greater value on our collective power to coordinate and organize aspects of our life together.[109] Lucy is even more tentative about defining this realm of 'public project pursuit', but ventures that it includes the realization of certain public goods, and 'all that activity which is conducted through the various instruments of the state'.[110] The value that we associate with the realm of 'public' project pursuit, according to Lucy, has two distinct components. The first component consists of the value we place upon the substantive goal being pursued by the collectivity—the specific (and possibly transient) 'public interest' that is purportedly being advanced. The second component consists of the value we place upon the virtues and constraints in accordance with which we require our collective goals to be pursued—the 'public law' values of fairness, rationality and the like.[111] Since any one instance of conduct can have both private and public aspects, we can expect a 'constant tension' between the realms of collective project pursuit and individual project pursuit.[112] It is this tension that is embodied in the distinction between public law and private law.

The 'project-based' account of the public law–private law divide articulated by Simmonds and Lucy provides the theoretical starting point for this comparative study of the law of charities. It is a compelling starting point, I claim, because the tension that the authors identify between individual/private project pursuit and collective/public project pursuit maps on very closely to the central tension between charity law's twin goals—the goal of enabling property owners to improve the world in accordance with their own individual vision, and the goal of setting limits on that ability to ensure conformity with a more collective ideal of the good. 'The Philanthropic Motive is in practice a specialist motive', William Beveridge once declared, in the context of his famous post-war report on voluntary action; 'it drives men to combat a particular evil or meet a particular need that arouses their interest'.[113] Specialist motives and idiosyncratic acts of generosity have been responsible for much of the charitable sector's wealth since the earliest days of the common law tradition. Throughout charity law's history, however, the individuality of these motives and acts has had to be balanced against a variety of competing public interests—in properly administered and effectively applied charity property, in the integrity of the tax base, in a society without discrimination, and in other collective goals. We shall see that the tension between these competing priorities—protecting the autonomy of donors and charities and protecting the public interest in their activities—is a deep and recurring theme of the

[109] ibid 61.
[110] ibid 60–61.
[111] ibid 61–62.
[112] ibid 64.
[113] WH Beveridge, *Voluntary Action: A Report on Methods of Social Advance* (Great Britain, G Allen & Unwin, 1948) 125.

law of charities. Moreover, it is a tension that mirrors what Simmonds and Lucy identify as the profound tension between private law and public law.

Lucy's claim that we require public, but not private, projects to manifest additional virtues in pursuing their goals also resonates strongly within the charity law domain. While Lucy himself does not explain the rationale for this phenomenon, Christopher Stone has offered a compelling explanation, based on what he calls the 'moral exemplar model'.[114] Virtues such as fairness, Stone claims, are public goods. Nevertheless, a legal system that went too far in requiring individual citizens to be virtuous would both suffer from incoherence, and unacceptably extend the reach of government. Our solution to this predicament is to assign the role of moral exemplar to certain 'public' bodies, and to require them to exemplify these virtues for the benefit of the collectivity. Government is the paradigmatic moral exemplar.[115] However, this book will suggest that charities and charity trustees, who are often said to enjoy higher levels of public trust than politicians,[116] may also be assigned this moral exemplar role.

In adopting the outlines of Simmonds's and Lucy's account of the public law–private law divide as a lens through which to understand the law of charities, I make a number of additional claims. A first relates to Lucy's identification of public project and private project 'realms'. Based on the tentativeness with which he describes these realms,[117] Lucy may be taken to accept that there is a significant border zone between them. Taken on its own, however, the language of realms tends to suggest that all projects are readily classifiable as *either* collective *or* individual projects, a position this book has already rejected. While it will often be convenient to speak of the 'realms' of individual project pursuit and collective project pursuit, therefore, it is likely more accurate to envision them as two opposing poles, with a spectrum of projects extending between them.[118] Archetypal projects of each variety are identifiable at each pole—a person's decision to enter an amorous relationship, say, versus a government's decision to impose a tax for the national defence—but many projects, including charitable projects, will sit somewhere on the spectrum between.

A second claim concerns the relationship between the overarching project-based account of the divide, and the various versions of the public–private distinction that were earlier alluded to. While the broad concepts of collective project pursuit and individual project pursuit capture something essential about the law's regulation of charitable projects, there are actually several notions of the public and the private that reverberate within the charity law domain. Two of

[114] Stone (n 77) 1493–96.

[115] ibid 1492.

[116] See Lord Hodgson of Astley Abbotts, *Trusted and Independent: Giving Charity back to Charities—a Review of the Charities Act 2006* 2012) (Hodgson Review 2012) 15.

[117] Lucy (n 76) 58–61.

[118] For a similar argument, see A Grear, 'Theorising the Rainbow? The Puzzle of the Public-Private Divide' (2003) 9 *Res Publica* 169.

these parallel the public–private distinctions identified by Lucy: the distinction between matters of general concern and individual concern, and the distinction between the state and the non-state realms. However, there are at least two further ways of distinguishing public and private that are highly relevant to the law of charities. A first is to contrast altruistic or other-regarding projects (public) with projects that are perceived to be self-regarding (private). A second is to contrast projects that have no cognizable owner (public) with those that do (private). These various notions of the public and the private must be distinguished if we are to improve our charity law map.

Finally, the assertion that we may envision spectrums of projects, institutions, procedures and rules extending between the respective poles of collective and individual project pursuit within the various dimensions of the public law–private law divide raises an important question about this mapping endeavour: how are we to determine where on these spectrums charities, and the laws governing charities, lie? One might answer this question by reference to liberal theory;[119] one might alternatively choose to advance a normative view about how charitable projects should be understood. However, the primary concern of this book is to map the extent to which, and the ways in which, different regulatory regimes in fact treat charitable projects as either collective or individual projects. This concern requires that we adopt some theory of how the law typically responds to projects at the collective project and individual project poles.

While a comprehensive treatment of this issue lies beyond the scope of this introduction, there are strong indications that within the common law tradition, the spectrum of individual/collective projects exists in parallel with a spectrum of regulatory impulses, which also extend between two poles.[120] At the individual project/private law end of the spectrum, where the law's normative commitment is to protecting the freedom and personality of the individual, the law's impulse is to regulate lightly so as to maximize that freedom.[121] At the collective project/public law end, where there is a perceived public interest in the activity in question, the law's impulse is to regulate more intensively, with a dual view to protecting whatever *specific* public interest the collective project is understood to raise, and to protecting a perceived *general* public interest in having entities that carry out collective projects model virtues such as fairness, rationality and the like. The public law–private law *hybrid*, I argue, occurs at a point on this spectrum where these

[119] Along the lines proposed by Matthew Harding: see generally Harding, *Liberal State* (n 3).

[120] Evidence of this general spectrum of regulatory impulses can be identified very early in the common law tradition, suggesting that the impulse to regulate more intensely in cases of perceived public interest existed long before the terms 'public law' and 'private law' were in common use: see, eg, P Craig, 'Constitutions, Property and Regulation' (1991) *PL* 538; M Taggart, '"The Peculiarities of the English": Resisting the Public/Private Law Distinction' in P Craig and R Rawlings (eds), *Law and Administration in Europe: Essays in Honour of Carol Harlow* (Oxford, Oxford University Press, 2003) 110.

[121] Taggart speaks of 'the private law's instinctive privileging of self-regarding behaviour': see Taggart, (n 57) 5.

two sets of regulatory impulses bear down with comparable weight on a project, institution, procedure or rule.

V. The Law of Charities as a Public Law–Private Law Hybrid

Based on the foregoing account of the public law–private law divide, we are now in a position to set out in further detail the analytical and comparative hypotheses that will be explored in the remainder of the work. The analytical hypothesis of this book is that we can regard the law of charities as a hybrid legal discipline in both a *general* or *categorical* sense, and in a *context-specific* or *functional* sense. The charitable trust is a public law–private law hybrid in the general sense that it represents the adaptation of a private law institution (the trust) to a variant which is more of a public law nature, in cases where there is deemed to be a public interest in, or public benefit arising from, the trust. Where that condition is satisfied, the settlor's project is specially privileged—the conditions for the validity of the trust are loosened, and the project is generally permitted to endure forever, but on the other hand the donor's project is specially regulated in ways more akin to how the projects of public authorities or actors are controlled by public law. The charitable corporation was historically also a public law–private law hybrid in this general sense, although, as we shall in Chapter 2, its constituent public law and private law elements were somewhat different.

Within this framework of general hybridity, charities also function and are regulated as a public law–private law hybrid in a *context-specific* or *functional* sense. By this I mean that within particular regulatory contexts, both the conditions for obtaining charitable status and its attendant fiscal benefits, and the regulation of the conduct of charities and their trustees, are continually being adjusted in such a way as to maintain in a broad sense a functional equilibrium between individual project pursuit and collective project pursuit; that is to say, an equilibrium between the protection of the autonomy of property-owning individuals to control and direct their own wealth (and, by extension, the protection of the autonomy of the trustees appointed by those individuals), and the furtherance of competing public interests or visions of the good. While each regulatory regime will reflect its own constellation of public interests, it is nonetheless possible to identify a general dichotomy in this regard between jurisdictions that assign primary responsibility for the regulation of charities to their revenue authority, and jurisdictions that do not.

In any specific regulatory context, we find equilibrium adjustments occurring within various dimensions of the law of charities:

(i) First, within the law's substantive dimension, we witness adjustments in the detailed working out of the definition of charity, the laws regulating the conduct of charity trustees, and particularly the public benefit doctrine. These adjustments occur along at least four notional continuums:

(a) a continuum between wholly altruistic projects and wholly self-regarding projects;
(b) a continuum between projects that have no cognizable owner and projects that do;
(c) a continuum between projects that are a matter of general concern and projects that are a matter of individual concern; and
(d) a continuum between projects which are fully aligned to the public welfare goals of the state or polity in question, and projects which, although altruistic, are nevertheless at variance with those public welfare goals—in shorthand, public-welfare-compliant projects and public-welfare-deviant projects.

(ii) Second, we witness equilibrium adjustments in the very regulatory institutions and procedures that make and maintain these substantive equilibrium adjustments to the doctrines of the law of charities. These regulatory institutions and procedures, whether administrative, legislative or judicial, may in various ways manifest 'public law-leaning' or 'private law-leaning' tendencies in the texture of their processes.

This scheme of analysis shapes the comparative hypothesis that will be pursued in the following chapters: namely, that while contemporary regimes of charity regulation continue to treat charities as hybrids in the general sense, they exhibit different public-leaning and private-leaning tendencies at the context-specific level. The book will argue, first, that the common law charities tradition that originated in England and Wales was a true hybrid of private law and public law, in the general sense that it accorded comparable importance to the autonomy interests of persons who create and manage charities, and to the public interest in properly and effectively administered charity property. This hybridity was evident in the common law's approach to supervising and remedying the actions of charity trustees, in its approach to applying charity property *cy-près*, and in its approach to the public benefit criterion. The rules of *locus standi* that determined who could sue for a misuse of charity property in the Court of Chancery suggest that certain *procedural* features of the common law of charities were historically more 'public' than 'private'. Even in this procedural dimension, however, the common law of charities has partaken in selective ways of private law.

The English Charity Commission regime was created in the image of the English common law,[122] and reflects the same duality of focus on the autonomy interests of benevolent property owners, and the public interest in properly administered charity property. However, the regime was created for the explicit purpose of protecting this public interest better than the common law had done. Its develop-

[122] Meaning, in this context and in the remainder of the book, the English law of equity as fashioned by the Chancery Courts.

ment also reflected a growing political consensus that charities, and the trustees that manage them, should be models of virtue to rival the state. Certain recent developments have demonstrated a swing back towards the protection of charity autonomy in England and Wales, while others have demonstrated the extent to which other public interests are now bearing down on the field. Overall, however, we may say that while the Charity Commission regime continues to balance the same interests as the common law tradition, and thus treats charities as hybrids in the general sense we have identified, it has shifted the equilibrium between these interests in a way that privileges the public interest in charity property, as well as the public interest in the advancement of equality norms. The retrenchment of the UK welfare state and the related development of a culture of the contracting out of public welfare services have placed additional pressures on the charitable sector to be public-welfare-compliant. However, the Charity Commission regime evidences some commitment to resisting those pressures on the sector's behalf.

In countries that have opted for a tax-based regulator, like Canada and the United States, the trajectory from the common law tradition to a contemporary regime of charity regulation has been markedly different. This divergence is evident in Canada, a jurisdiction that received the English law of charities in its common law provinces but has integrated only limited substantive elements of that tradition into its regulatory regime. Unlike the Charity Commission regime, Canada's primary regime of charity regulation was not created to protect a perceived public interest in properly administered charity property, but rather to protect a perceived public interest in the elimination of tax abuses by donors and charities themselves. Embedded in the federal system of tax administration, the registered charity regime pursues a different public–private equilibrium than the common law of charities, and requires Canadian charities to be significantly more public-welfare-compliant than their English counterparts. While Canadian charity law is like English charity law in treating charities as public-leaning hybrids, its equilibrium adjustments are not tied to the 'charitable' collective project that the common law has always been concerned to protect.

We have already noted the potentially vast scope of this project; the discussion thus far has done little to alleviate concerns about breadth, and it is important to clarify the project's parameters. This book does not purport to conduct an exhaustive survey of the law of charities in either England and Wales or Canada. Rather, after sketching out in broad terms the history and nature of the common law charities tradition and the contemporary English regulatory regime, the book applies the public law–private law lens to an eclectic set of charity law issues, which are intended to shed light on the analytical and comparative hypotheses that have already been set out. Certain of these issues, in particular the evolution of the public benefit doctrine, have been selected because of their particular centrality to charity law's hybrid character. Others, such as charity law's rules of *locus standi*, have been selected in part because they have so far received comparatively little attention. The selection of 'institutional', 'doctrinal', 'procedural' and 'functional' charity law issues is also designed to cast some light on, or at least take seriously, the multidimensional nature of the public law–private law divide.

The book thus proceeds in the following way. Chapter 2 introduces the regulatory institutions that have historically had primary responsibility for the oversight of charities in England and Wales, tracing in broad strokes the transference of supervisory functions from the Court of Chancery to the Charity Commission for England and Wales. This story provides us with the best sense of the *general* public–private hybridity of the common law charities tradition. It distinguishes the two principal forms of charities, the charitable trust and the charitable corporation, and identifies the unique mixture of public law and private law elements that was embodied in each. The chapter also introduces the concept of *context-specific* hybridity by setting up an initial contrast between 'civil' and 'tax-based' regulatory regimes, and by identifying the particular interests that the civil Charity Commission was created to protect.

Following Chapter 2's overview of the Charity Commission regime, Chapters 3 and 4 consider two distinctive features of English charity law, examining the ways in which private law and public law impulses have come to bear on these features in specific regulatory contexts. Chapter 3 pursues the hypothesis that the public benefit rule is a *doctrinal hybrid* within which the strength of public law and private law thinking are felt in comparable measure. It identifies the particular public law and private law impulses that are at play in the common law doctrine, and examines how the equilibrium between these impulses has repeatedly been adjusted since the enactment of the Charities Act 2006. Chapter 4 examines an important procedural feature of the law of charities, the rules of *locus standi*, which determine who may seek relief for misapplications of charity property. The chapter establishes a two-pronged distinction between the quintessential 'public law' and 'private law' approaches to the question of who can sue, and then seeks to identify the 'public law-leaning' and 'private law-leaning' tendencies in charity law's standing rules, both at common law and under the Charity Commission regime.

The book changes gear somewhat in Chapter 5, identifying the different axis of public and private interests that inheres in Canada's tax-based regime of charity regulation, and exploring how that public–private axis reverberates throughout the institutional, substantive and procedural dimensions of Canadian charity law. Chapter 6 addresses the comparatively modern issue of the governmental co-optation of charitable resources, arguing that modern pressures associated with the retrenchment of the welfare state threaten to destabilize charity law's hybrid equilibrium, and considering what protections English and Canadian law offer against those pressures. In Chapter 7, the book turns to the emerging phenomenon of social enterprise, arguing that shifts to the functional equilibrium between charity law's public law and private law elements may explain the emergence of this 'post-charitable' legal form. The book concludes in Chapter 8 with some final observations on the law of charities as a public law–private law hybrid, and on the different functional equilibriums between individual project pursuit and collective project pursuit that have been reached by English and Canadian charity law.

2

Charity Regulators and the Institutional Public Law–Private Law Divide

I. Introduction

In its introductory chapter, this book suggested that it is useful to envisage the public law–private law divide as a spectrum of regulatory impulses, which parallels a spectrum of projects that extend between two opposing poles. Archetypally 'individual projects'—those we consider ourselves entitled to formulate and pursue without regard to the value placed upon the projects by others—are situated at one of these poles, while archetypally 'collective projects'—those in which every member of society is understood to have an interest or a stake—are situated at the other. Where an activity is understood to be part of an individual project, I argued, the law's impulse is generally to regulate lightly, so as to maximize the individual project pursuer's autonomy and his or her capacity for creativity and innovation. Where an activity is understood to be part of a collective project, on the other hand, the law's impulse is to regulate more intensively, both to protect the perceived public interest in that collective project, and to ensure that the project is pursued in a 'virtuous' way. These conflicting impulses exist in multiple legal dimensions, I claimed, and may often be used to measure the particularly 'private' or 'public' character of a project, institution, procedure or rule.

This chapter focuses on the nature and disposition of the regulatory institutions historically tasked with the primary oversight of charities in England and Wales, with a view to situating them within this notional public law-private law framework. To this end, the chapter has three main objectives. First, it seeks to lay the groundwork for the remainder of the book by tracing the transference of supervisory functions from the Court of Chancery to the Charity Commission for England and Wales and outlining the contemporary regulatory paradigm. Second, the chapter makes the case for the *general* hybridity of the common law charities tradition by identifying some of the ways in which this tradition historically partook of private law and public law. Finally, the chapter introduces an argument for the *context-specific* hybridity of 'civil' and 'tax-based' regimes of charity regulation, examining the extent to which the primary commitment of England and Wales's civil charity regulator is to protecting the autonomy interests of benevolent property owners, on the one hand, or to intervening in an identified public interest, on the other.

The chapter pursues these objectives as follows. By way of background, Section II introduces the common law's concept of a charity and the tradition's 'charity regulators', the Crown and the Court of Chancery. It reviews the court's inherent jurisdiction to administer and control charities, and the extensive remedial powers ensuing from such jurisdiction. It also draws attention to the distinction between charitable trusts and charitable corporations, and to the unique mixture of public law and private law elements that was embodied in the law of charitable corporations. Section III sets out my claim regarding the dichotomy between civil and tax-based models of charity regulation. It introduces the modern regulators that I have chosen to illustrate this dichotomy, the Charity Commission for England and Wales and the Canada Revenue Agency's Charities Directorate, and explains the reasons for their selection. Section IV then describes the origins of the Charity Commission for England and Wales in some detail, with a view to highlighting the distinct mischief that the regulatory body was created to address. It outlines the supervisory and remedial powers of the modern Commission, and the regime's relationship with the common law tradition. I conclude with some observations on the context-specific 'public-private' character of England and Wales's charity regulator, and the nature of the public interest that it seeks to protect.

II. The Common Law's Charity Regulators

The English Crown has, since at least the seventeenth century, been recognized as having a 'superintending power' over charities,[1] which is a legacy of the feudal relationship of ligeance between the English people and the Crown. Just as the law of nature required that every subject obey and serve the King, so it required that the King maintain and defend his subjects, particularly those who could not defend themselves. Charities, and the objects of charity, were included in this latter category, along with children and the infirm.[2] As the King could not appear in his own courts,[3] it fell to his law officers to carry out the advocacy aspects of this *parens patriae* prerogative. Thus it came to be accepted, 'by long and immemorial custom', that it was the right and duty of the Attorney General, as the chief law officer of the Crown, to enforce rights of a charitable nature in the courts in order to ensure the realization of their charitable objects.[4]

[1] H Picarda, *The Law and Practice Relating to Charities*, 4th edn (Hayward's Heath, Bloomsbury Professional, 2010) 727.

[2] See *Calvin's Case* (1608) 7 Co Rep 1a, 5a; J Warburton and others, *Tudor on Charities*, 9th edn (London, Sweet & Maxwell, 2003) 367; see also *National Anti-Vivisection Society v IRC* [1948] AC 31 (HL) 63.

[3] See, eg, *R v Austen* (1821) 9 Price 142n.

[4] *A-G v Magdalen College, Oxford* (1854) 18 Beav 223, 241, 52 ER 88, 96. See also *Wallis v Solicitor-General for New Zealand* [1903] AC 173 (HL) 181–82 (Lord MacNaghten).

The bulk of the Crown's superintending power over charities, however, has been delegated to the courts themselves.[5] From almost its inception, the Court of Chancery exercised a broad, remedial jurisdiction over charities; this 'inherent jurisdiction' is now vested in the English High Court.[6] The court's jurisdiction over charities is generally portrayed as a branch of the court's jurisdiction over the administration of trusts.[7] There is considerable overlap between these two jurisdictions. As Jones has established, however, the ecclesiastical courts enjoyed an authority to 'cure' uncertain charitable legacies of personal property and apply them *cy-près* well before the trust was even a recognized legal form.[8] Only gradually, as the use of the trust increased and the Chancellor came to assume jurisdiction over a growing number of charitable dispositions, did the Chancellor begin to adopt many of these ecclesiastical practices as his own.[9]

Jones's comments on the lineage of the charities jurisdiction remind us that charities have long existed in more than one legal form. The trust was for a long period the legal structure of choice for charitable activity, since it allowed private individuals to devote property to specific charitable purposes, appoint trustees, and dictate how those trustees should manage the property, free from state intervention.[10] However, the 'corporate' charity, which today plays a central role in the charitable sector, also features prominently in the history of the common law tradition. The charitable trust and the charitable corporation were each composed of a distinctive blend of public law and private law elements, and our doctrinal map should reflect these differences. In what follows, therefore, I will seek to distinguish between the judicial powers that flow from the court's inherent jurisdiction over trusts in general, and those that flow from its 'charities jurisdiction' to protect resources devoted to charitable purposes. I will also highlight the differences between the supervisory regimes applicable to charitable corporations and trusts. First, however, I will provide a very brief summary of the common law meaning of charity, to paint a more detailed picture of the institutions of which we speak.

A. The Common Law Meaning of Charity

It is a unique feature of the common law of charities that the label 'charity' attaches to institutions by virtue not of their form, but of the purposes that they

[5] Picarda (n 1) 727; *A-G v Lady Downing* (1767) Wilmot 1, 97 ER 1 (Ch) 24.

[6] Picarda (n 1) 729. In Canada, as we shall see in Chapter 5, the Court of Chancery's charities jurisdiction is now vested in the provincial superior courts.

[7] ibid, noting that the 8th edition of *Tudor on Charities* suggested that the inherent jurisdiction depended exclusively on the existence of a trust. See also *Construction Industry Training Board v A-G* [1973] Ch 173 (CA) 176.

[8] GH Jones, *History of the Law of Charity, 1532–1827* (Cambridge, Cambridge University Press, 1969) 59. See also MR Fremont-Smith, *Foundations and Government: State and Federal Law and Supervision* (New York, NY, Russell Sage Foundation, 1965) 17.

[9] Jones (n 8) 59.

[10] M Chesterman, *Charities, Trusts, and Social Welfare* (London, Weidenfeld and Nicolson, 1979) 3.

carry out.[11] In the very early days of the English charity law tradition, the meaning of charity was 'fluid and relatively unformulated'.[12] In 1601, however, the Parliament of Queen Elizabeth I passed an Act entitled the Statute of Charitable Uses (commonly and hereafter known as the Statute of Elizabeth), the Preamble to which set out the following list of 'good, godly and charitable' objects:

> The relief of aged, impotent, and poor people; the maintenance of sick and maimed soldiers and mariners, schools of learning, free schools, and scholars in universities; the repair of bridges, ports, havens, causeways, churches, seabanks, and highways; the education and preferment of orphans; the relief, stock, or maintenance of houses of correction; marriage of poor maids; supportation, aid, and help of young tradesmen, handicraftsmen, and persons decayed; the relief or redemption of prisoners or captives; and the aid or ease of any poor inhabitants concerning payment of fifteens, setting out of soldiers, and other taxes.

The Preamble did not purport to establish a definition of charity for all purposes. Rather, it sought to delineate the jurisdiction of the Commissioners who, under the Act, were empowered to inquire into and remedy breaches of charitable trust. Over time, however, the courts came to accept that the objects enumerated in the Statute of Elizabeth 'and all other objects which by analogy are deemed within its spirit and intendment and no other objects' were legally charitable.[13] Through this process, the English courts of equity converted the Preamble definition into a general rule of law.[14]

With the passage of time and the process of judicial interpretation, the common law concept of charity expanded, evolving from its legislative roots. In the 1891 *Pemsel* decision, the House of Lords effectively created a new starting point for the common law definition by identifying what have come to be known as the four 'heads' of charity: the relief of poverty, the advancement of education, the advancement of religion and 'other purposes beneficial to the community, not falling under any of the preceding heads'.[15] A substantial case law and commentary developed around each of the four *Pemsel* heads, full consideration of which is beyond the scope of this work. However, the Statute of Elizabeth and *Pemsel* remain the dual touchstones of the common law definition.[16] To be charitable, a purpose must also benefit the community or a substantial segment of the community within the meaning of the public benefit doctrine.[17]

[11] The label 'charitable' may equally attach to gifts and bequests, but I will focus on charitable institutions in this work.

[12] Chesterman (n 10) 24.

[13] *Gilmour v Coats* [1949] AC 426 (HL) 443.

[14] For a similar observation, see Picarda (n 1) 10.

[15] *Commissioners for Special Purposes of Income Tax v Pemsel* [1891] AC 531 (HL) 583. The Supreme Court of Canada has taken the position that *Pemsel* is now the starting point: see *Vancouver Society of Immigrant & Visible Minority Women v MNR* [1999] 1 SCR 10, 169 DLR (4th) 34 [144].

[16] *Vancouver Society* (n 15) [144].

[17] See, for example, *Oppenheim v Tobacco Securities Trust Co Ltd* [1951] AC 297 (HL) 307. The public benefit doctrine is the subject of Chapter 3.

B. Supervisory Jurisdiction over the Charitable Trust

The court's inherent jurisdiction to control the administration of a trust at the request of an appropriate person was described by Lord Eldon in the nineteenth century as a 'main part, originally almost the whole' of the Court of Chancery's jurisdiction.[18] It was also a defining feature of the trust. As the Master of the Rolls stated in *Morice v Durham*, 'there can be no trust, over the exercise of which this court will not assume a control; for an uncontrollable power of disposition would be ownership, and not trust'.[19] Charitable trusts fell within this inherent jurisdiction, as we will see, but were subject to an even higher standard of judicial control than private trusts.

The precise scope of the court's general trusts jurisdiction is notoriously difficult to define.[20] However, its key characteristics—remedial flexibility and a 'rigorous standard of judicial control over the use and management of property'[21]—are well known. The stringent standard of judicial control is reflected in the wide range of actions that constitute a breach of trust; the court has the authority to remedy any act or omission by a trustee that is contrary to the duties imposed upon him, whether or not the breach is deliberate, and whether or not it causes any harm.[22] Even where no breach of trust has been established, the court may sometimes exercise control over the discretionary decisions of trustees. While the court does not generally review discretionary decisions reached honestly and in good faith, there are a number of circumstances in which it will intervene.[23]

The second characteristic of the trusts jurisdiction, its remedial flexibility, is equally pronounced. In the exercise of its inherent jurisdiction over trusts, the Court of Chancery may either appoint[24] or remove[25] trustees, depending on whether they will promote the execution of a trust. It may sanction departures from the terms of the trust instrument in certain circumstances, and prevent trustees from exercising any power without the sanction of the court in others.[26] The court has the inherent jurisdiction to cure a formal defect in a trustee's execution of a power by ordering the making good of the defect.[27] And where trustees fail to

[18] *A-G v Brown* (1818) 1 Sw 265, 36 ER 384 (Ch) 291.

[19] *Morice v Bishop of Durham* (1804) 9 Ves 399 (Ch) 404–05.

[20] *Re Royal Society's Charitable Trusts* [1956] Ch 87, 91, cited in D Waters, 'Changing the Purpose of Gifts: the Fate of Administrative and Cy-Pres Judicial Schemes in Canada' (2010) 23 *The Philanthropist* 93, 96.

[21] J McGhee (ed), *Snell's Equity*, 32nd edn (London, Thompson Reuters (Legal) Limited, 2010) 19.

[22] DJ Hayton and C Mitchell, *Commentary and Cases on the Law of Trusts and Equitable Remedies*, 12th edn (London, Sweet & Maxwell, 2005) 704.

[23] *Re Beloved Wilkes' Charity* (1851) 3 Mac & G 440 (Ch). For a fuller discussion of the judicial control of trustees, see Hayton and Mitchell (n 22) 651–73.

[24] *Re Tempest* (1866) LR 1 Ch 485, 35 LJ Ch 632 (CA).

[25] *Letterstedt v Broers* (1884) 9 AC 371, 51 LT 169 (PC). This applied even where no misconduct was proven.

[26] See generally J Mowbray and others, *Lewin on Trusts*, 18th edn (London, Sweet & Maxwell, 2008) 1110, 1854–56.

[27] ibid 1053.

exercise an imperative power to distribute funds under a discretionary trust, the court can exercise the power by authorizing representative beneficiaries to prepare a scheme of distribution, or by preparing one itself.[28]

The rules and principles that constitute the court's trusts jurisdiction are, for the most part, equally applicable to private and charitable trusts.[29] Nevertheless, it has long been recognized that in the case of charitable trusts, the courts exercise a 'power and discretion that does not belong to them in the case of a private trust'.[30] A court may direct the errant trustees of either a private or a charitable trust to rectify errors in the application of trust funds or to take steps towards the fulfilment of the trust objects.[31] In the charitable trust context, however, the court also has the inherent jurisdiction to confer powers on trustees that they lack under the trust instrument,[32] and to discharge trustees from their trust obligations.[33] The courts have tended to apply a heightened level of judicial control to the discretionary decisions of charity trustees, ordering trustees to account for the distribution of charitable funds for which they are responsible, and even retaining custody of charity funds.[34] The court's jurisdiction to regulate the administration of a charity has been described as 'unlimited',[35] and may be invoked in any case where the court deems that an administrative change is advisable.[36] Charitable trusts and trustees are specially regulated at common law, in other words, in a manner reminiscent of the special regulation of public authorities and actors by public law.

If charitable projects are specially regulated within the common law tradition, they are also specially favoured, in ways which evoke the special privileges and protections that may attach to the projects of government.[37] The charities jurisdiction encompasses a number of specific curative powers, which allow the courts to remedy formal and substantive defects in charitable trusts in order to ensure the application of their resources to charitable purposes. Equity has always taken the position that where a settlor manifests a general intention to give to charity, the failure of the particular 'mode' in which the charity is to be put into effect should

[28] *McPhail v Doulton* [1971] AC 424 (HL) 456–57.

[29] McGhee (ed) (n 21) 684.

[30] *Andrews v M'Guffog* (1886) LR 11 AC 313 (HL). See also *A-G v Gleg* (1738) Amb 584 ('the court has a particular free and extensive jurisdiction in the case of a charity').

[31] *A-G v Coopers Co* (1812) 19 Ves 186, 34 ER 488 (Ch).

[32] In *Re Royal Society*, for example, the court extended the range of investments that trustees were permitted to make under the trust document. This was not possible in private trusts until a statutory amendment in the mid-twentieth century: see Waters (n 20) 95–96.

[33] *Re JW Laing Trust* [1984] Ch 143.

[34] Picarda (n 1) 528, citing *A-G v Gleg* (n 30) and *M'Coll v Atherton* (1848) 12 Jury 1042. See also *A-G v Governors of Harrow School* (1754) 2 Ves Sr 551, 28 ER 351 (Ch), and *Re Devlin's Estate* (1889) 23 LR Ir 516.

[35] See, eg, the argument of the Attorney General in *Re JW Laing* (n 33) 146.

[36] Warburton and others (n 2) 374, citing *A-G v Dedham School* (1857) 23 Beav 350 (Ch).

[37] On the 'special treatment' that charity has always received under English law, see *Gaudiya Mission v Brahmachary* [1998] Ch 341, 350. On the special treatment that government may receive, see A Davies, *The Public Law of Government Contracts* (Oxford, Oxford University Press, 2008) ch 3.

not destroy the charity.[38] From early times, therefore, where a settlor's transfer of property to a charitable use was defective, for example because the appointed trustee lacked capacity to hold property at common law, the Chancellor could intervene to perfect the transfer and enforce the use.[39] Where a settlor intended to establish a charitable trust, but failed to prescribe all the details of its administration, the court would direct an appropriate scheme.[40]

The court's curative powers with respect to charitable trusts apply to substantive as well as formal defects. While private trust documents must be interpreted according to ordinary rules of construction, a court may give a benignant construction to a document in order to save a charitable trust.[41] A private trust for uncertain objects is necessarily void.[42] However, where property is given in trust for charity generally, absent any directions as to the specific objects to be carried out, a court may apply the fund in the manner it deems most expedient.[43] In earlier times, where the designated object of a fund was illegal or superstitious, the court could likewise apply the fund to another charitable purpose at its discretion. The court's ability to 'fill in' the intention of a benevolent settlor in order to perfect an uncertain or illegal trust was always controversial, it must be noted, particularly since the courts often justified the exercise of this power as a way of fulfilling the settlor's intent. Lord Eldon called it a 'strange doctrine' that one could 'find a charitable purpose in a purpose that is to fail altogether', or discover an intention to build a Foundling Hospital in a declared intention to build a Jewish synagogue.[44] Nevertheless, the curative jurisdiction of the court remains exercisable at common law, provided there is a clear intention that property be held on trust for charitable purposes; where there is no trust, but only an uncertain absolute gift to charity, the power to direct the gift's application devolves to the Crown.[45]

Finally, the charities jurisdiction encompasses a unique judicial power to alter the objects of a trust. Pursuant to the *cy-près* doctrine, if property is given in trust for a particular charitable purpose, which is or becomes impossible or impracticable to carry out, and the settlor demonstrated a paramount charitable intention to devote the property to charity, a court may direct that the property be applied to a purpose 'as near as possible' to that intended by the testator.[46] The origins of *cy-près* are debated, but by the early seventeenth century it was a 'sophisticated

[38] *Moggridge v Thackwell* (1803) 7 Ves 36, 32 ER 15 (Ch) 69.

[39] Jones (n 8) 60–68. It was originally thought that this jurisdiction flowed from the Statute of Elizabeth, but by the late seventeenth century it was accepted that imperfect transfers could be perfected in Chancery, even if the proceedings were brought by bill or information.

[40] *Wellbeloved v Jones* (1822) 57 ER 16; *A-G v Stepney* (1804) 10 Ves 22, cited in Picarda (n 1) 512.

[41] See, eg, *Houston* v *Burns* [1918] AC 337, 341–42.

[42] Mowbray and others (n 26) 99.

[43] *A-G v Syderfen* (1683) 1 Vern 224. See also *Re Gott* [1944] Ch 193.

[44] *Moggridge* (n 38) 81, 87.

[45] ibid 83.

[46] In earlier times, the court's substitution of a new mode to carry out the settlor's charitable intention was considered as part of *cy-près*, but most authors now restrict the doctrine to situations where a particular purpose cannot be carried out: see Jones (n 8) 73; Picarda (n 1) 438.

and mature doctrine'[47] which allowed a court to redirect charity funds where the amount of a gift was insufficient to carry out the donor's intentions, or there was no suitable site for the charitable project, or the object of the gift had already been achieved.[48] Unlike later statutory versions of the doctrine, however, the common law *cy-près* doctrine did not authorize a court to redirect charity funds on the basis that it could identify a more expedient or beneficial application of the property.[49] The court's duty was to 'carry into effect the intentions expressed by the founders so far as those intentions are not inconsistent with any existing law'.[50]

The foregoing paragraphs represent only a brief overview of the court's inherent jurisdiction over charitable trusts. Nonetheless, they demonstrate the manner in which the primarily private law institution of the trust and its governing laws were adapted to reflect a perceived public interest in charitable projects, producing a variant which is more of a public law nature. The *cy-près* doctrine provides a particularly good illustration of the general hybridity of the common law of charitable trusts, and the deep tension within its canon between the value placed on individual project pursuit and collective project pursuit. Like the other curative powers that make up the charities jurisdiction, the court's ability to apply charity property to purposes not specifically envisaged by the charity's settlor manifests a distinctly *public law* impulse to protect the public interest in the use of property for charitable purposes. On the other hand, the strict limitations on the *cy-près* power, and the court's frequent reliance on the settlor's intentions as a way to justify the exercise of the power,[51] manifest a distinctly *private law* impulse to protect the autonomy and will of the settlor. The *cy-près* doctrine thus provides a compelling example of the general hybridity of the common law tradition, in the sense that it accords comparable importance to the autonomy interest of benevolent property owners, and the public interest in properly and effectively administered charity property.

C. Supervisory Jurisdiction over the Charitable Corporation

Although the exact parameters of the court's jurisdiction to control and administer charitable trusts have always been somewhat obscure, the existence of the jurisdiction and its broad and remedial character are not open to doubt. The relationship between the courts and the charitable *corporation*, on the other hand, has always been more complex. A charitable corporation is a corporation whose corporate

[47] Jones (n 8) 74.

[48] See Picarda (n 1) 446–54, and the cases cited therein.

[49] *Philpott v St George's Hospital* (1859) 27 Beav 107, 111. Compare Charities Act (CA) 2011, s 62(1)(e).

[50] *A-G v Boucherett* (1858) 25 Beav 116, 53 ER 580 (Ch) 583.

[51] For a discussion of this and other justifications for the *cy-près* doctrine, see J Garton, 'Justifying the Cy-Près Doctrine' (2007) 21 *Trust Law International* 134.

purposes are charitable.[52] Historically, charitable corporations were created either by Royal Charter, by a grant of letters patent, or by a special Act of Parliament.[53] Prior to the development of the Charity Commission regime, the supervision of charitable corporations was carried out primarily through the exercise of a private jurisdiction, based on legal rules created by the corporation's founder. However, the court enjoyed a 'residual' jurisdiction over charitable corporations, which it exercised where there was no one else to ensure that charitable funds were properly administered, or where the court's intervention could be justified by the existence of a clear and distinct trust. We will examine these unique features of the supervisory regime for charitable corporations in the ensuing section, with a view to gaining a fuller, more nuanced picture of the public law–private law hybridity of the common law charities tradition.

The common law historically treated charitable corporations as 'the creatures of the founder'.[54] The connection between a founder and his founded property was elemental: Coke opined that foundership (the role of being the founder) was 'so inseparably incident to the blood of the founder' that it could not be transferred to anybody else.[55] In recognition of this connection, the common law allowed the founder of a charitable corporation to dictate the objects to which his property and the property of subsequent supporters would be directed, and the 'laws' that would govern his foundation. The founder of a charitable corporation also had the power to appoint a 'visitor' to interpret and apply his foundation's laws.[56] The visitor was said to enjoy a 'domestic jurisdiction', which authorized him to interpret not only the foundation's laws, but also the 'internal powers and discretions' that derived from them.[57] If a founder failed to appoint a visitor, the law presumed that the foundation was to be visited by the founder and his heirs.[58]

This unique power of the founder of a charitable corporation to establish the legal regime governing his entity set the charitable corporation apart from other corporations. Ecclesiastical corporations, which also generally owed their existence to gifts of property from private individuals, were subject to the visitation of the Ordinary, while civil corporations were subject to the visitation of the ordinary courts.[59] Charitable corporations, on the other hand, could have as their visitor any private individual, although those founded by the Crown were generally visited by the sovereign or his or her appointee.[60] In *Philips v Bury*, the *locus classicus*

[52] Picarda (n 1) 267.

[53] ibid 270.

[54] *St John's, Cambridge v Toddington* (1757) 1 Burrow 158, 97 ER 245.

[55] S Kyd, *A Treatise on the Law of Corporations*, vol 1 (J Butterworth, 1793) 51.

[56] The settlor of a charitable trust could apparently also appoint a visitor of the charity, but this was not a common practice: Warburton and others (n 2) 412. Trusts, as we have seen, remained under the court's control: *Morice* (n 19); *A-G v St Cross Hospital* (1854) 18 Beav 475, 52 ER 187 (Ch).

[57] *Thomas v University of Bradford* [1987] AC 795 (HL) 820–21.

[58] *Philips v Bury* (1694) Holt 715. See also Picarda (n 1) 736.

[59] CA Cooke, *Corporation, Trust and Company; An Essay in Legal History* (Manchester, Manchester University Press, 1950) 69.

[60] JW Bridge, 'Keeping Peace in the Universities: The Role of the Visitor' (1970) 86 *LQR* 531, 534.

of the law of visitors,[61] Holt CJ summed up this distinction by declaring that while corporations were subject to the general laws of the realm, the charitable corporation was '*entirely private*, and wholly subject to the rules, law, statutes and ordinances which the founder ordains, and to the visitor whom he appoints, and to no others'.[62]

The fact that charitable corporations were generally governed not by the common law, but by a private law system established by their founder, had the effect of significantly insulating charitable corporations from the supervision of the courts.[63] There was no right of appeal from the decisions of a visitor, and the High Court would intervene only where the visitor dealt with a matter outside his jurisdiction, or refused to deal with a matter within his jurisdiction.[64] In 1747, Wright J put the matter starkly, stating: 'Visitors have an absolute power; the only absolute one I know of in England'.[65] Two and a half centuries later, the House of Lords reaffirmed the near-absolute power of English visitors to decide matters deriving from the founder's laws.[66]

However, the relative insulation of charitable corporations from judicial supervision was not attributable solely to the entitlements of their property-owning founders, and the private jurisdiction that arose therefrom. The autonomy of charitable corporations and the self-governance they exercised were also related to the role of the Crown in their establishment. Until the general corporate laws of the nineteenth century made incorporation the automatic consequence of stipulated, preliminary acts, the granting of corporate status was a royal prerogative in English law. Consequently, the foundation of charitable corporations could typically only be accomplished by the sovereign's consent.[67] A charitable corporation could be created by a grant of letters patent, or the enactment of a special parliamentary Act.[68] In the early days, however, it was most often the sovereign alone that performed the creative act of incorporation, through the instrument of the Royal Charter.[69] The usual practice was for a body of persons to draft the contents of a Royal Charter, and then present a petition for the Charter to the Crown.[70]

[61] *R v Hull University Visitor, ex parte Page* [1993] AC 682, 698.

[62] *Philips v Bury* (n 58) 903–04.

[63] *ex parte Page* (n 61) 698, 700.

[64] *Thomas* (n 57) 825.

[65] *R v Bishop of Chester* (1748) 1 W Bl 22, 96 ER 12, cited in *ex parte Page* (n 61) 698.

[66] *Thomas* (n 57) 811–14; *ex parte Page* (n 61) 704.

[67] 1 Bl Comm 271–73, 472. Even special Acts required royal assent, but as we will discuss further in Chapter 6, charitable corporations created by special Act are likely best understood as creatures of the legislature.

[68] Picarda (n 1) 270.

[69] 1 Bl Comm 473. See also LCB Gower, *Gower's Principles of Modern Company Law*, 4th edn (London, Stevens & Sons, 1979) 22, noting that it was not until the latter part of the eighteenth century that it became the practice for Acts of Parliament actually to effect incorporation.

[70] Picarda (n 1) 270. See also *A-G v National Hospital for the Relief and Cure of the Paralysed and Epileptic* [1904] 2 Ch 252, 256.

Ultimately, however, it was the sovereign who either dictated or approved the powers exercisable by the corporation, the ends towards which those powers would be used, and the manner in which the powers would be exercised. It is perhaps for this reason that Blackstone compared charitable corporations to republics, and wrote that 'the founder of all corporations, in the strictest and original sense, is the King alone'.[71]

The Crown's involvement in the foundation of charitable corporations vested them with a certain public authority, which was reflected in the limitations on the judiciary's authority to supervise them. Thus, a number of eighteenth-century cases confirm that the court has no inherent jurisdiction to alter the trusts of a charity founded by Royal Charter, because such charities owe their existence to the authority of the Crown, which is a 'higher authority than [the] court'.[72] The court also has no jurisdiction to alter the trusts of a charity that is comprehensively regulated by statute, unless it is given that jurisdiction under the Act.[73] Today, of course, individuals may create corporate charities by their own acts and association. Historically, however, these common law rules placed significant limits on the court's ability to supervise charities that were not charitable trusts.

Until the development of the Charity Commission regime, then, the private jurisdiction of the visitor served as the primary mode of supervision for the charitable corporation in England and Wales. Nevertheless, there were circumstances in which questions regarding the administration of such corporations were understood to fall within the inherent jurisdiction of the courts. First, the courts were prepared to exercise a supervisory jurisdiction over charitable corporations if they could find a trust, within the corporate structure, upon which their authority could be based. The judicial usage of this technique increased, Maurice Cullity has argued, as it became apparent that corporate law was inadequate to prevent abuses in the use of charitable funds.[74] Thus, in the nineteenth-century case of *Attorney-General v St Cross Hospital*, Sir John Romilly MR found that a twelfth-century charter for a hospital foundation constituted 'as clear and distinct a trust for the general support of charity as ever was created'.[75] As a result, he concluded, the visitorship of the Bishop of Winchester did not curtail the court's jurisdiction,

[71] 1 Bl Comm 468, 480–81.

[72] *A-G v Smart* (1748) 1 Ves Sen 72 (Ch); *A-G v Middleton* (1751) 2 Ves Sr 327, 28 ER 210 (Ch). See also Warburton and others (n 2) 371. The CA 2011 extends the court's jurisdiction to make schemes for chartered charities, but provides that such schemes may not take effect until Her Majesty thinks fit to amend the charter: CA 2011, s 68.

[73] *Re Shrewsbury Grammar School* (1849) 1 Mac & G 324, 333. See also Warburton and others (n 2) 372–73. Where a charity is established by Royal Charter or by statute, the court may not exercise its jurisdiction in any way that conflicts with those instruments: *Construction Industry* (n 7) 187. See also *Re Whitworth Art Gallery Trusts* [1958] Ch 461, [1958] 1 All ER 176, 176.

[74] M Cullity, 'The Charitable Corporation: a "Bastard" Legal Form Revisited' (2001) 17 *The Philanthropist* 19.

[75] *A-G v St Cross Hospital* (1853) 17 Beav 435, 51 ER 1103 (Ch) 459.

for it was the court's duty to administer and enforce the performance of a trust 'as much where there is a visitor as where there is none'.[76]

Even where no trust could be identified, the Court of Chancery sometimes interfered with the administration of a charitable corporation where such interference was 'necessary', in the sense that there was no other person to ensure that corporate funds were properly administered in furtherance of the corporation's charitable objects.[77] Thus, in the eighteenth-century case of *Attorney-General v Middleton*, the Court of Chancery held that while a foundation that had a charter with proper powers would provide 'no ground to come into this court', a foundation with no charter would fall within its jurisdiction as a matter of necessity.[78] A charitable corporation with no visitor could likewise be the subject of an administrative scheme.[79] And where the 'visitor' of a charitable corporation was also the person charged with the management of its estate and revenues, the courts were willing to supervise that management, since there must somewhere be a power to regulate, and no person should be allowed to judge his own cause.[80] While the court's jurisdiction over the charitable corporation was subject to substantial limits, therefore, it appears that the court's impulse to protect property devoted to charity sometimes prevailed over its impulse to protect the settlor's private supervisory regime, even where there was no trust.

As the foregoing paragraphs indicate, the 'regulatory regime' that was applicable to charitable corporations at common law differed substantially from that associated with charitable trusts. Like its trust law counterpart, however, the regime bore the weight of the respective regulatory impulses of public and private law in comparable measure. The common law provided an unrivalled protection of the autonomy interests of the founders of charitable corporations, allowing them not only to formulate their own charitable projects, but also to establish the framework and the arbiter for their continued regulation. Because charitable corporations were all creatures of the royal prerogative, however, it is arguable that the common law in fact viewed all charitable corporations as *public* projects, and the sovereign as their true founder. Whether or not this is the case, the efforts made by the courts to exercise a residual jurisdiction over charitable corporations, in the face of significant limitations on their power, demonstrate that the impulse to protect the public interest in charity property attached to charitable corporations as well as trusts. While the existence of separate supervisory regimes for charitable trusts and corporations necessarily complicates our doctrinal map, therefore, it does not undermine our claims about the general hybridity of the common law charities tradition.

[76] Ibid 466. See also *A-G v Dedham School* (n 36) 356 ('this Court does not interfere with the visitatorial power, unless it finds a breach of trust').
[77] See further Cullity (n 74) 23.
[78] *A-G v Middleton* (1751) 2 Ves Sr 327, 28 ER 210 (Ch).
[79] This is implicit in *A-G v The Governors of the Foundling Hospital* (1793) 2 Ves J 42, 30 ER 514, 47.
[80] ibid. See also *A-G v Lock* (1744) 3 Atk 164 (Ch); *Middleton* (n 78).

III. The Modern Charity Regulators: Comparing 'Civil' and 'Tax-based' Regulatory Regimes

In many common law jurisdictions, the functions of the Crown and the superior courts as charity regulators have today been replaced, supplemented or delegated to other regulatory institutions in a modern regime of charity regulation. A major purpose of this book is to begin mapping these regimes' interface with the common law, and with the public law–private law divide. However, charity law has become increasingly complex since the time of its inception in Chancery. Areas of law that were unknown to early Chancery judges, such as human rights law and the law of public contracts, have encroached upon the field. The tax treatment of charity property has emerged as a central consideration, raising persistent questions about whether the fiscal implications of charitable status should influence charity law's development. Most significantly, perhaps, the English common law of charities has been exported to a variety of common law jurisdictions, where it has been transformed through its interaction with different doctrines, institutions and constitutional norms.

To pursue our comparative mapping goal amidst such complexity, we must establish principles of division that distinguish between various *classes* of charity regulation in the contemporary common law world.[81] In pursuit of that aim, this work puts forward a first, basic division between what I will call 'civil' and 'tax-based' regulatory regimes.[82] A civil regime of charity regulation, in my account, is one in which decisions about charitable status and the ongoing regulation of charities are made independently of the tax consequences that attach to the status. Civil charity regulators typically have a charity-specific statutory mandate, and operate at a substantial level of independence from government. A tax-based regime of charity regulation, on the other hand, is one in which decisions about charitable status and the ongoing regulation of charities are embedded within a general framework of tax administration. Tax-based charity regulators typically have a statutory mandate that reflects their general tax administration purposes, and operate in a much closer relationship with government. Civil charity law regimes can be found in jurisdictions such as England and Wales, Scotland, Ireland, Singapore and Australia, while tax-based charity law regimes dominate in Canada and the United States.

This book explores the suggested dichotomy between civil and tax-based charity regulation with primary reference to two modern charity regulators: the Charity

[81] On the structure of classification, see J Weinrib, 'What Can Kant Teach Us about Legal Classification?' (2010) 23 *Canadian Journal of Law and Jurisprudence* 203.

[82] The use of the term 'civil' to describe a type of regulatory regime for charities is somewhat less than ideal, given the multiple meanings of the term. However, the term is user friendly and sometimes used by the Charity Commission to describe its own character: see Charity Commission, *Tackling Abuse and Mismanagement 2014–15—Annex 1* [4].

Commission for England and Wales, which administers the Charities Act 2011 (UK), and the Canada Revenue Agency's Charities Directorate, which administers the 'registered charity regime' set out in the Canadian Income Tax Act. The Charity Commission and registered charity regimes share a number of common traits. Both emerged against the background of the common law of charities, and continue to rely heavily on many of its substantive doctrines. Both operate in jurisdictions that grant substantial (though distinct) tax privileges to charitable institutions and gifts.[83] Both constitute in fact the *primary* regimes of charity regulation within their respective jurisdictions,[84] although they coexist with other bodies of law.

Despite these common features, this book argues, the Charity Commission and Charities Directorate are fundamentally dissimilar charity regulators. The Charity Commission is a civil regulator, a non-ministerial government department with a charity-specific mandate. It can generally be understood as the inheritor of the charities jurisdiction of the English Crown and the superior courts. The Commission employs procedures and remedies that are broadly aligned with those of the common law tradition and, like the common law, balances the autonomy interests of donors and charities primarily against the public interest in properly and effectively administered charity property. The Charities Directorate, by contrast, is a tax-based regulator, or more specifically an internal administrative unit of Canada's federal revenue authority. The Directorate employs procedures and remedies that are often at odds with the common law charities tradition, and pursues a different kind of public–private balancing that weighs the autonomy interests of donors and charities against the public interest in the integrity of the tax base.

In these and other ways, the civil and tax-based regulatory regimes that are the focus of this work interact in very different ways with the common law of charities, and with the respective spheres of public law and private law. The following chapters seek to shed light on these different relationships by examining select institutional, doctrinal and procedural features of English and Canadian charity law. The challenges of this comparative exercise will be further considered in Chapter 5. However, it is important to emphasize from the outset that both regimes exist in relationship with other bodies of domestic law. For example, while the Charity

[83] To take one example, individual taxpayers in the UK make charitable gifts out of after-tax income, and the government then transfers to the recipient charities an amount roughly equal to the bottom-rate tax payable on the gift. In Canada, by contrast, individuals claim tax credits for charitable gifts directly from the government. The tax treatment of charitable gifts in the UK is covered in a number of leading texts, including Picarda (n 1) ch 55, and J Kessler and S Kamal, *Venables and Kessler on the Taxation of Charities*, 6th edn (Oxford, Key Haven, 2007). The leading text in Canada is ABC Drache, RB Hayhoe and DP Stevens, *Charities Taxation, Policy and Practice. Taxation* (Toronto, Thomson Carswell, 2007).

[84] This is not a controversial proposition in England and Wales, nor, I would argue, in Canada: see P Monahan and E Roth, *Federal Regulation of Charities: A Critical Assessment of Recent Proposals for Legislative and Regulatory Reform* (Toronto, York University, 2000) 7; Drache, Hayhoe and Stevens (n 84) 1.2 and ch 10.

Commission for England and Wales remains the jurisdiction's primary charity regulator, it coexists with a revenue authority that has an increasingly strong presence in the field. The role of UK tax authorities in English charity regulation was historically relatively limited, due in large part to a long-standing provision in the Charities Act that makes the Charity Commission the presumptive arbiter of charitable status for all purposes other than rectification of the register.[85] However, this presumption has been displaced by the Finance Act 2010, which sets out four conditions that an institution must now meet in order to be recognized as a charity for tax purposes in the UK.[86] The new provisions define charitable purposes by reference to the Charities Act 2011, and continue to require charities to register with the Charity Commission. However, the provisions also require a charity to establish that its managers are 'fit and proper persons' to manage the body or trust, effectively giving Her Majesty's Revenue and Customs (HMRC) the last word on whether an institution is administered well enough to benefit from charitable tax reliefs. HMRC has a growing number of other regulatory tools that can be used to prevent the misadministration of charitable resources, including restrictions on tax relief for non-charitable expenditures, and the general anti-abuse rule.[87] These legislative developments have altered the relationship between the Charity Commission and HMRC, and raised concerns that HMRC may usurp part of the Commission's traditional regulatory role.[88]

If England and Wales's civil charity regulator must increasingly jostle with the UK tax authority for regulatory dominance over the field, Canada's tax-based charity regulator must contend with the limits of Canada's constitutional structure, as well as an increasing number of provincial regulatory regimes. As we shall see in Chapter 5, Canada has 10 provinces, three territories, and a constitutional structure that assigns to the provinces the exclusive authority to make laws regarding the establishment, maintenance and management of charities. While most of the provinces have made only minimal use of this authority to date, the provincial legislatures do exercise their authority over matters that intersect with charity law, including corporate law and human rights law. Canada's largest province (Ontario) also has a statutory regime of charity regulation that is based loosely on the English Charity Commission model. Aspects of these supplemental provincial regimes will be examined in Chapter 5. For now, however, we turn to examine the origins and present disposition of the Charity Commission for England and Wales.

[85] CA 1960, s 5(1); CA 1993, s 4(1); CA 2011, s 37.

[86] Finance Act 2010, s 30 and sch 6. See generally J Smith, 'Notes on the Finance Acts: Section 30 of and Schedule 6 to the Finance Act 2010: Charity Re-defined' [2010] *British Tax Review* 415.

[87] D Morris, 'Recent Developments in Charity Taxation in the United Kingdom: The Law Gives and the Law Takes Away' in M Harding and others (eds), *Not-for-Profit Law: Theoretical and Comparative Perspectives* (Cambridge, Cambridge University Press, 2014) 206–07.

[88] ibid 257.

IV. The Charity Commission for England and Wales

A. Origins

We have seen that at common law, a charity could be subject to either a public or private supervisory jurisdiction, depending on its legal form and the manner of its establishment. While all charitable trusts fell within the inherent jurisdiction of the courts, the mode of supervision of a charitable corporation depended on the directions of its founder, who could both establish the charity's laws and appoint the person who would apply them. In any case where a charity encompassed a trust or lacked a competent regulator, however, the Crown could invoke the court's inherent jurisdiction to control and administer charity property. If a uniting principle underlay this web of common law rules, it was that there must always be some competent person with broad powers to oversee the administration of charitable funds.

The common law's commitment to the competent oversight of charities appears to have been shared by many English citizens and politicians, whose efforts over the course of two centuries culminated in the creation of the Charity Commission regime. In the eighteenth century, a number of English communities carried out local charity inquiries, hoping that by publicising and documenting charitable gifts, they would protect themselves against the disappearance of charitable funds.[89] In 1786 a parliamentarian named Thomas Gilbert successfully introduced a Bill that required churchwardens to provide the authorities with details of charitable donations given in their parishes for the benefit of the poor.[90] The majority of parishes responded to the Gilbert survey. However, the responses were far from complete, and the survey did not result in any legislative action.[91] Nonetheless, as Owen notes, the Gilbert survey did 'arouse some slight interest in endowments as a national asset and public problem', and laid the foundation for 'a more rational and responsible attitude [to charitable resources] on the part of the State'.[92] It was followed, in 1812, by the enactment of two charity statutes, which sought to simplify the common law procedure for remedying breaches of charitable trusts.[93] These statutes also required charities to register declarations of their property and income with the local Clerk of the Peace and the Chancery Court.

[89] RS Tompson, *The Charity Commission and the Age of Reform* (London, Routledge & Kegan Paul, 1979) 78–81.

[90] 26 Geo III c 58. A similar, earlier Bill introduced by Gilbert was defeated in the House of Lords: see Tompson (n 89) 83.

[91] Tompson (n 89) 84.

[92] DE Owen, *English Philanthropy, 1660–1960* (Oxford, Oxford University Press, 1965) 86–87.

[93] An Act to provide a summary remedy in cases of Abuses of Trusts created for Charitable Purposes (52 Geo III c 101); Charitable Donations Registration Act 1812 (52 Geo III c 102).

The immediate story of the establishment of the Charity Commissioners for England and Wales begins with Henry (later Lord) Brougham, a Scottish advocate and Opposition Member of Parliament with a 'consuming interest in the education of the poor'.[94] In 1816, Brougham persuaded the House of Commons to appoint a Select Committee to inquire into the education of the 'lower orders' in London. The Committee included several active charity law reformers. In its first report in June 1816, it alluded to evidence it had received 'which show[ed] the necessity of Parliament as speedily as possible instituting an inquiry into the management of charitable donations and other funds for the instruction of the Poor'.[95] The need for a distinct body to inquire into charity abuses emerged as a central theme in the Committee's reports, and in the spring of 1818 Brougham introduced a Bill to the House of Commons for the creation of such a body. By August 1818 the Tory government had appointed the first 'Commissioners to inquire concerning Charities in England for the Education of the Poor'.[96] One year later, the Commissioners' jurisdiction was expanded to encompass all of the charities in England and Wales.[97] The question that took another 35 years to answer was whether Parliament should create a *permanent* charity regulator.

The records of the legislative proceedings that preceded the appointment of the first Charity Commissioners indicate some of the propositions upon which advocates based their case for a permanent regulatory authority. The first was that the property devoted to charitable uses in England and Wales was a valuable resource that was worthy of protection. This does not appear to have been a matter of great debate. The Gilbert survey, which had twice been republished since its completion, came to be seen as evidence of the enormity of the true value of the nation's charitable trusts,[98] and the parliamentary records contain references to how 'amply' the English poor had always been provided for 'by the pious munificence of individuals'.[99]

The second proposition underlying the case for a permanent charity regulator was that the nation's valuable charitable resources were being abused, whether by design or neglect or because of defects in trust instruments and in the law. The 1818 report of the Select Committee on Education documented multiple instances of charity funds being misapplied and misappropriated, which Brougham invoked, to great effect, in parliamentary debate.[100] Brougham then wrote a widely read public letter to Sir Samuel Romilly, in which he catalogued many egregious cases of abuse and neglect within English charities.[101] The gifted politician's descriptions

[94] CW New, *The Life of Henry Brougham to 1830* (Oxford, Clarendon Press, 1961) 211.

[95] Tompson (n 89) 95–96.

[96] ibid 107.

[97] 59 Geo III c 81, s V.

[98] HC Deb 8 May 1818, vol 38, cols 595–96.

[99] HC Deb 8 May 1818, vol 38, cols 596, 610. See also HC Deb 22 May 1845, vol 80 noting that the Report of the Commissioners identified 25,000 charities with an annual income of less than 50 pounds.

[100] HC Deb 8 May 1818, vol 38, cols 596, 599, 610. See also HC Deb 8 May 1818, vol 38, col 596, 609.

[101] J Fishman, 'Charitable Accountability and Reform in Nineteenth-Century England: the Case of the Charity Commission' (2005) 80 *Chicago-Kent Law Review* 723, 734.

of charity abuse were likely exaggerated.[102] Nevertheless, they were not challenged in either House, and played an important role in causing Parliament to expand the Select Committee into a commission.[103]

The third pillar of the reformers' case for a permanent charity regulator was that the existing remedies for breaches of charitable trusts, and the existing mechanisms for modifying charitable trusts, were grossly inadequate. In his early speeches in support of a charity commission, Brougham chronicled the demise of the Statute of Elizabeth, whose provisions, though once the accepted procedure for the investigation of charitable abuses, had fallen into disuse.[104] However, he reserved his harshest words for the Court of Chancery, which, in addition to its inherent jurisdiction over charitable trusts, had final authority over any decrees made by a commission under the Elizabethan statute.[105]

Brougham's assertion that the Court of Chancery was neither an effective nor an affordable body for the resolution of disputes over charitable property proved considerably more controversial than his tales of charity abuse. Lord Chancellor Eldon was greatly vexed by the criticisms of his court, and responded by endorsing a wide range of legislative amendments that significantly reduced the powers of the first Commissioners.[106] The view that Chancery procedure was cumbersome and ineffective gained widespread acceptance, however, and by 1835 even the Crown's representatives were attesting to the 'prejudicial delay and destructive costs' incident to Chancery proceedings.[107]

The three main pillars of the case for charity law reform—the value attached to the nation's charitable resources, the abuse to which they were subject, and the perceived inability of Chancery to protect them—are all well evidenced in the legislative records of the time. However, the legislative records also suggest that from the earliest days of the debate over the Charity Commissioners, the political field was split between those who saw charity property as *private* property, and thus prioritized the autonomy interests of charity founders and trustees, and those who saw charity property as *public* property, and thus prioritized the public interest in the usage of those resources. Brougham offered a provocative summation of this debate in Parliament:

> ... let me here notice the clamour which has already been raised against the powers proposed to be conferred upon the commissioners charged with this important inquiry. I hear it said, that they are inconsistent with the rights of private property. Under the flimsy pretence of great tenderness for those sacred rights, I am well aware that the

[102] Tompson (n 89) 96–97.
[103] Fishman (n 101) 734–36.
[104] HC Deb 8 May 1818, vol 38, col 607.
[105] HC Deb 8 May 1818, vol 38, cols 607–08.
[106] Owen (n 92) 186; Tompson (n 89) 106.
[107] SC on Public Charities (1835) vi. Lord Chancellor Lyndhurst, in introducing the Charitable Trusts Bill, took the view that the Court of Chancery was well suited to deal with large endowments but not with small charities: HC Deb 22 May 1845, vol 80. For further discussion of criticisms of the Chancery during this period, see Jones (n 8) 163–65; Fishman (n 101).

> authors of the outcry conceal their own dread of being themselves dragged to light as robbers of the poor, and I will tell those shameless persons, that the doctrine which they promulge, of charitable funds in a trustee's hands being private property, is utterly repugnant to the whole law of England. That law regards the inheritance of the poor as a matter of public, not of private jurisdiction, and deals with it as it does with the rights of the Crown and the Church ... I therefore again assert, that a more gross abuse of language never was committed by ignorant or by willful perversion, than the statement that charitable funds are of a private nature.[108]

Other early proponents of charity law reform joined Brougham in describing charities as the 'property of the public',[109]and in 1846 the Lord Chancellor defended the Charitable Trusts Bill on the ground that charity trustees were '*public* officers, invested with *public* powers and *public* duties', who should be treated as such by the law.[110] Other powerful politicians disagreed, however, and fought to protect the autonomy of donors and trustees by opposing the Bill or seeking to exempt their constituents from the Commissioners' domain.[111]

In 1853, some 35 years after Brougham began his quest to remedy the abuse of charity resources, Parliament finally created a 'public and permanent authority' to oversee the administration of charitable trusts in England and Wales. Due to the strong arguments in favour of protecting the autonomy of wealthy individuals, however, the statute was far narrower than Brougham had hoped. The Charitable Trusts Act 1853, which authorized the appointment of four Charity Commissioners, provided those officers with only a limited mandate to 'examine and inquire' into the administration of charities in England and Wales, and the management and application of their resources.[112] It also excluded places of worship, charities maintained by voluntary subscriptions, and a number of the nation's most powerful charities from its scope.[113] In 1860, Parliament substantially expanded this mandate by granting the Charity Commissioners concurrent jurisdiction with the Lord Chancellor over certain matters of charity administration, but the Commissioners could not make orders with respect to charities whose annual income exceeded 50 pounds except upon application of the trustees.[114] Thus began the Commissioners' role as the *alter ego* of the Court of Chancery in matters related to poor charities,[115] and a statutory regime of charity regulation that builds upon, and seeks to improve, the common law tradition of the judicial supervision of charities at the behest of the Crown.

[108] HC Deb 8 May 1818, vol 38, cols 603–04.

[109] HC Deb 27 May 1818, vol 38, col 976, per Lord Earl of Rosslyn.

[110] HL Deb 27 March 1846, vol 85, cols 155–56, per Lord Lyndhurst; see also HL Deb 22 May 1845, vol 80, cols 766–80.

[111] See, eg, HL Deb 27 March 1846, vol 85, cols 150, 153. See also Owen (n 92) 306–07.

[112] CTA 1853, s 9; see also LA Sheridan and GW Keeton, *The Modern Law of Charities*, 3rd edn (Cardiff, University College Cardiff Press, 1983) 253.

[113] CTA 1853, s 66; Charitable Trusts Amendment Act 1855 (18 & 19 Vict c 124) s 49.

[114] CTA 1860, s 2. Jurisdiction over these matters had already been devolved to lesser judicial authorities under the 1853 Act: see CTA 1853, ss 28, 32.

[115] Owen (n 92) 308.

B. Nature and Orientation

In order to shift our focus from the origins of the Charity Commissioners for England and Wales to the nature and orientation of the contemporary Charity Commission, we must skip over 150 years of developments in the field. The basic trajectory runs from the Commission's humble beginnings as the 'poor man's Chancery' to its current status as the powerful, if underfunded, regulator of most English charities. Since these developments have been chronicled in great detail elsewhere,[116] only the briefest sketch will be offered here. The statutory framework governing the Charity Commissioners remained relatively static from 1860, when the Commissioners were endowed with concurrent judicial powers, until the middle of the twentieth century. Change began to occur in 1952, however, when the government, concerned to consider the impact of the developing welfare state on the role of the charitable sector, appointed Lord Nathan to report on the changes to the law of charitable trusts 'which would be necessary to enable the maximum benefit to the community to be derived from them'.[117] The Charities Act 1960 implemented many of the Nathan Report's recommendations, introducing the first charities register, modifying the *cy-près* rule to allow charitable resources to be used more effectively, and reforming the three-person board of Charity Commissioners into a larger, more independent and more powerful body. It also amended the statutory definition of charity, thereby extending the jurisdiction of the Charity Commissioners to charities that were not trusts.[118] The Charities Act 1992 effected further changes, extending the registration requirements for charities and further enhancing the Commission's supervisory powers.[119] These and other changes were consolidated in the Charities Act 1993.

The most recent phase in the evolution of the Charity Commission regime began in 2001, when then-Prime Minister Tony Blair announced that the Cabinet Office's Strategy Unit would undertake a major review of charities and the not-for-profit sector.[120] The Strategy Unit had a broad mandate, and its final consultation paper, *Private Action, Public Benefit: A Review of Charities and the Wider Not-for-Profit Sector*, contained a number of recommendations for regulatory reforms. *Private Action, Public Benefit*, together with the consultation and consequent government response, formed the basis of the reform measures that were

[116] For a concise summary of these developments, see Hodgson Review (2012) 10–12. A more detailed history of the Charity Commission can be gleaned from old editions of charity law textbooks: see, for example, OD Tudor, LS Bristowe and WI Cook, *The Law of Charities and Mortmain Being a Third Edition of Tudor's Charitable Trusts*, 3rd edn (London, Reeves and Turner, 1889); S Maurice, *The Charities Act, 1960* (London, Sweet & Maxwell, 1961).

[117] Report of the Committee on the Law and Practice related to Charitable Trusts (Cmd 8710, 1952) (Chaired by Lord Nathan) (Nathan Report) 1.

[118] CA 1960, s 45(1).

[119] Charities Act 1992, ss 2–3, 6–12.

[120] See generally Hodgson Review (2012); A Dunn and CA Riley, 'Supporting the Not-for-Profit Sector: the Government's Review of Charitable and Social Enterprise' (2004) 67 *MLR* 632, 632–33.

proposed in the Charities Bill 2004 and eventually enacted as the Charities Act 2006. The Charities Act 2006 represented a comprehensive overhaul of the English law of charities; as a result, Parliament built an automatic review procedure into the legislation, requiring that the statute be reviewed within five years.[121] This review was completed by Lord Hodgson of Astley Abbotts in 2012 and provides a valuable perspective on the first five years of the Act. The provisions of the Charities Act 2006 and earlier charity law statutes have subsequently been consolidated into the Charities Act 2011,[122] a lengthy statute that articulates the functions and powers of the contemporary Charity Commission in great detail. My intent in what follows is not to comprehensively summarize those provisions, but rather to highlight provisions that clarify the Commission's relationship to the common law's charity regulators, and those that shed light on the nature of the Commission's regulatory impulse towards charities and their trustees.

The nature and orientation of the modern Charity Commission are in large part dictated by Part 2 of the Charities Act 2011, which contains a detailed articulation of the institution's composition, objectives, functions and duties. Pursuant to Part 2, the Charity Commission is now a corporate body, whose members are appointed by the Minister for the Cabinet Office.[123] The Charity Commission has a chief executive appointed by the Commission itself, a staff of approximately 300 persons, and an annual budget of approximately 25 million pounds sterling.[124] Although the functions of the Commission are performed on behalf of the Crown, the Act specifies that the Commission itself is not subject to the direction or control of any Minister of the Crown or other government department.[125]

Pursuant to section 14 of the Act, the Commission has five statutory objectives:

1. to increase public trust and confidence in charities (the 'public confidence objective');
2. to promote awareness and understanding of the operation of the public benefit requirement (the 'public benefit objective');
3. to promote compliance by charity trustees with their legal obligations in exercising control and management of the administration of their charities (the 'compliance objective');
4. to promote the effective use of charitable resources (the 'charitable resources objective'); and
5. to enhance the accountability of charities to donors, beneficiaries and the general public (the 'accountability objective').[126]

[121] Charities Act 2006, s 73; Hodgson Review (2012).

[122] Unless otherwise specified, future references to the English Charities Act will be to this consolidating statute.

[123] CA 2011, s 13(1), sch 1, para 1(1).

[124] The Commission's present and forecast future budget is set out in the Hodgson Review: Hodgson Review (2012) 45.

[125] Unless the control is provided for under another enactment: see CA 2011, s 13(3)–(5).

[126] CA 2011, s 14.

The Act also establishes the functions of the Commission, which include determining whether institutions qualify as charities; encouraging and facilitating the better administration of charities; and 'identifying and investigating apparent misconduct or mismanagement in the administration of charities and taking remedial or protective action in connection with' such misconduct or mismanagement.[127] Section 15 clarifies that the Commission may give advice or guidance with respect to the administration of charities in connection with its general functions, and that it must maintain an accurate and up-to-date charities register. Section 16 addresses the *manner* in which the Commission must perform these functions, stipulating (among other things) that the regulator must perform its functions in a way that is compatible with its statutory objectives. It also provides that the Commission must, so far as is practicable or appropriate, act in a way which is compatible with the encouragement of charitable giving, and the facilitation of innovation by or on behalf of charities.[128]

The Charities Act 2011 endows the Commission with extensive powers to carry out its statutory functions and duties. Some of these powers are best understood as an extension *to* the Commission of the historical charities jurisdiction of the Court of Chancery. Thus, pursuant to section 69, a provision that has existed in a similar form since 1860, the Commission may by order 'exercise the same jurisdiction and powers as are exercisable by the High Court in charity proceedings' for the purposes of establishing a scheme for the administration of a charity; appointing, discharging or removing a charity trustee; or vesting or transferring charity property.[129] The Commission has long had concurrent jurisdiction to make schemes for the application of charity property *cy-près*,[130]and now also enjoys the same power as the High Court to relieve a charity trustee of liability for a breach of trust or duty.[131] Despite these extensive powers, the Act does place certain restrictions on the Commission's concurrent jurisdiction. Most notably, the Commission does not have jurisdiction to determine title to a property as between a charity and an adverse party, nor to try or determine any question as to the existence or extent of any charge or trust.[132] While the Commission cannot confer charitable status on an institution in the context of such a dispute, however, the Commission routinely confers charitable status on trusts and companies in the context of its registration function. Overall, then, the Act provides the Commission with most of the supervisory and curative powers that make up the court's inherent jurisdiction over charities.

[127] CA 2011, s 15(1). The other general functions involve the issuance of public collections certificates, and the dissemination of information and advice relating to the Commission's other functions and objectives.

[128] CA 2011, s 16(2), (5).

[129] CA 2011, s 69(1). Disobedience to a section 69 order of the Commission may be dealt with as disobedience to an order of the High Court: s 336. For the original version of this provision, see CTA 1860, s 2.

[130] CA 2011, s 67.

[131] CA 2011, s 191.

[132] CA 2011, s 70(1).

Some of the Commission's powers may also be understood as an extension *of* the charities jurisdiction itself. For example, the Charities Act 2011 relaxes the common law rules that prohibited the courts from altering the trusts of a chartered or statutory charity; the Commission shares this expanded jurisdiction with the court.[133] The Act also extends the circumstances in which charity property may be applied *cy-près*. To this end, the Act allows the court and the Commission to consider whether the original purposes have ceased to provide a 'suitable and effective' method of using the property, regard being had to the spirit of the gift and the social and economic circumstances prevailing at the time of the proposed alteration.[134] The Commission, but not the court, can also authorize charity trustees to temporarily apply a limited amount of a charity's income *cy-près* in the absence of a scheme.[135] In these and other ways, the contemporary Charity Commission may be regarded as exercising a sort of 'charities jurisdiction plus'.

The powers described thus far are those that the Commission, like the courts, must generally exercise when an application is brought before it. As we will explore further in Chapter 4, however, the Charities Act 2011 also gives the Commission a variety of powers to regulate charities of its own motion. Pursuant to section 70(5), for example, the Commission may exercise its section 69 concurrent jurisdiction where it is satisfied that charity trustees ought in the interests of charity to apply for a scheme, but have unreasonably refused or neglected to do so.[136] Pursuant to sections 80 and 81, the Commission may remove and appoint charity trustees of its own motion in a variety of other circumstances, and make associated vesting orders. The Commission may order a charity trustee to reimburse to the charity any remuneration to which it is not entitled under the Act, also of its own motion.[137] And a new provision in the Charities Act 2011 empowers the Commission to order a person in control of charity property to apply that property in a specified manner, in cases where the Commission is satisfied that the person is unwilling to apply it properly for the purposes of the charity, and that it is necessary or desirable to make an order to secure a proper application of the property.[138]

Even more significantly, perhaps, the Commission has a broad discretion to 'institute inquiries with regard to charities or a particular charity or class of charities' of its own motion, either generally or for particular purposes.[139] There are no preconditions to the exercise of this power of inquiry, which is complemented by a wide array of powers to obtain documents and other information.[140] Moreover,

[133] CA 2011, ss 68, 69; see also Picarda (n 1) 787.

[134] CA 2011, ss 62, 67.

[135] CA 2011, s 75.

[136] The Commission must also have given the charity the opportunity to make representations: CA 2011, s 75(4).

[137] CA 2011, s 186.

[138] CA 2011, s 85.

[139] CA 2011, s 46(1).

[140] See, for example, CA 2011 ss 48, 52. A section 46 inquiry is, however, subject to review by the Charity Tribunal: see CA 2011, sch 6.

where the Commission is satisfied, at any time after the institution of an inquiry, that there has been misconduct or mismanagement in a charity's administration, or that it is necessary or desirable to act for the purpose of protecting charity property, it may of its own motion take one or more of a range of protective and remedial measures specified in the Act.[141] In other words, the Commission model builds upon the remedial flexibility of the common law tradition, but frees the Commission from depending on third parties for the exercise of its regulatory authority. In this important sense, the contemporary Charity Commission is a much more powerful charity regulator than the Court of Chancery.

What, then, may we posit about the general regulatory impulse of the contemporary Commission, based on the provisions of the Charities Act 2011? Certainly, the Act contains some provisions that promote the autonomy interests of charities and their trustees. Section 185 provides charities with a new power to remunerate their trustees where the charity's trusts do not expressly prohibit such remuneration.[142] Section 124 extends the circumstances in which charities can mortgage their land without an order of the Commission. Most notably, section 20 constrains the Commission's powers to intervene in a charity's operation by specifying that, with limited exceptions, the Act does not authorize the Commission to exercise functions corresponding to those of a charity trustee in relation to a charity, or otherwise to be directly involved in the administration of a charity.

In spite of these autonomy-enhancing provisions, there is little doubt that the regulatory body constituted by the Charities Act 2011 operates under strong public law impulses. It is institutionally oriented towards intervening in an identified public interest, namely the public interest in properly administered and effectively employed charity property. This conclusion flows from the Commission's statutory objectives, which are entirely silent on the autonomy interests of charity trustees. It is bolstered by the Commission's extended statutory powers to address misconduct and mismanagement in charities, and to alter a charity's original trust. And it is consistent with the Commission's own understanding of its 'core role': 'to protect the public's interest in the integrity of charity'.[143] In privileging this public interest, however, the Charity Commission places correspondingly less value on the autonomy of charities, including their ability to rely on their trustees' judgement. This counterbalance did not escape the notice of Lord Hodgson, who argued in his Review that the Act should go further in 'deregulating and freeing up charities', and in placing more control and responsibility in the hands of trustees.[144]

[141] CA 2011, ss 76, 78, 79, 84.

[142] There are other conditions precedent to the exercise of this power, including that the remuneration does not exceed what is reasonable: CA 2011, s 185.

[143] Charity Commission, *Strategic Plan 2012–15*, 2 ('Mission').

[144] Hodgson Review (2012) [2.17]–[2.18].

V. Conclusion

This chapter has outlined the nature and orientation of the regulatory institutions that have historically had primary responsibility for the oversight of charities in England and Wales. In so doing, it has started to make the case for the *general hybridity* of the common law charities tradition, and the *context-specific hybridity* of the contemporary Charity Commission regime. The common law tradition of the judicial supervision of charitable trusts and corporations was a hybrid in the general sense that it navigated the tension between protecting the autonomy of property-owning individuals to direct and control their own wealth, and protecting the public interest in properly and effectively administered charity property, and accorded these opposing interests comparable weight. In the case of the charitable trust, the common law achieved this balance by adapting a primarily private law institution to a variant that was more of a public law nature. In the case of the charitable corporation, the common law achieved this balance by developing a Crown-sanctioned institution that provided unparalleled protection of the autonomy interests of the private founder, and then tempering that protection with a reassertion of the supervisory role of the courts.

Our initial survey of the contemporary English regime of charity regulation suggests that it continues to reflect the common law's duality of focus on the autonomy interests of benevolent property owners, and the public interest in charity property. However, the survey has also qualified this picture of regulatory continuity in two important ways. The first qualification is that modern English charities are regulated as more public-leaning projects than English charities of the past. While the Charities Act 2011 does, in limited respects, require the Charity Commission to protect charity autonomy, its overall effect is to strongly orient the Commission towards intervening in the affairs of English charities to protect the public's interest in the proper and effective administration of charity property.

The second qualification is that the relative continuity between the common law tradition and the Charity Commission regime is not mirrored in every common law jurisdiction with a modern regime of charity regulation, and is thus better characterized as context-specific. The contemporary charity law landscape is marked by a great diversity of regulatory regimes, which can initially be classified according to whether they are of a civil or tax-based character. Even within the civil regulator class, the character of particular regulatory regimes will vary: each regime will assign a somewhat different weight to the public and private interests we have identified in this chapter, as well as incorporating additional interests that may be specific to the jurisdiction. In a tax-based regulatory regime, however, the very nature of the balancing exercise is different. For as we will see in Chapter 5, the basic public interest that a revenue authority is mandated to protect is not a public interest in properly and effectively administered charity property, but a public interest in the integrity of the tax base.

3

Public Benefit and the Substantive Public Law–Private Law Divide

I. Introduction

The rule that an institution must be 'for the public benefit' in order to be charitable is perhaps the most distinguishing, and the most controversial, substantive doctrine of the law of charities. The public benefit that a charity provides is the institution's most prominent 'public element',[1] and the element that is most often used to justify the special treatment that charities receive.[2] Much has been written about the public benefit doctrine during the years since its development, and particularly since the enactment of the Charities Act 2006.[3] This chapter seeks to add a new perspective to the existing literature by examining the public benefit doctrine through the lens of the 'substantive' public law–private law divide and testing out a claim about the doctrine's hybrid character. I will suggest that the public benefit doctrine is one of the central hinges upon which turns the whole notion of charity law's public law–private law hybridity.

The project of the public law–private law divide in its substantive dimension is first to identify and categorize specific rules and doctrines as 'public law' or 'private law' doctrines, and then to examine their interrelationship.[4] We saw in Chapter 1 that this project has received increasing attention in recent years, such that there is now a substantial body of literature examining areas where public law and private law doctrines intersect, and debating the merits of their cross-fertilization.[5]

[1] S Maurice, 'The Public Element in Charitable Trusts' (1951) 15 *The Conveyancer* 338.

[2] See, eg, *Dingle v Turner* [1972] AC 601, [1972] 1 All ER 878 (HL) 889–90.

[3] A non-exhaustive list of this literature includes Maurice (n 1); GHL Fridman, 'Charities and Public Benefit' (1953) 31 *Canadian Bar Review* 537; M Moran, 'Rethinking Public Benefit: The Definition of Charity in the Era of the Charter' in J Phillips, B Chapman and D Stevens (eds), *Between State and Market: Essays on Charities Law and Policy in Canada* (Montreal, McGill-Queen's University Press, 2001); J Hackney, 'Charities and Public Benefit' (2008) 124 *LQR* 34; J Warburton, 'Charities and Public Benefit—from Confusion to Light?' (2008) 10 *Charity Law and Practice Review* 1; J Garton, *Public Benefit in Charity Law* (Oxford, Oxford University Press, 2013); M Synge, *The New Public Benefit Requirement: Making Sense of Charity Law?* (Oxford, Hart Publishing, 2015).

[4] M Freedland, 'The Evolving Approach to the Public/Private Distinction in English Law' in M Freedland and J-B Auby (eds), *The Public Law/Private Law Divide: une entente assez cordiale?* (Oxford, Hart Publishing, 2006) 108.

[5] See Ch 1, text at nn 32–34.

As I previously suggested in the same chapter, however, it is also possible to imagine public and private colliding *within* a singular legal doctrine, such that the doctrine could not be said to have a single or even primary site of belonging within either the public law or private law sphere. Such a doctrine, I argued, would best be characterized as a *hybrid* legal doctrine, within which the strength of public law and private law thinking are felt in comparable measure.

This chapter explores the claim that the public benefit doctrine is such a legal hybrid. More specifically, it depicts the development of the public benefit doctrine as a prime example of the way in which charity law's substantive doctrines have continually been adjusted so as to maintain over the long term a functional equilibrium between the protection of the autonomy of property-owning individuals to control and direct their own wealth (and, by extension, the autonomy of the trustees appointed by those individuals), and the furtherance of competing public interests or public welfare goals. Charity law makes these equilibrium adjustments, I claimed in Chapter 1, along several different continuums. One of these continuums extends between projects that are perceived to be wholly *altruistic* (or other-regarding) and projects that are perceived to be wholly *self-interested* (or self-regarding). A second continuum extends between projects that are fully aligned with the public welfare goals of the state or polity in question, and projects that, although altruistic, are nevertheless at variance with those public welfare goals (in shorthand, public-welfare-compliant projects and public-welfare-deviant projects). The axiom that government must act in the public interest[6] is archetypally 'public' in both of the above-mentioned senses. The public benefit doctrine's relationship with each of these continuums is markedly more complex.

This chapter seeks to clarify the particular balance that the common law public benefit doctrine strikes between individual and collective project pursuit along these two continuums, and to trace the multiple equilibrium adjustments that public benefit has undergone in England and Wales since the enactment of the Charities Act 2006. It proceeds in the following manner. In Section II, I review the history of the common law public benefit doctrine and its basic constituting principles. I argue that while the common law doctrine has always required charities to be mostly 'other-regarding', and embodies public law thinking to this extent, it provides charities with considerable autonomy to define *what type* of benefit the charity will provide and *what 'public'* will receive that benefit. It does not require the founders and trustees of charities to have regard to the needs of *all* their fellow citizens, nor necessarily to treat them equitably. In relation to the continuum between public-welfare compliance and public-welfare deviance, therefore, the doctrine is largely public-welfare neutral, and experiences the substantial weight of private law thought. These public law and private law impulses have historically

[6] In the Western liberal tradition, it is generally accepted that government must act in the public interest: see, eg, D Oliver, *Common Values and the Public-Private Divide* (London, Butterworths, 1999) 13. The precise meaning of this principle is considerably more controversial, as we shall see in Section III.

borne down with comparable weight on the public benefit doctrine, producing what we may understand as a hybrid legal rule.

Following this discussion of the common law position, Section III examines the context-specific ways in which the equilibrium between the doctrine's public and private elements has been adjusted under the contemporary Charity Commission regime. I consider how the enactment of the Charities Act 2006 affected the public benefit criterion, focusing particularly on the Commission's 2008 Public Benefit Guidance, and two important decisions that were rendered in its wake. Finally, in Section IV, I consider whether these equilibrium adjustments have undermined claims about public benefit's public–private hybridity, by contrasting the criterion with the quintessentially public law rule that government must act 'in the public interest'.

II. Public Benefit at Common Law

A. History and Nature

The lineage of the rule that an institution must be 'for the public benefit' to be charitable is generally traced back to the 1767 case of *Jones v Williams*, in which Lord Hardwicke, referring to the Statute of Elizabeth, defined a charity as 'a gift to a general public use, which extends to the poor as well as to the rich …'.[7] Public benefit did not emerge as a separate doctrinal criterion of a charitable purpose until considerably later.[8] Nevertheless, recent authority has confirmed that public benefit was 'from early times' inherent in the concept of charity and thus in the objects that fell within the Preamble to the Statute of Elizabeth.[9]

The courts have never attempted to define comprehensively what is, or is not, of public benefit. The common law doctrine built up 'not logically but empirically',[10] with the result that it has proved highly resistant to rationalization. A particular set of issues arose from the courts' historical tendency to assume that a purpose was charitable where it appeared to be for the relief of poverty, the advancement of education or the advancement of religion. This tendency had several results. First, it meant that many cases did not consider the public benefit issue at all.[11] Second, those courts that did consider the public benefit issue applied 'markedly different'

[7] *Jones v Williams* (1767) Amb 651, 27 ER 422 (Ch). See also Warburton (n 3) 3.

[8] *R (Independent Schools Council) v Charity Commission* [2011] UKUT 421 (TCC), [2012] Ch 214 (*Independent Schools Council*) [42]–[51].

[9] *Independent Schools Council* (n 8) [42]. Indeed, the prominent seventeenth-century Chancery lawyer Sir Francis Moore described public benefit as 'the key to the statute': see MR Chesterman, *Charities, Trusts, and Social Welfare* (London, Weidenfeld and Nicolson, 1979) 26.

[10] *Gilmour v Coats* [1949] AC 426 (HL).

[11] Warburton (n 3) 4.

standards of public benefit to the different heads of charity.[12] The tendency also came to be widely understood as a rebuttable 'presumption' that charities under the first three heads benefited the public in the requisite way.[13] For these and other reasons, commentators have described the public benefit doctrine as 'difficult', 'artificial', 'intangible' and 'nebulous', and as producing 'variable and unpredictable' results.[14] It is sometimes said that the authorities provide only a 'series of examples' of when a particular purpose may benefit the public within the meaning of the common law.[15]

B. Governing Principles

Despite the 'variable and unpredictable' nature of the public benefit doctrine, its basic features are well known. These are commonly broken down into two basic requirements or 'pillars': first, the purposes of the institution must confer a *benefit* on the public, and second, the class of persons eligible to benefit from the institution's purposes must constitute *the public*, or a sufficient section of it.[16] The first question—does the institution confer a benefit?—is to be answered by the court on the basis of the evidence before it. The intention of the donors cannot be taken into account.[17] Indirect and intangible benefits may satisfy the requirement, but any benefit must be capable of proof in a court of law.[18] The common law's conception of what purposes benefit the public is not static and may evolve to reflect society's changed habits, knowledge and laws.[19] Nonetheless, the concept tends to favour the status quo, since courts are hesitant to disrupt public benefit decisions of 'respectable antiquity', even where such decisions are confusing or out of date.[20]

Many of the finer points of the common law's conception of what constitutes a charitable 'benefit' can be traced back to the House of Lords' decision in *National Anti-Vivisection Society v IRC*.[21] In that case, a society that sought the abolition

[12] *Gilmour* (n 10) 449.

[13] See, for example, Warburton (n 3) 4. Both the Supreme Court of Canada and the Charities Directorate have taken the position that the English common law contained such a presumption: see *Vancouver Society of Immigrant & Visible Minority Women v MNR* [1999] 1 SCR 10, 169 DLR (4th) 34 [41]; *Guidelines for Registering a Charity: Meeting the Public Benefit Test* (CPS-024, March 2006) (*CRA Public Benefit Guidelines*) [3.3]. For a view that such a presumption never existed, see H Picarda, *The Law and Practice relating to Charities*, 4th edn (Hayward's Heath, Bloomsbury Professional, 2010) 39B.

[14] *Oppenheim v Tobacco Securities Trust Co Ltd* [1951] AC 297 (HL) 307; Fridman (n 3); Maurice (n 1).

[15] *Independent Schools Council* (n 8) [44].

[16] J Warburton and others, *Tudor on Charities*, 9th edn (London, Sweet & Maxwell, 2003) 7. There are competing analyses of the public benefit requirement: for two important accounts, see Garton (n 3); Synge (n 3).

[17] *Re Hummeltenberg* [1923] 1 Ch 237, 242, affirmed in *National Anti-Vivisection Society v IRC* [1948] AC 31 (HL) 44.

[18] *Gilmour* (n 10) 446.

[19] *Anti-Vivisection* (n 17) 74 (Lord Simonds).

[20] *Oppenheim* (n 14) 309.

[21] *Anti-Vivisection* (n 17).

of vivisection in all its forms sought an exemption from income tax on the basis that it promoted 'other purposes beneficial to the community' within the meaning of the fourth head of charity. In considering this request, the tax commissioners found as a fact that experiments on living animals had produced valuable scientific knowledge, and that any assumed public benefit related to the advancement of morals and education was greatly outweighed by the detriment to medical research and public health that would follow if the society achieved its goal. On appeal, the society argued that the protection of animals was a purpose beneficial to the community because of the moral benefit it produced, and that the court could not weigh this moral benefit against the material benefits of vivisection. However, the majority of the House of Lords ultimately decided it could weigh the relative value of these benefits, and in doing so held that the material benefits of vivisection were to be greatly preferred.

The *Anti-Vivisection* decision is generally understood to establish at least four principles related to the benefit criterion. First, it is the court, not the public or any interested party, which is the ultimate arbiter of what is beneficial for purposes of charity law.[22] As Lord Wright noted, a determination of charitable status is not a determination of the public consensus on the alleged worth of an institution's aims. The community's views on whether a purpose is beneficial may sometimes be taken into account, but ultimately it is for the courts to weigh advantage against disadvantage, even where the purpose relates to a controversial ethical or political issue.[23] The test, purportedly objective,[24] is whether the purpose reflects the 'true interests of mankind'.[25] Second, while a court may sometimes take the views of the people into account in determining public benefit, only the 'enlightened' opinions of the community are generally considered.[26] In practice, as the *Anti-Vivisection* case showed, enlightened views may be attributed to 'the people' without their direct input;[27] the personal value judgements of judges also play a role.[28]

The third principle that is often associated with the *Anti-Vivisection* case is that a charitable purpose must confer a 'net benefit' on the public in order to meet the public benefit test. This concept of a 'net benefit' can be derived from the general structure of the court's reasoning, and from Lord Wright's statement that courts must imagine the whole complex of circumstances, good and bad, that may result from the pursuit of objects in order to estimate whether an object will cumulatively benefit the community.[29] Finally, the *Anti-Vivisection* case establishes that

[22] *Anti-Vivisection* (n 17) 41; see also *Everywoman's Health Centre Society (1988) v MNR* [1992] 2 FC 52 (CA).

[23] *Anti-Vivisection* (n 17) 49, 72–73.

[24] *IRC v City of Glasgow Police Athletic Association* [1953] AC 380 (HL) 396.

[25] *Anti-Vivisection* (n 17) 73 (Lord Simonds).

[26] ibid 49 (Lord Wright).

[27] ibid 47 (Lord Wright) ('a man who has a beefsteak for dinner, if he thinks at all about the slaughter of the beast, reflects that that is inevitable in the present constitution of society').

[28] ibid 48. See also *McGovern v A-G* [1982] Ch 321, 336.

[29] *Anti-Vivisection* (n 17) 47.

objects that are 'contrary to the law' cannot be regarded as beneficial. Lord Wright took specific note of the situation of religious societies, stating that such a society 'may fail to satisfy the test if it is unlawful, and the test may vary from generation to generation ...'.[30] As we will see, the significance of these latter two principles has greatly increased in England and Wales since the enactment of the Human Rights Act 1998 and the Charities Act 2006.

The second pillar of the public benefit doctrine asserts that in order for a purpose to be charitable, the persons it benefits must be sufficiently numerous, and identified in such a way, as to constitute what the authorities have variously described as 'the public', 'a sufficient section of the public'[31] or 'an appreciably important class of the community'.[32] There is, however, no general or a priori rule as to what constitutes a sufficient section of the public.[33] In fact, the points of consensus on the limitations imposed by the common law authorities are relatively few. These points of consensus are as follows. First, a charity's benefit must be to some section of the *human* community.[34] Second, any 'private' benefit that a charity confers on individuals that are not proper beneficiaries must be merely incidental to its charitable functions.[35] Finally, there is consensus that the quality that distinguishes a charity's beneficiaries from other members of the public must not depend on their relationship to a particular person or employer.[36] However, this 'personal nexus' rule does not apply to charities for the relief of poor relations, nor does it prevent the settlor of an educational trust from suggesting that the trustees give preference to her descendants or employees.[37]

In addition to these agreed limitations on a charity's ability to define its public at common law, various additional possible limitations have been the subject of debate. A first point of debate is whether a charity with numerically few possible beneficiaries benefits a sufficient section of the public. Lord Simonds suggested in *Oppenheim* that the potential beneficiaries of a charitable trust should not be 'numerically negligible',[38] but subsequently stated in *Baddeley* that a valid charity might 'by its very nature' benefit only a limited number of people.[39] A second point of debate is whether a charity is entitled to accord a benefit to 'a selected few out of a larger number equally willing and able to take advantage of it'.[40]

30 ibid 41 (Lord Wright).
31 *Oppenheim* (n 14) 314, 318.
32 *Verge v Sommerville* [1924] AC 496, 499.
33 *Oppenheim* (n 14) 309. The standard varies for each head of charity: see *IRC v Baddeley* [1955] AC 572, 615.
34 *Anti-Vivisection* (n 17) 41 (Lord Wright).
35 *IRC v Oldham Training and Enterprise Council* [1996] STC 1218, 1234.
36 *Oppenheim* (n 14) 306; *Re Compton* [1945] Ch 123 (CA).
37 *Re Koettgen's Will Trusts* [1954] 1 Ch 252; see also Peter Luxton, *The Law of Charities* (Oxford, Oxford University Press, 2001) 178.
38 *Oppenheim* (n 14) 306 (Lord Simonds).
39 *Baddeley* (n 33) 592.
40 ibid 592.

The issue was classically illustrated by Lord Simonds's dictum in *Baddeley* that a bridge that could only be crossed by 'impecunious Methodists' would not be for the public benefit.[41] Charity regulators have tended to read Lord Simonds's comments broadly, relying on *Baddeley* for the proposition that no charity's benefiting 'public' may be unreasonably restricted in relation to the purposes of the charity.[42] However, the jurisprudence contains multiple examples of cases where courts have upheld trusts that defined their 'public' in a way that had no evident relationship to their charitable purposes.[43] As a result, some commentators have endorsed the narrower view that at common law, the requirement of a rational relationship between a charity's 'public' and its purposes is only applicable to charities established for purposes of general public utility.[44]

A final 'second pillar' issue that has historically created great controversy is whether a charity's benefiting 'public' may rightly exclude the poor. The early common law tradition appears to have taken the view that such exclusion was impermissible; indeed, in his 1607 Reading on the Statute of Elizabeth, Sir Frances Moore, a leading Chancery lawyer, declared that poverty was 'the principal and essential circumstance' for bringing a gift within the compass of the statute.[45] In the ensuing centuries, however, a long line of ambiguous and conflicting judicial decisions cast doubt on Moore's position.[46] In the 1969 case of *Re Resch*, the Privy Council waded into the debate by upholding the validity of a charitable bequest for the general purposes of a private hospital that charged substantial fees, thereby excluding poor persons who were not in receipt of medical benefits from access to its services.[47] In his decision, Lord Wilberforce stated that while a nursing home that limited its admission to the rich would not be charitable, a trust for the provision of medical facilities could be charitable, despite the fact that 'by reason of expense they could only be made use of by persons of some means'.[48] Indirect as well as direct benefit had to be taken into account, and in the case before him the element of public benefit was 'strongly present', for reasons that included the relief to the public system that flowed from the services of the private hospital.[49] The reasoning of the Privy Council allowed for a wide range of defensible positions on what degree of inclusion of the poor the common law required.[50] Lord Phillips

[41] ibid 615.

[42] See, eg, Charity Commission, *Charities and Public Benefit* (January 2008) [F3]; *CRA Public Benefit Guidelines* (n 13) [3.2.2].

[43] See, eg, *Re Koettgen's Will Trusts* (n 37).

[44] Adam Parachin makes this argument: see A Parachin, 'Public Benefit, Discrimination and Charity' in K Barker and D Jensen (eds), *Private Law: Key Encounters with Public Law* (Cambridge, Cambridge University Press, 2013) 171, 189–92. Peter Luxton cites *Baddeley* for the proposition that fourth-head charities must not impose two sets of restrictions on the beneficiary class: Luxton (n 37) 180.

[45] Chesterman (n 9) 26.

[46] For an extensive review of these cases, see *Independent Schools Council* (n 8) [118] and onwards.

[47] *Re Resch's Will Trusts* [1969] 1 AC 514 (PC).

[48] ibid 544.

[49] ibid.

[50] Compare Warburton and others (n 16) 11; M Synge, 'Poverty: An Essential Element in Charity Law After All?' (2011) 70 *Cambridge Law Journal* 649.

captured the position well when he referred to *Re Resch* during the parliamentary debates over the Charities Act 2006: 'read, and read, and read ye may, but a certain conclusion you will not find …'.[51]

The various principles that have been associated with the common law public benefit doctrine over the years provide initial support for our claim that the doctrine is a public law–private law hybrid. The doctrine cannot comfortably be described as a *private law* doctrine, for it is primarily concerned with furthering the public's interest in deriving a tangible benefit from charity property by limiting the autonomy of property-owning individuals to define their own benevolent projects. On the other hand, the doctrine cannot comfortably be described as a *public law* doctrine, for it neither requires charities to benefit a particularly large or representative section of the political community, nor does it categorically prohibit them from conferring private benefits. The common law public benefit doctrine appears to self-consciously balance individual project pursuit and collective project pursuit in setting the parameters of charitable projects. In order to map its particular hybrid character more accurately, however, we need to consider where public benefit situates charities on the continuum between altruistic and self-regarding projects, and where it situates them on the continuum between public-welfare-compliant projects and public-welfare-deviant projects. We can then reassess the relative strength of the public law and private law impulses that bear down upon the doctrine.

It is important at this point to describe in somewhat further detail two of the continuums along which I have claimed charity law repeatedly moves. For purposes of this work, I accept the assertion of the Ontario Law Reform Commission (OLRC) that *altruism* involves the doing of good works for strangers, 'strangers' being taken in this context to mean persons that are 'remote in our affections [and] to whom we are not otherwise obligated'.[52] Therefore, our first continuum can be seen as extending from projects that are intended to benefit total strangers, to projects that are intended for the sole benefit of those who pursue them. Most projects, of course, lie somewhere in mid-continuum; projects that are intended to benefit family members or persons with whom we have various emotional or obligational connections generally fall within this range.

The continuum between public-welfare-compliant projects and public-welfare-deviant projects is somewhat more difficult to define, and will be the subject of further discussion in Chapter 6. As a starting point, however, we may posit that government is the paradigmatic champion of the public welfare; indeed, along with the public interest, the 'public welfare' is a concept that government largely defines. In defining and pursuing the public welfare, however, it is generally

[51] HL Deb 7 June 2005, vol 672, col 794, cited in S Lloyd, *Charities—The New Law 2006: A Practical Guide to the Charities Acts* (London, Jordans Publishing, 2007) 25.

[52] Ontario Law Reform Commission, *Report on the Law of Charities* (Canada, 1996) 150 (OLRC Report).

understood that democratic government must 'bear *the interests of the community as a whole* constantly in mind'.[53] This characteristic of democratic government allows us to suggest that when it comes to the pursuit of projects, an important (if not exclusive) condition of public-welfare compliance is that a project's benefits be *accessible and useful to the entire political community.* We will refine the concept of public-welfare compliance in due course.

How do the various components of the public benefit doctrine relate to each of these two continuums? Of the three rules that are conceded to limit public benefit at common law, two appear to be primarily concerned with affirming and protecting the *altruistic* quality of charitable projects. We have seen that one of these, the personal nexus rule, prohibits the founder of a charity from defining the charity's beneficiary class by reference to a personal relationship. The effect of this rule, as the OLRC Report pointed out, is to ensure that the founder of a charity has a measure of emotional and obligational distance from the beneficiaries he or she selects.[54] As Matthew Harding has noted, the personal nexus rule is not perfectly congruent with a commitment to altruism in its operation.[55] The poor relations cases treat projects that are intended to benefit family members as being for the benefit of the public, while in *Oppenheim* the court denied the 'public' benefit of a project where the founder arguably had a substantial degree of emotional and obligational distance from his proposed beneficiaries.[56] Notwithstanding these tensions, the most convincing justification for the personal nexus rule is that it prevents individuals who have a 'special interest' in the welfare of a particular class from constituting a charity in their favour.[57] The judicial suggestion that the poor relations exception may be justified because poverty relief is 'so altruistic … that the public element may be necessarily inferred thereby'[58] is consistent with the conclusion that the personal nexus rule is primarily concerned to preserve the altruistic quality of charitable projects.

The rule that charities may not confer 'private benefits' also evidences a primary concern with protecting the *altruistic* quality of charity. The private benefit rule, as we have seen, functions to prevent a charity from conferring benefits on an individual other than as a beneficiary.[59] Occasionally, the application of

[53] P Cane, *Administrative Law*, 4th edn (Oxford, Oxford University Press, 2004) 15. See also *Aston Cantlow and Wilmcote with Billesley Parochial Church Council v Wallbank* [2003] UKHL 37, [2004] 1 AC 546 [62] (Baroness Hale).

[54] This was the expression used by the OLRC: OLRC Report, 176. Parachin describes this as the 'stranger or arm's length function' of the public benefit rule: Parachin (n 44) 6–9.

[55] M Harding, *Charity Law and the Liberal State* (Cambridge, Cambridge University Press, 2014) 95–98.

[56] See OLRC Report, 179.

[57] See *Oppenheim* (n 14) 39 (per Lord MacDermott). For a similar argument, see Harding (n 55) 94, 101.

[58] *Re Scarisbrick* [1951] Ch 622, 639.

[59] *Incorporated Council for Law Reporting for England and Wales v A-G and others* [1972] Ch 73 (CA). The Charity Commission now refers to this as 'personal benefit': Charity Commission, *Public Benefit: The Public Benefit Requirement (PB1)* (2013) pt 6.

the rule may result in an institution that benefits only 'strangers' being denied charitable status.[60] However, the private benefit rule arises most often where an institution seeks to pursue educational or other purportedly charitable objects in a field in which most of its members have a commercial or professional interest.[61] The question that the court will consider in such a case is whether the institution will benefit its own members in a way that is more than merely incidental to the institution's 'public object'.[62] In this way, the private benefit rule, like the personal nexus rule, manifests the common law's view that if an institution's benefits accrue to persons with whom the founder has an emotional or obligational connection, that institution will lack the 'element of unselfishness' that is a crucial aspect of charity.[63]

The remaining elements of the common law doctrine—the human community rule, the numerical negligibility test, the 'reasonable restriction' test, and the concern with the exclusion of the poor—are arguably less concerned with protecting the altruistic quality of charitable projects, and more concerned with ensuring that charitable projects are aligned with the public welfare goals of the state. The rule requiring that charities benefit the human community, to take a first example, is not directed at the protection of altruism in the sense that we have defined it—indeed, it prohibits the conferral of charitable benefits on species with which humans generally have *no* obligational connection. Its function is presumably to ensure that charitable benefits be accessible and useful to the members of the political community itself. Similarly, if one seeks to explain why the common law will not condone an educational trust for the benefit of three persons, or a trust for the construction of a bridge that may only be crossed by Methodists, it does not appear to be because those projects are necessarily self-regarding, but because they are too far out of alignment with the state's public welfare goal of making such benefits accessible to the entire political community. The common law's concern with the exclusion of the poor, though reflective of a long-standing association between altruism and poor relief, also requires more than that charities benefit the stranger. It reflects a concern, more reminiscent of the public welfare policy of governments, that those most in need should not be excluded from the benefits of charitable gifts.

If certain elements of the common law public benefit doctrine can therefore be seen to reflect, in a basic sense, a desire for charities to be public-welfare-compliant, these elements are comparatively weak. The human community rule, while generally uncontroversial, only limits individual project pursuit to the extent of preventing charities from being constituted for the sole benefit of non-human

[60] See, eg, *Helena Partnerships Ltd v Revenue and Customs Commissioners* [2012] EWCA Civ 569.

[61] See Luxton (n 37) 189–90, and the cases cited therein.

[62] *Royal College of Nursing v St Marylebone Borough Council* [1959] 1 WLR 1077 (CA) 1085, citing *Geologists' Association v IRC* (1928) 14 TC 271, 283.

[63] *Incorporated Council for Law Reporting* (n 59) 86. In this context, Russell LJ used the descriptor in reference to the non-profit-making character of a charity.

entities. The numerical negligibility test has almost never functioned to deny an institution charitable status.[64] And while a prohibition on the exclusion of the poor and a 'reasonable restriction' test would both seem to reflect a concern that charities improve the well-being of all members of the political community, the status and scope of these principles are unclear. In sum, while the common law public benefit doctrine feels the greater weight of public law thinking in regard to the altruistic quality of charitable projects, private law thinking dominates on the continuum between public-welfare compliance and public-welfare deviance, such that charity founders and trustees retain substantial autonomy to define what type of benefit their charity will provide and who will receive that benefit.

III. Public Benefit Under the Charities Act 2011

A. The Charity Commission's Public Benefit Guidance

The uncertain state of the common law public benefit doctrine was an important factor in the debates leading to the enactment of the Charities Act 2006. The Cabinet Office's 2002 report, *Private Action, Public Benefit*, had recommended that public benefit should remain 'at the heart of the definition of charity'. It was also widely accepted that the government wanted to make the public benefit criterion more stringent in its application.[65] In the period following the release of the Cabinet Office report, there were calls for the government to provide a statutory definition of public benefit, as the Scottish Parliament had proposed, or to enumerate statutory public benefit criteria.[66] The idea of replacing the public benefit requirement with a 'public character test' was also proposed.[67] Ultimately, however, Parliament rejected all of these approaches, determining that the existing public benefit case law should stay in place.

Despite Parliament's decision not to 'replace' the common law authorities with a statutory definition, the enactment of the Charities Act 2006 (which has since, it will be recalled, been consolidated into the Charities Act 2011) marked the beginning of a new public benefit era in England and Wales. Now, for the first time since the creation of the Charity Commission regime, the statutory definition of charity explicitly provides that a charitable purpose is a purpose that is 'for the public benefit'.[68] The content of the public benefit requirement is addressed in

[64] M Synge, 'Charitable Status: Not a Negligible Matter' (2016) 132 *LQR* 303.

[65] Peter Luxton, *Making Law? Parliament v the Charity Commission* (London, Politeia Publishing, 2009) 25.

[66] Francesca Quint, 'Schools and the Reform of Charity Law: the Draft Charities Bill' [2004] *Education Law Journal* 151, 153. Scotland did enact a partial definition of public benefit in its charities legislation: see Charities and Trustee Investment (Scotland) Act 2005, s 8.

[67] Picarda (n 13) 39.

[68] Charities Act (CA) 2011, s 2(1)(b).

subsection 4(3), which states that 'any reference to the public benefit is a reference to the public benefit as that term is understood for the purposes of the law relating to charities in England and Wales'. However, subsection 4(3) is explicitly made subject to subsection 4(2), which states that in determining whether the public benefit requirement is satisfied in relation to any otherwise charitable purpose, 'it is not to be presumed that a purpose of a particular description is for the public benefit'. Prior to the *Independent Schools Council* decision, this provision was widely understood to represent a change in the law for religious, education and poverty charities, which had (it was understood) previously benefited from a presumption of public benefit at common law.[69]

The Charities Act 2011 places the challenge of elucidating the statutory public benefit requirement squarely in the hands of the Charity Commission. We have already seen that promoting awareness and understanding of the public benefit requirement's operation is one of the Commission's five statutory objectives.[70] In pursuance of this objective, the Act specifically requires the Commission to issue and revise public benefit guidance, following public and other consultation.[71] Charity trustees are obliged to 'have regard to' such guidance when exercising any powers or duties to which the guidance is relevant.[72] In their annual report, charity trustees must confirm that they have complied with this duty, and identify the activities undertaken by their charity during the year to further its charitable purposes for the public benefit.[73] These obligations have only heightened the controversy surrounding the Charity Commission's public benefit guidance in the years since the statute's enactment.

The Charity Commission published its initial public benefit guidance in January 2008, following a four-month consultation that produced nearly 1,000 responses. *Charities and Public Benefit*, a 40-page document that was made available with an accompanying legal analysis on the Charity Commission website, summarized the regulator's views on the common law authorities, and on what charity trustees were required do to meet their public benefit duties under the Act.[74] It was followed by the issuance of several supplementary guidance documents addressing public benefit's application to particular types of charities, including religious, educational and fee-charging charities.[75] We shall see that following the release of the *Independent Schools Council* decision in 2011,[76] the

[69] Lloyd (n 51) 24.

[70] CA 2011, s 14.

[71] CA 2011, s 17.

[72] CA 2011, s 17(5).

[73] Charities (Accounts and Reports) Regulations 2008, SI 2008/629, pt 5.

[74] Charity Commission, *Charities and Public Benefit* (January 2008) (since withdrawn) The guidance was authored by staff in the Commission's Policy Division, with input from legal staff, and signed off by the Commission's board: see Synge (n 3) 12.

[75] See, in particular, Charity Commission, *Public Benefit and Fee-Charging* (December 2008) (since withdrawn).

[76] *Independent Schools Council* (n 8).

Commission's public benefit guidance was substantially revised. However, since my aim in this chapter is to trace the equilibrium shifts that the public benefit doctrine has undergone since 2006, we will begin with the original guidance. For ease of reference, I will italicise those sections of *Charities and Public Benefit* that were subsequently withdrawn.

The starting point of the Commission's understanding of the statutory public benefit requirement, as communicated in *Charities and Public Benefit*, was that *all* organizations wishing to be recognized as charities must explicitly demonstrate to the Commission that their aims are for the public benefit.[77] In extrapolating that requirement, *Charities and Public Benefit* put forward seven public benefit principles, which were structured around the two pillars of the common law rule. With regard to the rule that a charity must confer an identifiable *benefit*, the following principles were identified by the Commission as 'important factors' to be considered in all cases:

a. It must be clear what the benefits are.
b. The benefits must be related to the charitable aims of the organization.
c. The benefits must be balanced against any detriment or harm.[78]

In expanding upon factor (c), the Commission stated that where the detrimental or harmful consequences of an organization's aims outweighed its benefits, the organization would not be charitable.[79] Damage to the environment was given as one example of a relevant harm; the promotion of hatred towards others was another.

With regard to the 'second pillar' rule that any benefit must be to *the public*, or a sufficient section of it, *Charities and Public Benefit* identified four principles:

a. The beneficiaries must be appropriate to the aims.
b. Where benefit is to a section of the public, the opportunity to benefit must not be unreasonably restricted by geographical or other restrictions, or *by ability to pay any fees charged.*
c. *People in poverty must not be excluded from the opportunity to benefit.*
d. Any private benefits must be incidental.

With regard to principle 2(b), the guidance asserted that the 'usual' starting point for a charity would be 'to provide as much benefit as possible, given the nature of its aims and what resources it has'.[80] Any restrictions on who could benefit from a charity had to be 'legitimate, proportionate, rational and justifiable' given the nature of the organization's charitable aims.[81] Where an organization restricted its beneficiary class based on the personal characteristics of its beneficiaries, *Charities and Public Benefit* warned that the Commission would have regard to the effects of

[77] Charity Commission, *Charities and Public Benefit* (n 75) 8.
[78] ibid 7.
[79] ibid 13–16.
[80] ibid 18.
[81] ibid 18.

non-discrimination legislation in determining the organization's public benefit.[82] This was a predictable regulatory response to the recently enacted Human Rights Act 1998, which requires all domestic legislation to be read and given effect, so far as possible, in a way that is compatible with the rights set out in the European Convention on Human Rights (ECHR).[83] The warning nevertheless signalled a departure from the traditional deployment of the public benefit criterion, since the courts had not historically used the public benefit doctrine to deny 'discriminatory' trusts.[84]

More controversial, as it turned out, was the guidance's assertion that an organization that excluded people from the opportunity to benefit based on their inability to pay fees charged by the organization would not meet the public benefit test.[85] 'Not excluding' people who were unable to pay the fees meant allowing them to benefit 'in some material way related to the charity's aims'.[86] *Charities and Public Benefit* gave a number of examples of how such other benefits might be provided. In line with its stated approach to interpreting the law in the light of changing social and economic conditions, the Commission also asserted that in assessing whether the 'other benefits' provided by fee-charging charities fulfilled the public benefit requirement, it would consider whether the service or facility provided was one for which there was a public need.[87] These sections of *Charities and Public Benefit* were supplemented by a further, 40-page guidance entitled *Public Benefit and Fee-charging* (also since withdrawn), which was designed to help the trustees of fee-charging charities to find ways of maximizing the benefits their charities provided to persons who could not afford the fees. For present purposes, I will refer to these two policy documents as the 2008 Public Benefit Guidance.

The 2008 Public Benefit Guidance created a great deal of controversy within the charitable sector and beyond. Several influential commentators disputed the Commission's starting position that the effect of section 3(2) was to require all charities to positively show that their purposes were for the public benefit in both the 'first pillar' and 'second pillar' senses of the rule.[88] Others contested the Commission's scrutiny of charitable activities, labelling this an 'unwarranted departure' from the common law's focus on charitable purposes.[89] Peter Luxton emerged as the most vociferous critic of the 2008 Guidance, charging that the Commission had crossed the line between applying the law and making new law in order to further the political intentions of the government, and had thus fatally

[82] ibid 20.
[83] Human Rights Act 1998 (UK), s 3.
[84] A possible exception is *Canada Trust Co v Ontario Human Rights Commission* (1990) 69 DLR (4th) 321 (Ont CA): see generally Parachin (n 44).
[85] Charity Commission, *Charities and Public Benefit* (n 75) 23.
[86] ibid.
[87] ibid 10, 25.
[88] Luxton (n 65) 17. See also Hackney (n 3) 348; Picarda (n 13) 37–39F.
[89] A Iwobi, 'Out With the Old, In With the New: Religion, Charitable Status and the Charities Act 2006' (2009) 29 *Legal Studies* 619. See also Synge (n 3) 62–63.

compromised its independence.[90] The detail of these critiques, each significant in its own right, lies beyond the scope of the present work. However, the very volume and intensity of the criticism generated by the Commission's position reflects the substantial degree to which the 2008 Guidance appeared to alter the equilibrium that the common law public benefit doctrine had traditionally set between individual and collective project pursuit. It is debatable whether responsibility for this equilibrium shift belongs in greater measure to Parliament, which imposed the duty to issue public benefit guidance upon the Commission, or the Commission, which produced the voluminous regulatory response.[91] In either case, the 2008 Guidance marked a shift towards a more heavy-handed and 'public-law-oriented' approach to the public benefit criterion, which restricted charity autonomy in furtherance of several competing public welfare goals.

In terms of the specific, substantive ways that the 2008 Public Benefit Guidance limited the autonomy of donors, charities and trustees, two are particularly worthy of note. First, in confirming that the 'benefit' charities provide and the 'public' they serve would be evaluated by reference to human rights legislation, the Commission limited the autonomy of charities whose projects were targeted at persons sharing a protected characteristic, such as ethnicity, sexual orientation or creed. In doing so, the Commission sought to align English charities with a particular public welfare goal that was at that point largely external to the charity law tradition—the goal of eliminating discrimination in all its human forms. Second, in extracting from an ambiguous line of common law authorities a set of rules regarding fee-charging and the exclusion of the poor, the Commission limited the autonomy of charities whose projects were targeted at persons of some wealth. In doing so, the Commission arguably sought to align English charities with a different, and apparently more controversial public welfare goal—the goal of creating a society in which all citizens are able to benefit from opportunities for human flourishing, and in which the benefits of charitable activity correspond to financial need. The courts have had occasion to respond to both of these regulatory limitations on charity autonomy in the years since *Charities and Public Benefit* was published. We will examine the judicial response to each limitation in turn.

B. The *Catholic Care* Decisions

The first challenge to the Charity Commission's interpretation of the public benefit doctrine in the post-Charities Act 2006 era related to the Commission's move to evaluate public benefit by reference to human rights law. By 2008, the ECHR law on discrimination had already come to bear on the difficult

[90] Luxton (n 65) 27–28, 34.

[91] C Decker and M Harding, 'Three Challenges in Charity Regulation: the Case of England and Wales' in M Harding, A O'Connell and M Stewart (eds), *Not-for-Profit Law: Theoretical and Comparative Perspectives* (Cambridge, Cambridge University Press, 2014) 314, 323.

relationship between queer communities and religious institutions. In 2007, the UK Parliament approved the Equality Act (Sexual Orientation) Regulations 2007, making it unlawful for any person to discriminate on the grounds of sexual orientation in the provision of goods, facilities and services. Faith-based adoption and fostering agencies were particularly targeted by these regulations, which included transitional protection for publicly funded agencies of this type.[92] Like many of the UK's human rights instruments, however, the Regulations also included an exemption for persons who acted pursuant to a charitable instrument. Regulation 18 provided that the Regulations did not make it unlawful for a person to provide benefits only to persons of a particular sexual orientation, if (a) that person acted in pursuance of a charitable instrument, and (b) the restriction of benefits was imposed by reason of or on the grounds of the provisions of the charitable instrument. It was a dispute over the scope of this charitable instrument exemption that led to the High Court decision in *Catholic Care v Charity Commission for England and Wales*.[93]

Catholic Care was a charitable company, funded partly by payments from local authorities and partly from charitable gifts raised through the Roman Catholic Church, which provided the services of an adoption agency in the diocese of Leeds.[94] As a consequence of its religious beliefs, it did not offer its adoption services to same-sex couples or civil partners.[95] Following the approval of the Equality Act (Sexual Orientation) Regulations, Catholic Care sought to bring itself within the Regulation 18 exemption by amending its objects clause to clarify that it would only provide adoption services to heterosexuals in accordance with the tenets of the Catholic Church. Pursuant to the requirements of the Charities Act 1993,[96] it sought the Charity Commission's consent to this amendment. The Commission refused to consent, on the ground that the proposed amendment would not bring the charity within the Regulation 18 exemption in any event. Catholic Care appealed the Commission's decision to the Charity Tribunal, and then the High Court.

In considering whether the tribunal had erred in concluding that Catholic Care could not lawfully decline to provide adoption services on the basis of sexual orientation even if it adopted the proposed objects, the High Court focused much of its attention on the proper interpretation of Regulation 18. In this regard, the court held that the proper 'ECHR right compatible' interpretation of Regulation 18 was that it permitted charities to provide benefits on the basis of differential

[92] Equality Act (Sexual Orientation) Regulations 2007, reg 15, cited in *Catholic Care (Diocese of Leeds) v The Charity Commission for England and Wales* [2010] EWHC 520 (Ch) [40]. These regulations have subsequently been embodied in the Equality Act 2010.

[93] *Catholic Care* (HC) (n 92).

[94] ibid [2].

[95] ibid [4].

[96] Under then s 64 of the CA 1993, any alteration of the objects clause of a charitable corporation required the prior written consent of the Commission in order to be effective. This provision is substantially reproduced in the CA 2011: see CA 2011, s 198.

treatment *only* where such provision would be justified under Article 14, the ECHR's non-discrimination provision. Based on the Article 14 case law, this meant that a charity could distribute benefits on the basis of a protected ground of discrimination only where such provision constituted a proportionate means of achieving a legitimate aim.[97]

Because the High Court considered that Regulation 18 had to be interpreted in terms of its relationship with charity law and the regulatory role of the Charity Commission, however, it also articulated a number of general principles concerning the proper relationship between public benefit and UK human rights law. First, the High Court confirmed that the ECHR compatibility rule applies to the statutory definition of public benefit.[98] Second, it affirmed the Commission's approach to the weighing of a potential charity's benefits and harms, stating that an organization that proposes to fulfil a purpose for the public benefit will only qualify as a charity 'if, taking into account any dis-benefit arising from its *modus operandi*, its activities nonetheless yield a net public benefit'.[99] Finally, the High Court stated that a charity that discriminated otherwise than as a proportionate means of achieving a legitimate aim—the test for the justification of differential treatment under Article 14—would not likely meet the public benefit test, 'precisely because of the large public dis-benefit likely to flow from any unjustified, and therefore discriminatory treatment'.[100] In the result, the court remitted the matter to the Charity Commission to be decided according to the principles it had set down.[101]

While the High Court in *Catholic Care* declined to go so far as to draw a 'precise equation' between the public benefit criterion and the non-discrimination norms established by the ECHR,[102] subsequent developments in England and Wales have bolstered that position. In 2010, the various statutory exemptions that had previously authorized many charities to confer benefits on groups of persons defined by a protected personal characteristic without justification were consolidated into one, ECHR-compliant, charitable instrument exemption. Pursuant to section 193 of the Equality Act 2010, a charity may restrict the provision of benefits to persons who share a protected characteristic only if such provision is a proportionate means of achieving a legitimate aim, or is for the purpose of preventing or compensating for a disadvantage linked to the protected characteristic.[103] Based on this provision and the High Court ruling in *Catholic Care*, the Charity Commission issued a further supplement to its public benefit guidance in 2011, clarifying that an institution that restricts its beneficiaries to people who share a protected characteristic, and cannot justify the restriction under the Equality Act

[97] *Catholic Care* (HC) (n 92) [56], citing *Schmidt v Germany* (1994) 18 EHRR 513.
[98] *Catholic Care* (HC) (n 92) [70].
[99] ibid [68], [97].
[100] ibid [97]–[99].
[101] ibid [111].
[102] ibid [99].
[103] Equality Act 2010, s 193.

test 'will not be able to show that it is for the public benefit and cannot therefore be a charity'.[104] The Commission's Equality Act guidance has not been challenged in England and Wales, though the Scottish Charities Appeal Panel has indicated that it disagrees with the Commission's position.[105]

The Commission's re-evaluation of Catholic Care's request to amend its charitable objects took place against the backdrop of these developments. The regulator again turned down Catholic Care's application, and was confirmed in its decision by two appellate courts.[106] The nine decisions that have emerged from the Catholic Care litigation have raised a number of difficult issues,[107] and demonstrated the strength of the opposing views on matters that pit equality rights against the autonomy of religious institutions. From the perspective of our concern with equilibrium shifts, however, the most striking feature of the extended litigation may be that Catholic Care did not deem it advisable to even raise the argument that its seemingly evident interest in protecting its institutional autonomy and controlling its own wealth should prevail over the public interest in eliminating discrimination. On the contrary, adapting its position to the dominant human rights framework, Catholic Care conceded that the religious convictions that allegedly lay at the heart of its charitable project would *not* justify the denial of its adoption services to same-sex couples.[108] Instead, the charity argued that the amendment of its objects would serve a more public goal—the 'legitimate aim' of increasing the number of hard-to-place children placed with adoptive families. The case boiled down to a debate about whether this legitimate aim, which was of 'importance to society generally', would actually be achieved by the proposed amendment, and whether the proposed discrimination on the grounds of sexual orientation would constitute a 'proportionate means' of achieving this legitimate aim.[109]

Together with the Equality Act guidance, the *Catholic Care* decisions provide the first part of our story about how the equilibrium that the public benefit doctrine traditionally set between individual and collective project pursuit has shifted in England and Wales since the enactment of the Charities Act 2006. The story is a dramatic one, in which a doctrine that almost never functioned to deny discriminatory trusts at common law has come to be defined by reference to a

[104] Charity Commission, *Equality Act Guidance for Charities: Restricting Who Can Benefit from Charities* (2011) 10.

[105] *St. Margaret's Children and Family Care Society v Office of the Scottish Charity Regulator* (Scottish Charity Appeals Panel, January 2014). Scotland's charities legislation contains a specific provision on weighing benefit and dis-benefit: Charities and Trustee Investment (Scotland) Act 2005, s 8.

[106] Charity Commission, *Catholic Care (Diocese of Leeds)—Decision Made on 21 July 2010: Application for Consent to a Change of Objects under s 64 of the Charities Act 1993*; *Catholic Care (Diocese of Leeds) v Charity Commission for England and Wales*, CA/2010/0007 (First Tier Tribunal (Charity)); *Catholic Care (Diocese of Leeds) v Charity Commission for England and Wales* [2012] UKUT 395 (TCC).

[107] For a discussion of these issues, see Debra Morris, 'Charities and the Modern Equality Framework—Heading for a Collision?' (2012) 65 *Current Legal Problems* 295, 306.

[108] *Catholic Care* (TCC) (n 106) [15].

[109] ibid [21].

powerful non-discrimination norm. It is tempting to minimize *Catholic Care*'s impact, in part because of its formal consistency with earlier common law authority. The *Anti-Vivisection* decision established that objects contrary to the law are not for the public benefit, and *Catholic Care* is, on one view, merely an application of that principle. What *Catholic Care* has made clear, however, is that with the development and ascendance of human rights law, public benefit's 'illegality' rule has become a far greater limitation on the autonomy of property-owning individuals than it has been for a very long time.[110] Parliament and the High Court have come down in support of the position implicitly taken by the Charity Commission in the 2008 Public Benefit Guidance—namely, that the autonomy interest of charity founders and trustees in defining their own beneficiary group will generally be required to yield to a competing public interest—the public interest in eliminating discrimination.

C. The *Independent Schools Council* Decision

The second part of our story about the changing equilibrium between individual and collective project pursuit in the public benefit context is best illustrated by examining the initiation and resolution of the conflict between the Charity Commission and England and Wales's independent schools. The Commission's guidance on public benefit and fee-charging, as developed and applied in its public benefit assessment reports,[111] was seen by many in England and Wales as a direct challenge to the autonomy of the nation's fee-charging charities, and particularly its independent schools. Few were surprised, therefore, when an umbrella body for independent schools applied for judicial review of the guidance, seeking to have several of its sections quashed. In January 2011 the Attorney General also entered the fray, employing for the first time the Attorney General's statutory power to refer any question regarding the operation or application of charity law to the Charity Tribunal.[112] The Attorney General's reference set out a series of

[110] Ironically, perhaps, the last time that the illegality rule played a major role in constraining the autonomy of the founders of charity in England and Wales was during the period of religious intolerance: see GH Jones, *History of the Law of Charity, 1532–1827* (Cambridge, Cambridge University Press, 1969) 10–11.

[111] In 2008, the Charity Commission began carrying out 'public benefit assessments' of a number of individual charities, in order to illustrate to the broader charitable sector how the Commission would apply its guidance in practice. Two independent schools failed the assessment, in part because they did not make sufficient provision for the poor to participate by way of means-tested bursaries. See Charity Commission, *Public Benefit Assessments—Emerging Findings for Charity Trustees from the Charity Commission Public Benefit Assessment Work: 2009–11* (March 2011).

[112] This power is now set out in the Charities Act 2011, s 236. On 27 January 2011, the Attorney General lodged a separate reference to determine whether trusts with a restricted pool of beneficiaries defined by a relationship to an individual or a company and established for the purpose of relieving poverty, satisfied the public benefit test following the implementation of the Charities Act 2006. The Upper Tribunal answered this question in the affirmative: see *AG v Charity Commission for England and Wales* [2012] UKUT 420 (TCC).

fact-specific questions that were designed to determine what types and levels of benefits provided by independent schools to persons who could not afford the school fees would be in accordance with the law of charities.[113]

A three-judge panel of the Upper Tribunal (Tax and Chancery Chamber) heard the reference and the judicial review claim alongside each other in May 2011. The end result, as already indicated, was that the Commission withdrew substantial portions of the 2008 Public Benefit Guidance, including the sections of *Charities and Public Benefit* that appear in italics above, and the whole of the Fee-Charging supplement.[114] *Independent Schools Council v Charity Commission for England and Wales* is a lengthy and detailed decision, which contains an extensive review of the common law public benefit authorities and a commentary on many of the hypothetical scenarios set out in the Attorney General's reference.[115] Among other things, the Upper Tribunal held that the common law had never in fact 'presumed' institutions falling within the first three heads of charity to be for the public benefit: while judges were in practice 'predisposed' to reach this conclusion, it could be displaced by argument or by the judge's own consideration of the purpose before the court.[116] As a result, the Upper Tribunal confirmed, the declaration in section 4(2) that 'it is not to be presumed that a purpose of a particular description is for the public benefit' had not substantially changed the law.

For present purposes, however, the most important feature of *Independent Schools Council* lies in the Upper Tribunal's approach to the vexed question of the ability of charities to target their services at persons of some wealth. Prior to *Independent Schools Council*, as we have seen, there was little consensus on whether and to what extent the public benefit doctrine required charities to make provision for the poor. Contrary to the position of the Charity Commission, many charity lawyers took the view that in the education context, the public benefit requirement was satisfied where the class of beneficiaries met the criteria of not being connected by a personal nexus, and not being unreasonably restricted in relation to the charity's objects. This, indeed, was the position of the Independent Schools Council at trial.[117] In its submission, where a school's purpose was to offer educational services upon payment of its fees, the only relevant question was whether those who could pay the fees were disqualified by these negative tests. The public benefit doctrine, the Council argued, was simply a finite set of prohibitions, *not* a source of positive obligations designed to ensure reasonable access to charitable

[113] For a list of the questions, see *Independent Schools Council* (n 8) Annex A.

[114] The Tribunal was prepared to make a direction quashing the relevant parts of the guidance, but agreed to let the Commission withdraw it instead: *Independent Schools Council* (n 8) supplementary judgment [25]–[26].

[115] For a more extensive review of the decision, see M Synge, 'Case Note: *Independent Schools Council v Charity Commission for England and Wales* [2011] UKUT 421 (TCC)' (2012) 75 *MLR* 624.

[116] *Independent Schools Council* (n 8) [67]–[68].

[117] Statement of Facts and Grounds Relied Upon by the Claimant, the Independent Schools Council [63].

benefits 'for the entire public'.[118] If an institution met the negative criteria, the Council submitted, nothing more was required.[119]

The Upper Tribunal firmly rejected the Council's submissions regarding the purely negative character of the public benefit doctrine, and in so doing suggested that the doctrine *is* a source of positive obligations to benefit certain sections of the public.[120] *Independent Schools Council* describes the personal nexus rule as 'no more than … one test' by reference to which a purpose might be excluded from the ranks of charitable purposes, and makes clear that even where the link between a charity's beneficiaries is impersonal and the class of potential beneficiaries is not numerically negligible, the public benefit requirement may not be satisfied.[121] More specifically, *Independent Schools Council* declares that an institution that excludes the poor from benefit as a matter of its governing instrument cannot be a charity.[122] The Upper Tribunal agreed that no previous case had decided the point, but 'consider[ed] it right as a matter of principle, given the underlying concept of charity from early times'.[123]

Independent Schools Council's pronouncement that no charity may exclude the poor from benefit by the terms of its governing instrument is an important pronouncement, with significant rhetorical weight. Taken in context, however, its effect is somewhat more limited. As the Upper Tribunal itself recognized, it is not by the terms of their governing instruments that institutions generally exclude the poor.[124] The poor are most often excluded by *practice*, and this observation applied equally to the independent schools involved in the litigation in question. The charitable nature of these institutions was not in issue, since charitable status in England and Wales is generally assessed without reference to the activities an institution carries out.[125] Instead, the debate over the 'public benefit' of fee-charging schools focused on the public benefit duties of their charity trustees. The Upper Tribunal's treatment of this debate in *Independent Schools Council* illustrates the type of judicial decision that may ensue when private law and public law impulses come to bear with comparable force on a substantive legal rule.

In considering the nature of the duties that charity trustees must satisfy to 'operate in a way which [is] for the public benefit', the Upper Tribunal appeared equally concerned to protect the autonomy of the trustees to whom charity

[118] ibid [64].

[119] The Council also argued that indirect benefits were just as important to an assessment of public benefit as direct benefits, and that ensuring a reasonable level of direct access for poor persons to the charity's core services was not a prerequisite to any indirect benefits being taken into account: ibid [3], [82].

[120] See *Independent Schools Council* (n 8) [213].

[121] ibid [141].

[122] ibid [162], [178].

[123] ibid [178].

[124] ibid [186], noting that it 'highly unlikely' that any schools actually do exclude the poor as a matter of their constitution.

[125] ibid [187], [191], [228].

founders entrust the management of their property, and to further the public welfare goal of creating a society in which all citizens have reasonable access to the benefits of charitable activity. On the one hand, the tribunal emphasized that charity trustees are not under a legal obligation to act in a way which the Charity Commission or anyone else would consider 'reasonable' or 'appropriate'.[126] The courts have never imposed their view of what is reasonable on the trustees of private trusts, the Upper Tribunal stated, 'and the same should apply to charities'.[127] In the context of fee-charging schools, the Upper Tribunal stated that it was not possible to be prescriptive about either the nature or the extent of the benefits a school must provide to the poor.[128] Both the level of benefit and the method of its provision were properly 'matter[s] of judgment for the trustees'.[129]

On the other hand, the Upper Tribunal emphasized that the law has always limited the range of actions that charity trustees can properly take in a given situation.[130] The Upper Tribunal stressed that these limits are not based on a reasonableness test, but nonetheless suggested that the autonomy of charity trustees to determine the nature of their charity's benefits is limited by the requirement that they make 'adequate provision for … certain sub-classes of the potential beneficiary class', other than fee-paying students.[131] The fact that an institution saves the government money through the private provision of an otherwise public service is unlikely to supply the requisite public benefit.[132] The standard, the Upper Tribunal emphasized, is not a *de minimis* standard, but rather a question of 'what a trustee, *acting in the interests of the community as a whole*, would do in all the circumstance[s] of the particular school under consideration'.[133] In an ensuing paragraph, the Upper Tribunal framed the public dimension of the duty even more strongly:

> [Trustees] need to consider the question of access more generally and how to treat all their potential beneficiaries fairly. This is not to say that trustees cannot properly make policy decisions which have the effect of ruling out of consideration large numbers of potential beneficiaries. But such policy decisions must be rational and justifiable *in the promotion of the public interest.*[134]

The Upper Tribunal, as Mary Synge notes, did not name the public interest that such decisions would promote.[135] Nevertheless, the passage strongly suggests that to the extent that the public benefit doctrine allows charity trustees to exclude large numbers of potential beneficiaries by charging fees for their charity's services, it

[126] ibid [221].
[127] ibid [220].
[128] ibid [217].
[129] ibid [220].
[130] ibid [220].
[131] ibid [214].
[132] ibid [207].
[133] ibid [215] (emphasis added).
[134] ibid [218] (emphasis added).
[135] Synge (n 115) 632.

does so on the basis of that unnamed public interest, and not out of respect for the autonomy and judgment of charity founders and trustees.

What, then, does *Independent Schools Council* add to our understanding of the hybridity of the English public benefit doctrine, and the changing equilibrium between that doctrine's public and private elements since the enactment of the Charities Act 2006? Aside from its regulatory repercussions, *Independent Schools Council* provides a valuable illustration of the instability attaching to hybrid legal phenomena. Indeed, the Upper Tribunal decision displays many of the qualities that we associated with hybrid texts in chapter one. It is a 'locus of conflict' between competing values—the relieving of human need, equity, individual and institutional autonomy—which are not entirely reciprocal. It looks backwards at a historical legal doctrine and suggests that it 'never really was' the way it used to be viewed. *Independent Schools Council* is marked by dissonances, demonstrated in its holding that a charity that excludes the destitute does not thereby exclude the poor.[136] And it is plagued by a lack of cohesion, such that both parties to the litigation were able to declare the decision a victory for their side, while charity trustees continue to struggle to understand what public benefit means.[137]

Of course, the meaning of a legal decision is often subsequently clarified by the patterns of 'commitment, resistance and understanding' that it generates.[138] Such has proved to be the case with *Independent Schools Council*. As Synge predicted, the Charity Commission has displayed little enthusiasm for enforcing the public law-oriented passages of the Upper Tribunal's decision, or for engaging in further battles with the independent schools.[139] Subsequent to the forced withdrawal of most of its guidance on public benefit and fee-charging, the Charity Commission has published substantially revised public benefit guidance, which gives the trustees of fee-charging charities very broad discretion to set the amounts they charge for their services, and to determine what provision is made for the poor.[140] In practice, therefore, it appears that the Commission has been forced to pull back from its public law-oriented position on public benefit's role in ensuring a more accessible and equitable distribution of charitable benefits in England and Wales. Despite the hybrid nature of the *Independent Schools Council* decision, and notwithstanding the equilibrium shifts in the anti-discrimination context, the autonomy interest of charity founders and trustees in defining their own beneficiary group has largely prevailed over the competing public interest in a society where the entire political community has reasonable access to charitable benefits, and where the distribution of those benefits conforms more closely to financial need.

136 *Independent Schools Council* (n 8) [173].

137 Synge (n 115) 624, 638. Synge herself declared the decision a 'compromise'.

138 On the generation of legal meaning by communities, see Robert M Cover, 'Foreword: *Nomos* and Narrative' (1983–84) 97 *Harvard Law Review* 4.

139 Synge (n 115) 636.

140 Charity Commission, *Public Benefit: Running a Charity (PB2)* (2013), particularly Annex C: *Charging for Services*. However, the Commission's publications suggest that it still aims to ensure that trustees carry out their duty to carry out purposes for the public benefit: Synge (n 3) 229.

IV. Conclusion

We are now in a position to draw some conclusions about the public benefit doctrine, and about its suggested hybridity across the substantive public law–private law divide. Based on what we have learned about what it means for a charity to be 'for the public benefit' at common law, we may claim to have identified a common law doctrine without a single or even primary site of belonging within either the public law or the private law sphere. In relation to the continuum between altruistic and self-regarding projects, the public benefit doctrine treats charitable projects as resolutely *altruistic* projects, purposefully insulating the sector from self-regarding behaviour through a strict application of the personal nexus rule and the prohibition on 'private benefits'. Public law thinking prevails, such that the doctrine's concern with protecting the 'other-regarding' quality of charitable projects outweighs its concern to protect the individual autonomy of charity founders and their appointed trustees. In relation to the perceived spectrum between public-welfare-compliant projects and public-welfare-deviant projects, on the other hand, the common law doctrine treats charitable projects, for the most part, as public-welfare-neutral, only rarely limiting the types of benefits a charity can pursue, and placing only a minimal number of restrictions on an individual's ability to direct a charitable benefit to a group of his or her choosing. Private law thinking prevails, such that the doctrine's concern with protecting the ability of individuals to formulate their own benevolent projects outweighs its concern with ensuring that charitable benefits are reasonably available to all citizens in a political state.

Given the comparable force of these public law and private law impulses, it is not unreasonable to conclude that the public benefit doctrine is, or was, a 'true hybrid' at common law. The more difficult question is whether the doctrine *remains* a true hybrid in light of the various equilibrium adjustments that it has undergone within the contemporary Charity Commission regime. We have previously noted that hybrid phenomena are *dynamic* phenomena, whose subject components may be alternately dominant and subsidiary.[141] If we conclude that the dominance of one component of the public benefit doctrine has become complete and permanent, however, we may also conclude that the term hybrid is no longer apt.

We have seen that under the contemporary English regime of charity regulation, additional public law impulses have come to bear on the public benefit rule. Whether or not the common law ever 'presumed' charities under the first three heads to be for the public benefit, the Charities Act 2011 and accompanying Commission guidance have clearly occasioned an operational shift in the degree and quality of public benefit evidence that charity trustees must provide. The Commission has promoted a more equitable interpretation of the public benefit doctrine, and the Upper Tribunal has partly, though not entirely, affirmed the

[141] See Ch 1, text at n 47.

Commission's position. Finally, the evolving anti-discrimination law has come to bear with full force on public benefit in England and Wales, such that an institution that defines its beneficiary class in a manner inconsistent with the Equality Act 2010 will not be for the public benefit and thus will not be registered as a charity. In all of these ways, the public law elements of public benefit are on the rise.

So ascendant is the public element of the public benefit doctrine, in fact, that judges and scholars have begun to equate the doctrine with another, unquestionably public law rule. As we shall see in Chapter 6, the development of the concept of a 'hybrid public authority' under the Human Rights Act 1998 has given rise to judicial disputes over the circumstances in which a charity may be considered sufficiently 'of or like' government to incur human rights obligations. The test that the courts have developed for hybrid public authority status is multi-factoral, but in *Aston Cantlow*, Lord Nicholls held that an 'obligation to act only in the public interest' constitutes one indicator of a body whose nature is governmental.[142] Subsequent courts have relied on this factor to distinguish charities from other kinds of institutions, suggesting that charities are 'like the government' in this way. In *YL v Birmingham City Council*, for example, the House of Lords contrasted the profit motivation of the alleged hybrid public authority before it with the 'public interest' motivation of a charity: the fact that the defendant for-profit care home, *unlike a charity or philanthropist*, had no obligation to act in the public interest contributed to the House of Lords' decision that it was not a person with a function of a public nature.[143] In *Weaver*, a majority of the Court of Appeal also appeared to link the public interest criterion to charitable status, stating that the fact that a housing trust was 'acting in the public interest and [had] charitable objectives' reinforced the conclusion that its functions were public under the Human Rights Act 1998.[144] Recent charity law scholarship contains similar suggestions that governments and charities are in fact 'in the same business … to enable the pursuit of, or even directly to pursue, the common good'.[145]

These recent suggestions that charities must act 'in the public interest' or 'for the common good' offer another way of thinking about the equilibrium that public benefit sets between individual and collective project pursuit, and the adjustments that this equilibrium has undergone under the contemporary English regime. For unless the English courts are in fact seeking to introduce a new criterion of charitable status, their comments suggest they view the 'public interest' and 'public benefit' as substantially equivalent concepts. Is this correct? Has the rule that charities must act 'for the public benefit' become so public law oriented in recent years that it can be equated with the 'public interest' concept that applies to the conduct of government? This is the issue that the final section of this chapter seeks to address.

[142] *Aston Cantlow* (n 53).

[143] *YL v Birmingham City Council* [2008] 1 AC 95 (HL) [116] (Lord Mance), [26] (Lord Scott). But compare [135] (Lord Neuberger).

[144] *R (Weaver) v London and Quadrant Housing Trust* [2010] 1 WLR 363 (CA) [71].

[145] M Harding, 'Distinguishing Government from Charity in Australian Law' (2009) 31 *Sydney Law Review* 559. Harding identifies voluntarism as the key feature distinguishing charity from government.

There is general agreement that one of the 'distinguishing features' of democratic government, and one that may be used to justify the existence of separate public law rules, is that the government acts not in its own interest, but in the public interest.[146] However, the meaning of the term 'public interest' has long been the subject of intense debate. 'Not only do scholars disagree on the defining of the public interest', Frank Sorauf wrote in 1955, 'they disagree as well about what they are trying to define: a goal, a process, or a myth'.[147]

In the years since Sorauf's pronouncement, political science has developed a range of competing theories on how the public interest should be defined. Early theories put forward a 'normative' or 'unitary' view of the public interest, asserting that it represented a moral standard that was capable of being judged according to a coherent, unitary set of values.[148] A more recent and more widely accepted set of theories equate the public interest with the interests of the democratic majority,[149] asserting that in a democracy, the public interest must continually be defined through a process of citizen consent.[150] A third, competing group of public interest theories, often called common interest theories, equate the public interest with the interests that *all* members of a polity may share, and focus on values of societal unanimity, compatibility and fraternity.[151] Half a century after Sorauf's pronouncement, then, the meaning and usefulness of the principle that government must act 'in the public interest' is still not entirely clear.[152] Enough points of consensus exist, however, to allow us to compare the public interest concept with charity law's public benefit rule.

The first point of relative consensus on the public interest concept is that 'the public' whose interests the government must consider consists of the whole political community.[153] The position of certain groups on the periphery of this community, such as as-yet unborn citizens and residents with less than full citizenship status, have been matters of debate.[154] However, it is clear that a government would not be 'acting in the public interest' if it focused exclusively on the interests of a community in a foreign jurisdiction. Nor would government be acting in the public interest if, in reaching its policy decisions, it considered the interests of only

[146] A Davies, *The Public Law of Government Contracts* (Oxford, Oxford University Press, 2008) ch 3.

[147] F Sorauf, 'The Conceptual Muddle' in CJ Friedrich (ed), *The Public Interest* (Chicago, IL, Committee to Advance Original Work in Philosophy, 1959), cited in V Held, *The Public Interest and Individual Interests* (New York, NY, Basic Books Inc, 1970) 1–2.

[148] Held (n 147) 135. See also C Cochran, 'Political Science and "The Public Interest"' (1974) 36 *The Journal of Politics* 327, 330.

[149] Held (n 147) 49–98. Held's category of 'preponderance theories' overlaps with what Cochran calls 'process theories', where the public interest is identified with the result of the democratic interest-conflict process, or with the process itself: Cochran (n 148) 339–47.

[150] Cochran (n 148) 330.

[151] Held (n 147) 99–134. See also RE Goodin, 'Institutionalizing the Public Interest: The Defense of Deadlock and Beyond' (1996) 90 *American Political Science Review* 331.

[152] See, for example, M Feintuck, *The Public Interest in Regulation* (Oxford, Oxford University Press, 2004).

[153] Held (n 147) 151–52.

[154] Cochran (n 148) 347, citing JR Pennock, 'The One and the Many: a Note on the Concept'.

a subset of the political community, defined in geographical, ethnic or religious terms.[155] As we have previously noted, the representative role of democratic government requires that it 'bear *the interests of the community as a whole* constantly in mind'.[156]

If we compare this conception of the public with the 'public' that charities are obliged to benefit under contemporary charity law, the continuing distinction between the two concepts becomes apparent. In the wake of *Independent Schools Council*, it is clear that English charities, like government, must at least consider the needs of an important section of the political community, namely the 'not-so-well-off'. In the wake of the *Catholic Care* decisions, it is also clear that English charities, like government, must act in the interests of the *entire* political community to the extent that they must refrain from acts of unlawful discrimination that may 'dis-benefit' any of the political community's members. Subject to these important qualifications, however, the public benefit doctrine still does not require charities to benefit the whole political community, nor to bear the interests of the community as a whole in mind. Charities may quite legitimately focus on the needs of a community defined by geography, religion or a particular affliction; they may even devote all of their resources to assisting a foreign community such as German veterans or the 'native inhabitants of Dacca'.[157] In essence, as Lord Hobhouse observed of the church council whose public authority status was at issue in *Aston Cantlow*, charities may act 'in the sectional not the public interest'[158] without damage to the public benefit rule.

A second distinction between the public interest and public benefit concepts relates to the nature of each concept's arbiter. There is relative consensus that in a democracy it is the democratically elected representatives of the political community that are charged with determining the substantive content of the 'public interest' at any time. This point, which is generally assumed in the political science literature, was confirmed by the House of Lords in *R (Alconbury Developments Ltd)*. This case considered whether the Human Rights Act 1998 required that an impartial tribunal, rather than the government executive, make decisions that affected rights to the ownership and enjoyment of land.[159] Lord Hoffmann was emphatic that in a democratic state such as the UK, 'decisions as to what the general interest requires are made by democratically elected bodies or persons accountable to them'.[160] A decision as to the public interest, he held, 'is not a

[155] This is not to say that government cannot pursue projects that target particular subsets of the political community: *R (Kaur and Shah) v Ealing LBC* [2008] EWHC 2062, cited in Morris (n 107) 9. Ultimately, however, government must have the interests of the whole political community in mind.

[156] Cane (n 53) 15. See also *Aston Cantlow* (n 53) [62] (Baroness Hale).

[157] *Re Robinson* [1931] 2 Ch 122; *Mitford v Reynolds* (1842) 1 Ph 185. The courts have sometimes, but not always, taken the view that such charitable works benefit in a general sense the community in the UK: see Picarda (n 13) 39F–H.

[158] *Aston Cantlow* (n 53) [86].

[159] *R (Alconbury Developments Ltd) v Secretary of State for the Environment, Transport and the Regions (SSETR)* [2001] UKHL 23, [2003] AC 295.

[160] ibid [69].

judicial or quasi-judicial act ... [i]t is the exercise of a power delegated by the people as a whole to decide what the public interest requires'.[161] In resolutely distancing the judicial branch of government from the realm of public interest, or 'policy' decisions, Lord Hoffmann reinforced earlier House of Lords' authority that decisions as to the public interest 'are not such as courts are fitted or equipped to make'.[162]

The paradigm described in *Alconbury Developments*, within which the legislative and executive branches are expected to make decisions about the public interest without interference by the judiciary, stands in stark contrast to the charity law paradigm within which the courts (and their regulatory alter egos) are expected to make decisions about the public benefit without assistance from the legislative or executive branch. This distinction does not *necessarily* speak to the public or private character of the public benefit rule; indeed, the courts are the primary arbiters of many legal concepts that fall squarely within the public law sphere. However, the fact that the public interest and public benefit concepts are interpreted and applied by different arbiters has implications for the nature of each concept. The legislative and executive branches determine the substantive content of the public interest on an ongoing basis, taking the will of the political community into account. The courts, on the other hand, modify the substance of the public benefit rule only where litigation demands it, and generally make only incremental adjustments to the types of benefits that charities can provide.[163] The effect of this different methodology is that the public benefit concept is more stable and less tied to the will of the public than the public interest that government is bound to pursue.

A final distinction between the public interest and public benefit concepts relates to the kinds of interests that each concept allows its subject to have and pursue. In their quest to construct a coherent theory of the public interest, philosophers and political scientists have often sought to define the public interest in contradistinction to other kinds of interests. The major conceptual division is between the public interest, on the one hand, and individual interests, on the other.[164] In 1966, however, Richard Flathman usefully distinguished *two* kinds of individual interests: individual self-regarding interests, and individual other-regarding interests. Individual other-regarding interests, according to Flathman, are such that 'if I have an other-regarding interest, it is *my* interest, but my interest is *in* the advantage, profit or welfare of others'.[165] Unlike self-regarding interests, they are always subjectively defined.

Flathman's division of the universe of interests into the public interest, individual self-regarding interests and individual other-regarding interests highlights another important difference between the public interest and public benefit

[161] ibid [74].

[162] *Gouriet v Union of Post Office Workers, sub nom AG v Gouriet* [1978] AC 435 (HL) 482.

[163] The meaning of public benefit doctrine could, of course, be determined by the legislative branch. As we have seen, however, England and Wales has not chosen this route.

[164] Held (n 147) ch 2.

[165] Richard Flathman, *The Public Interest* (New York, NY, Wiley, 1966), cited in Held (n 147) 23.

concepts, which recalls the two continuums with which we began. When we say that government must act 'in the public interest', what we mean is that government can have *neither* individual self-regarding interests, *nor* individual other-regarding interests in the advantage or welfare of a group of individuals that is other than the entire political community. The public interest rule requires the government to be *both* altruistic *and* public-welfare-compliant, in the sense that government must pursue projects that are ultimately aimed at improving the welfare of every member of the polity.

When we say that charities must be 'for the public benefit', on the other hand, we imply that charities may not have *individual self-regarding* interests,[166] but we do not deny that they may have *individual other-regarding* interests in the advantage, profit or welfare of a particular group. Indeed, as Lord Beveridge recognized, charities may be the paradigmatic manifestation of interests of this kind.[167] Unlike government, charities do not generally emerge as an embodiment of the will of the public; rather, they are the creation of individuals with a strong interest in a particular cause, such as the advancement of their own religion, or the relief of persons burdened by a particular need. These individual interests are embodied in a charity's governing documents, and become the foundation of the duties of the charity's trustees. The public benefit doctrine does not displace the centrality of individual other-regarding interests to charitable projects, although it does place limitations on the manner in which these interests are framed and carried out. In this sense, the public benefit doctrine diverges sharply from the rule that government must act in the public interest, or for the common good.

In the course of this chapter, I have sought to show that the public benefit doctrine has become a more 'public law-oriented' rule since the enactment of the Charities Act 2006. Through its public benefit guidance, the Charity Commission has demonstrated its impulse is to shift the traditional equilibrium of the common law public benefit doctrine, reducing the autonomy of charity founders and trustees in order to further a variety of competing public welfare goals. However, the public benefit doctrine continues to place significant value on the ability of individuals to define what type of benefit their charity will provide and what 'public' will receive that benefit. It allows the expression of most individual other-regarding interests, and still normally requires that charitable projects be public in only the altruistic, and not the public-welfare-compliant sense. To be for the public benefit, a charitable project is not required to further the public interest; it need only further a sectional interest that the charity defines with some constraints. Despite the ascendance of the doctrine's public components in recent years, therefore, the rule that charities must be for the public benefit remains a *hybrid* legal doctrine, and not a rule of public law.

[166] The individuals who found and contribute to charities, in contrast to charities themselves, *may* be motivated by an individual self-regarding interest: see, for example, *Incorporated Council for Law Reporting for England and Wales v A-G and others* [1972] Ch 73 (CA) 93.

[167] WH Beveridge, *Voluntary Action: A Report on Methods of Social Advance* (London, G Allen & Unwin, 1948) 125; see also Ch 1, text to n 113.

4

Charity Law Standing Rules and the Procedural Public Law–Private Law Divide

I. Introduction

We have, to this point, explored the general and context-specific hybridity of English charity law primarily from the perspective of the law's institutional and substantive dimensions. In Chapter 2 we examined the nature and disposition of the regulatory institution that is primarily responsible for the supervision of charities in England and Wales, its relationship to the common law tradition, and the nature of the public interest that it is concerned to protect. In Chapter 3 we focused on the public benefit doctrine, characterizing it as a doctrinal hybrid, and exploring how the equilibrium between its constituent 'public law' and 'private law' elements has shifted in the period since the enactment of the Charities Act 2006. Claims about the public law–private law hybridity of charity law may also be examined from the perspective of the law's *procedural* dimension. This chapter will consider one notable procedural feature of the law of charities, its rules of *locus standi*, and consider how those rules partake of the respective spheres of public law and private law.

The question of who may initiate legal proceedings against another, and the manner of answer to that question, are matters that may properly be considered as defining features of the procedural public law–private law divide.[1] The 'public law' and 'private law' approaches to the issue of entitlement to bring legal proceedings differ in at least two interrelated respects. First, each legal sphere poses the question 'who can sue?' at a different time and in a different manner. Within a quintessential private law paradigm, the question is generally integrated into the definition of individual causes of action. While certain private law concepts (such as privity of contract and the tort law duty of care) are directly concerned with determining who can sue, the inquiry is nestled within, and treated as part of, the substantive merits of the private law claim.[2] Within a quintessential public

[1] See, for example, P Cane, *Administrative Law*, 4th edn (Oxford, Oxford University Press, 2004) 62.
[2] ibid 62.

law paradigm, on the other hand, the question of a person's entitlement to seek judicial relief for a wrong is not fully integrated into the cause of action, and is still addressed as a partially independent matter.[3] The issue is described as an issue of 'standing', and determined by a self-standing body of rules that address 'who, in the circumstances of conduct that the law recognizes as wrongful, should be entitled to seek relief, and what sort of relief they should be permitted to seek, and for what purpose'.[4] As Peter Cane points out, this feature of the 'public law' approach to who can sue is a reflection of the fact that public law wrongs are 'first and foremost wrongs *against the public*', so that 'the wrong is defined in terms of the public interest whereas the right to sue in respect of it is described in terms of the claimant's interest in the matter'.[5]

A second distinction between the public law and private law approaches to the question of who can sue relates to *the basis upon which* potential litigants are permitted, or excluded from, judicial relief. This distinction is somewhat less clear cut, but its broad outlines may nonetheless be traced. Within a quintessential private law paradigm, a plaintiff's ability to sue another is rooted firmly in the plaintiff's personal rights and interests. As Peter Benson has explained, the juridical conception of rights that characterizes private law presupposes that, in order to establish a valid claim against a defendant, the plaintiff must have 'something that is by rights his or her own (*suum*), with which the defendant is duty-bound not to interfere'.[6] Without such a personal right or interest, the potential private law plaintiff has no entitlement to seek judicial relief.[7] Where a potential private law plaintiff *does* have a personal right or interest, however, and that interest is injured in a way that meets the conditions of an established cause of action, the question of the plaintiff's ability to sue is easily resolved. For within a quintessential private law paradigm, a plaintiff that can establish the elements of a cause of action has a *right* to bring that cause of action, and to obtain 'affirmative assistance' (in the form of judicial access) from the state.[8] The court generally has no discretion to refuse the private law plaintiff access to the courts on the basis of extraneous considerations.

Historically, personal rights and interests also played an important role in determining the entitlement of an individual plaintiff to sue in respect of a public wrong. The English law of standing for judicial review was marked by considerable diversity prior to 1978, with different rules of standing applicable to the

[3] There has been some movement towards the fusion of standing and merits in the administrative law field, but this movement has not been uniform. See P Craig, *Administrative Law*, 7th edn (London, Sweet & Maxwell, 2012) 779–82, 786.

[4] J Walker and L Sossin, *Civil Litigation* (Toronto, Irwin Law Incorporated, 2010) 55.

[5] Canew (n 1) 62.

[6] P Benson, 'Philosophy of Property Law' in J Coleman and S Shapiro (eds), *The Oxford Handbook of Jurisprudence & Philosophy of Law* (Oxford, Oxford University Press, 2002) 755. See also A Ripstein, 'Philosophy of Tort Law' in Coleman (ibid) 657.

[7] Benson (n 6) 755.

[8] B Zipursky, 'Philosophy of Private Law' in Coleman and Shapiro (eds) (n 6) 635.

various prerogative orders, and to the remedies of injunction and declaration that had been adopted from private law.[9] While the courts sometimes (though not always) allowed persons to seek an order of *certiorari* or prohibition on public interest grounds, an individual plaintiff could only bring an action for an injunction where she showed that the interference with the public right also infringed her private right or caused her special damage.[10] In *Gouriet* the House of Lords applied this 'conception of standing based on the vindication of private rights' to the declaration remedy, holding that private citizens had no role in enforcing public rights.[11] The courts might have some role in adjudicating matters of purely public interest, Lord Wilberforce asserted, but only at the instance of the officer to whom the Constitution had assigned the protection of the public interest—the Attorney General, the chief law officer of the Crown.[12]

As Paul Craig has noted in the English administrative law context, however, the general theme that has characterized recent developments in the law of standing is a movement *away* from this insistence on a private legal right.[13] The view that the primary function of the court's supervisory jurisdiction in the public law sphere is to redress individual grievances has been displaced, to a significant extent, by a view that the court should be concerned more broadly with the maintenance of the rule of law.[14] In a variety of public law contexts, therefore, courts have come to view the determination of *locus standi* as a more *discretionary* judicial task, a 'balancing act' that takes into account a variety of factors and concerns.[15] While the courts place weight on the applicant's personal rights and interests in carrying out this balancing act, they also consider other factors, such as the strength of the applicant's legal argument, the presence or absence of other challengers, and the value assigned to the specific public interest that is asserted in a particular case.[16]

A major impact of this development is that the standing rules in many paradigmatic public law contexts no longer require claimants to demonstrate a special interest in the matter they wish to litigate that goes beyond that 'shared with the generality of the public'.[17] A public interest claimant does not even need to belong to the section of the community that has been affected by the alleged breach.[18]

[9] For a discussion, see Craig (n 3) 769–90.

[10] *Boyce v Paddington BC* [1930] 1 Ch 109, 114. The Supreme Court of Canada cited *Boyce* with approval in the first half of the twentieth century: see *MacIlreith v Hart* (1908) 39 SCR 657, 663–64.

[11] Craig (n 3) 773.

[12] *Gouriet v Union of Post Office Workers, sub nom AG v Gouriet* [1978] AC 435 (HL) 482.

[13] Craig (n 3) 790. The Supreme Court of Canada has recently made a similar observation: see *Canada (AG) v Downtown Eastside Sex Workers United against Violence Society* [2012] 2 SCR 524 [1].

[14] H Woolf and others, *De Smith's Judicial Review*, 7th edn (London, Sweet & Maxwell, 2013) [2-003].

[15] ibid [2-021], citing *R v North Somerset DC ex p Garnett* [1998] Env LR 91. In Canada, see *Downtown Eastside Sex Workers* (n 13) [1]–[3], [35]–[36].

[16] Woolf and others (n 14) [2-029], [2-033]; *Finlay v Canada* [1986] 2 SCR 607 [31].

[17] Woolf and others (n 14) [2-032], citing *R (on the application of Dixon) v Somerset CC* [1997] EWHC Admin 393 [13].

[18] ibid, citing *R (on the application of Williams) v Surrey CC* [2012] EWHC 516 (Admin).

In recent years, for example, an English court has granted standing to a non-partisan English pressure group that sought to challenge a controversial government decision regarding the use of international aid funds, even though the group had no direct interest in the government's funding decision and was only purporting to represent the interest of potential overseas aid recipients.[19] The Supreme Court of Canada has adopted an equally liberal approach to 'public interest standing' in constitutional and administrative law, holding that the court has the discretion to grant standing to individuals with no personal interest in a matter after weighing certain identified criteria.[20] In response to these judicial developments, public law scholars have begun to develop a loose taxonomy for the law of *locus standi*. Peter Cane identifies four categories of standing: 'personal standing' (for applicants who seek to establish standing on the basis of their own personal interests), 'associational standing' (for applicants who seek standing to represent the interests of their members or constituents), 'surrogate standing' (for applicants who seek standing to represent another person who is not well placed to bring the action) and 'public interest standing' (for applicants who seek standing to represent the general public interest, rather than that of a group).[21]

In general, then, it seems possible to identify a two-pronged distinction between the quintessential 'private law' and 'public law' approaches to the question of who can sue: private law integrates the question into its causes of action and grants standing as a matter of right on the basis of the plaintiff's personal rights and interests, while public law considers the question separately and grants standing as a matter of discretion on the basis of a variety of factors. However, the boundary between the 'public law' and 'private law' approaches to who can sue is rather less neat than it might first appear. In particular, several areas of ostensibly 'private law' doctrine also address questions of entitlement to sue somewhat apart from questions of the substantive merits of the claim.[22] The most famous of these areas is likely the law of public nuisance, which provides remedies for activities that unreasonably interfere 'with the public's interest in questions of health, safety, morality, comfort or convenience'.[23] While public nuisance is a species of tort and thus generally classified as a 'private law wrong', a plaintiff who wishes to sue in public nuisance must either obtain the permission of the Attorney General to do so or establish some damage that is special or peculiar to him- or herself.[24]

Though less often mentioned in discussions of the law of *locus standi*, charity law also addresses the question of a plaintiff's entitlement to seek relief for a

[19] *R v Foreign Secretary, ex parte World Development Movement* [1995] 1 WLR 386.

[20] *Thorson v AG of Canada* [1975] 1 SCR 138; *Downtown Eastside Sex Workers* (n 13) [36].

[21] P Cane, 'Standing Up for the Public' [1995] *PL* 276.

[22] This is the basic formulation employed in TA Cromwell, *Locus Standi: A Commentary on the Law of Standing in Canada* (Toronto, Carswell Publishing, 1986) 7. In Cromwell's account, as in this one, standing excludes questions about the legal capacity of the plaintiff.

[23] L Klar, *Tort Law*, 4th edn (Toronto, Thomson Carswell Publishing, 2008) 715, citing OM Reynolds Jr, 'Public Nuisance: A Crime in Tort Law' (1978) 31 *Oklahoma Law Review* 318.

[24] See W Estey, 'Public Nuisance and Standing to Sue' (1972) 10(3) *Osgoode Hall Law Journal* 563.

wrong apart from questions of the substantive merits of the claim. This chapter aims to shed some light on this procedural feature of charity law by examining how our subject regulatory regimes approach the question of who can seek relief in matters relating to charity property, and by identifying the 'public law-leaning' and 'private law-leaning' tendencies that those approaches embody. We will see that there are detectable in this procedural domain two of the public–private continuums that we identified in Chapter 1 as continuums with resonance within the law of charities. One of these continuums extends between projects that have no cognizable owner (public) and projects that do (private). The other extends between projects that are matters of general concern (public), and projects that are matters of individual concern (private).

While issues of *locus standi* may arise in a number of charity law contexts, this chapter focuses solely on the question of who has standing to seek relief for legally recognized wrongs that involve a misadministration of charity property. On the other hand, the chapter extends its gaze beyond the issue of entitlement to sue, attempting instead to address the question of what *judicial and administrative* remedies persons are entitled to seek for misapplications of charity property in England and Wales. The answer to this question, I suggest in this chapter, is both more important and more informative than is generally recognized. At a general level, the law of standing is important because it determines the persons who do or do not have access to legal remedies, and the circumstances in which 'otherwise illegal action may go without redress'.[25] Within the specific context of a regime of charity regulation, the law of standing may also provide a number of interesting insights into charity law's *substantive* dimension. First, because the question of *locus standi* goes directly to the question of a decision maker's jurisdiction,[26] standing rules tell us something about how extensive and effective a regulator's supervisory authority over charities actually is. Second, standing rules tell us something about what manner of rights a legal regime perceives in charity property, and what manner of wrongs are created by that property's misuse. Finally, standing rules tell us something about the value that a particular regime of charity regulation attaches to the protection of those rights.

The chapter develops these arguments in the following way. Section I looks at the standing rules that traditionally limited access to charity proceedings within the English common law tradition, highlighting the constitutional role that the Crown's chief law officer historically played in enforcing charitable trusts, and the limited recognition of standing for other parties. Section II recounts how the Charity Commission regime ended the Attorney General's 'effective monopoly'

[25] LA Stein, 'The Theoretical Bases of Locus Standi' in LA Stein (ed), *Locus Standi* (Sydney, The Law Book Company Ltd, 1979) 4. See also K Schiemann, 'Locus Standi' [1990] *PL* 342.

[26] *R v Secretary of State for Social Services, ex parte Child Poverty Action Group* [1989] 1 All ER 1047 (CA) 1055 ('the question of *locus standi* goes to the jurisdiction of the court ... the parties are not entitled to confer jurisdiction, which the court does not have, on the court by consent ...)'. For the same principle in Canada, see *LIUNA Local 527 Members Training Trust Fund v R* [1992] 2 CTC 2410 (TCC).

over charity proceedings, and considers just how far the standing rules under the Charities Act 2011 have modified the common law position. Finally, in Section III, I draw some conclusions about the public law-leaning and private law-leaning tendencies of these rules of *locus standi* and consider what light these procedural tendencies shed on the substantive content of each regime.

II. Standing at Common Law

As we saw in Chapter 2, the court has always enjoyed rather extraordinary powers at common law to supervise the administration of charity property and to remedy its misuse. Under the authority of its inherent charities jurisdiction, the court has responded to misapplications of charity property by setting aside sales of the property, removing charity trustees or giving directions for an administrative scheme. The court has also sometimes ordered charity trustees to account for the distribution of charitable funds, or retained custody of a charitable trust fund itself. It was in this sense that we described the court's jurisdiction to regulate the administration of a charity as 'unlimited', and likened it to its extended jurisdiction over public authorities and actors.[27]

As in the sphere of judicial review, however, the court's broad, inherent authority to remedy abuses of charity property has always been subject to an important limitation: it can only be exercised at the suit of a person who has standing to invoke the court's powers. Who, then, does the common law recognize as being entitled to sue to remedy a misapplication of charity property? In private trusts, it is accepted that the trust beneficiary is the proper party to initiate proceedings against the trustees for breach or to recover trust property from a third party.[28] However, charitable trusts are constituted for purposes rather than persons, and generally do not establish ascertainable beneficiaries who are entitled to the trust's performance. In this situation, the common law has assigned to the Attorney General the primary role of seeking judicial relief for the misapplication of charitable funds. The more difficult question, as we shall see, is whether anyone else has standing to bring charity proceedings.

A. The Attorney General

It is a fundamental principle of the law of trusts that a court of equity will not uphold a trust that it cannot administer and control at the suit of a person who

[27] See Ch 2, s I(B).

[28] D Waters, MR Gillen and LD Smith, *Waters' Law of Trusts in Canada*, 4th edn (Toronto, Thomson Reuters Publishing, 2012) 173.

has standing to enforce the trustee's duties.[29] 'There must be somebody in whose favour the court can decree performance',[30] as *Morice v Durham* confirms; the operation of a trust cannot be made to rest upon the good will of the trustees. The general rule, therefore, is that 'a trust to be valid must be for the benefit of individuals'.[31] There are a limited number of cases where trusts for purposes have been upheld, irrespective of whether they could be actively enforced,[32] but these exceptions are generally regarded as anomalous and aberrant.

The major exception to the trust law requirement of individual beneficiaries is the exception for charitable trusts. This is because at common law, the Crown's chief law officer, the Attorney General, is charged with this vital enforcement function. The Attorney General's role in initiating proceedings to protect against the misadministration of charitable funds emerged during the seventeenth century, in parallel to the decline of the Charity Commission procedure established by the Statute of Elizabeth.[33] By the nineteenth century, the Attorney General's enforcement role with regard to charitable trusts was well established. As Lord Eldon stated in *A-G v Brown*:

> It is the duty of a court of equity, a main part, originally almost the whole, of its jurisdiction, to administer trusts ... From this principle has arisen the practice of administering the trust of a public charity: persons possessed of funds appropriated to such purposes are within the general rule; but no one being entitled by an immediate and peculiar interest to prefer a complaint, who is to compel the performance of their obligations, and to enforce their responsibility? It is the duty of the King, as *parens patriae*, to protect property devoted to charitable uses; and that duty is executed by the officer who represents the Crown for all forensic purposes.[34]

Thus, where a trustee of charity property is alleged not to be applying the property to its intended charitable use, the Attorney General may act to protect the interests of charity by initiating proceedings to bring the trustee to account and to ensure the charity property is properly applied.[35] In this way the trust law requirement of a person able to compel performance of the trust is met.

Prior to the enactment of the Judicature Acts and the fusion of the legal and equitable jurisdictions, the ordinary practice was for the Attorney General to institute charity proceedings in the Court of Chancery by way of an information, which

[29] DJ Hayton and C Mitchell, *Commentary and Cases on the Law of Trusts and Equitable Remedies*, 12th edn (London, Sweet & Maxwell, 2005) 201.

[30] *Morice v Bishop of Durham* (1804) 9 Ves 399 (Ch) 539; on appeal (1805) 10 Ves 522.

[31] *Bowman v Secular Society Ltd* [1917] AC 406 (HL) 441; *Re Endacott* [1960] Ch 232, 246.

[32] See, eg, *Re Astor's Settlement Trusts* [1952] Ch 534, 542–47; *Re Endacott* (n 31) 251.

[33] See GH Jones, *History of the Law of Charity, 1532–1827* (Cambridge, Cambridge University Press, 1969) 8, 16–21, and 52–56, noting at 21 that there is no evidence of the Crown bringing an information in Chancery to enforce a charitable gift prior to the enactment of the Statute of Elizabeth in 1601. Before that, interested or representative persons could petition the Chancellor or an ecclesiastical court to enforce a charitable use, but such suits were not common.

[34] *A-G v Brown* (1818) 1 Swans 265 (Ch) 290 (Lord Eldon LC).

[35] See, for example, *A-G v Compton* (1842) 1 Y & C 417, 62 ER 951 (Ch). For earlier instances, see *A-G v Newman* (1670) 1 Ch Ca 158; *A-G v Herrick* (1772) Amb 712, 27 ER 461 (Ch).

set out the acts of the defendant that were alleged to be injurious to those whose rights the Crown was charged to protect.[36] Then, as now, the Attorney General was entitled to begin proceedings against a charity in his or her own name, or at the request of a private individual, called a relator, who believed that a charity had been the subject of abuse.[37] Until the mid-nineteenth century, relator actions to enforce a charity were consented to as a matter of course, it being the apparent position of the Crown that the Attorney General could not 'with propriety refuse the use of his name, if there be any arguable question to be submitted to a court'.[38] However, it was extremely rare for the Attorney General to bring charity proceedings in his own name, because that would offend the convention that the Crown paid no costs.[39]

Historically, therefore, relator proceedings in Chancery constituted the primary procedure for addressing misapplications of charity property. The Crown brought relator proceedings against both charitable trusts and charitable corporations, though the jurisdiction of the court to remedy abuses by the latter type of charity depended, as we saw in Chapter 2, on whether there was an alternate supervisory mechanism in place. While relators often had a personal interest in the matter for which they sought a remedy, it was not necessary for a relator to have 'the least particle of private interest' in the due administration of a charity.[40] The law treated relators as persons 'aggrieved *in a matter of public interest* … who [had] satisfie[d] the Attorney General that the subject matter of the action [was] such as to justify the use of that officer's name'.[41] The relator historically assumed the liability for any costs arising out of the action,[42] and sometimes directed the conduct of the suit.[43] As a matter of law, however, it was the Attorney General who had control of relator proceedings, and determined how they should proceed.[44] Whether acting *ex relatio* or *ex officio*, the role of the Crown was to represent what was variously described as the interest of 'all persons beneficially interested in charity funds',[45] every object of a charity,[46] or charity in general,[47] and to ensure that justice was done, not only to the objects of charity, but to all of the subjects of the realm.[48]

[36] JF Redesdale, C Edwards, JW Smith and JW Moulton, *A Treatise on the Pleadings in Suits in the Court of Chancery, by English Bill*, 6th American, from the 5th London edn (New York, NY, JS Voorhies Publishing, 1849) 120.

[37] H Picarda, *The Law and Practice Relating to Charities*, 4th edn (Hayward's Heath, Bloomsbury Professional, 2010) 924–28.

[38] *Gouriet* (n 12) 478–79, citing *Shore v Wilson* (1842) 9 Cl & F 355, 407.

[39] Redesdale and others (n 36) 23, fn (d).

[40] *A-G v Vivian* (1826) 1 Russ 225, 38 ER 88 (Ch) 235–36.

[41] Picarda (n 37) 928.

[42] In a relator proceeding, the relator was personally liable for the defendant's costs if the proceeding failed, was deemed improper or unnecessary, or was brought for improper cause: see Jones (n 33) 161.

[43] *A-G v Vivian* (n 40) 236, citing Lord Redesdale.

[44] Picarda (n 37) 933.

[45] *Re Sekeford's Charity* (1861) 5 LT 488 (Ch).

[46] *A-G v St Cross Hospital* (1854) 18 Beav 475; *A-G v Bishop of Worcester* (1851) 9 Hare 328, 68 ER 530.

[47] *Ware v Cumberlege* (1855) 20 Beav 503 (Ch).

[48] *The Corporation of Ludlow v Greenhouse* (1827) 1 Bligh NS 17, 4 ER 780.

B. Other Parties

It is apparent, then, that at common law, the Attorney General is the party ordinarily entitled and expected to initiate legal proceedings to remedy misapplications of charity property. The Crown's legal officer is the constitutional defender of charity in general, and 'the only person who can represent a charity and sue on its behalf'.[49] To say that the Attorney General is the only person who can sue on *behalf* of a charity, however, is not necessarily to say that he is the only person with *standing* to sue to remedy a misapplication of charity property. The conventional position, articulated by Frederic Maitland in his famous lectures on Equity, is that charitable trusts have no *cestui que trust* and that no private person can enforce a charitable trust in his own name.[50] However, the cases suggest that the Court of Chancery took a more nuanced approach, occasionally allowing individuals with an identifiable ownership interest related to charity property to sue the charity's trustees.

As a first matter, it is clear that the trustees of a charitable trust (in whom ownership of the trust property is vested) have standing to apply for the advice or direction of the court on any question respecting its administration,[51] and that a single trustee may, for his own protection and that of the charity's beneficiaries, initiate proceedings against his co-trustees to recover and secure charity property. The latter proposition was confirmed in an early Canadian case in which the court held that members of a charitable corporation who were trustees of its funds were entitled to sue to correct breaches of trust by the corporation, and that the Attorney General was not a necessary party.[52] A charitable corporation may also sue certain of its directors and officers if they have breached their trust or fiduciary duties with regard to charity property.[53]

The jurisprudence also contains a limited number of cases where parties who were not trustees have been permitted to sue in their own names to remedy misapplications of charity property. These cases must be understood against the particular procedural rules that historically governed Chancery pleadings. Prior to the enactment of the Judicature Acts, we have seen, the Crown instituted proceedings in the Court of Chancery by filing an information; individuals, on the other hand, commenced Chancery actions by filing a bill. Any person with the requisite capacity was entitled to file a bill praying relief against another, provided the remedy

[49] *Strickland v Weldon* (1885) LR 28 Ch D 426 (Ch).

[50] FW Maitland, *Equity: A Course of Lectures* (Cambridge, Cambridge University Press, 1936) 51.

[51] At common law, this power was only available where a trustee paid trust funds into court and sought a judicial administration of the trust. Since the mid-nineteenth century, however, statutes in England and Wales and Canada have made the power independent of the institution of any action: Waters and others (n 28) 1154–55.

[52] *Boulton v Church Society of the Diocese of Toronto* (1867) 14 Gr 123 UC Ct (Ch). See also *Nash v Morley* (1842) 5 Beav 177, 49 ER 545 (Ch).

[53] *Charitable Corporation v Sutton* (1742) 2 Atk 400.

sought was one that would most effectually be provided by a court of equity.[54] However, a defendant could seek to have a plaintiff's bill dismissed on the basis that the plaintiff did not have the proper interest in the suit.[55] Thus, while almost any individual could initiate proceedings in Chancery to remedy a misapplication of charity funds, the issue of the plaintiff's entitlement to file the bill could be raised as a preliminary issue distinct from the bill's substantive merits. These rules produced a number of recorded cases where courts considered whether to grant standing to non-trustees to file a bill against a charity, either on the basis that they were cognizable beneficiaries of the charity (with equitable rights therein), or on the basis that they had some other ownership interest related to charity property.

The nineteenth-century case law evidences the courts going both ways on the issue of the standing of potential beneficiaries of a charity to sue. In *A-G v The East India Company*, for example, two almspersons who were entitled to receive the benefit of a charity were among a group that filed an information and bill seeking to set aside a lease of charity property on the basis that it was obtained fraudulently and did not benefit the charity. On a demurrer, Shadwell V-C held that the plaintiffs did not have the requisite interest to support a bill, since they sought no relief for themselves individually, and had not showed that they were 'individually entitled to anything'.[56]

The question of beneficiary standing resurfaced in a different context a number of years later, when the Attorney General brought an information at the relation of certain inhabitants of a parish, seeking to set aside an improper conveyance of charity property that was held for the benefit of the parish poor. The impropriety of the conveyance was not contested; the only issue was whether relief was barred by a statute of limitations, which provided that persons claiming some 'interest in land' were required to bring their action within 20 years. Sir John Romilly MR concluded that the statute had no application to the information, on the basis that neither the parish poor nor any other class of persons could, by themselves individually, have instituted any proceeding to redress the breach.[57] However, the House of Lords reversed the Master of the Rolls' decision as to the application of the statute, describing the parish poor as *cestuis que trust* with equitable rights in the trust property, and suggesting that a group of the parish poor, as representing themselves and all others entitled, could have sued the defendants on their own.[58] In *Lang v Purves* the Privy Council appeared to affirm this suggestion, stating, in the context of a dispute over church property:

> [I]f the Attorney General declines to interfere, and the *cestuis que trust* differ amongst themselves as to the proper mode of administration of the trust, a certain number may

[54] Redesdale and others (n 36) 38.

[55] ibid. 177–79.

[56] *A-G v The East India Company and Others* (1840) 11 Sim 380 (Ch) 387–88.

[57] *A-G v Magdalen College, Oxford* (1854) 18 Beav 223, 52 ER 88 (Ch) 242, 253–54.

[58] *The President and Scholars of the College of St. Mary Magdalen, Oxford v A-G* (1857) VI HL Cases (Clark's) 189, 210–12; 10 ER 1267, 1276–77.

> file a Bill on behalf of themselves and others, making some of the dissentients and the Attorney General, Defendants.[59]

The case law also shows the courts granting individuals standing to sue in their own name for the misadministration of charity property in circumstances where those individuals had some other ownership interest involving the charity property. In *Davis v Jenkins*, for example, the minister and owners of the pews inside a chapel for Protestant dissenters filed a bill seeking relief against a trustee who had allegedly claimed the chapel property as his own.[60] The defendant trustee brought a preliminary motion, arguing that the suit ought to have been instituted by information, but the Chancery Court dismissed his motion. Lord Eldon acknowledged that the question of what species of suit could proceed upon a bill presented 'a point of great Difficulty', but nonetheless rejected the view that a suit must be by information whenever the subject of the suit was a 'public Right'.[61] Where, as in the case before him, the pew owners had paid the expenses of the charity by voluntary contributions and rent from the pews, Lord Eldon concluded that they were entitled to bring a bill.[62]

If the nineteenth-century courts sometimes granted standing to parties that had a cognizable ownership interest related to allegedly misadministered charity property, they did not tend to grant standing to parties with less direct interests in the proper administration of a charity. In *A-G v Vivian*, for example, Parish Church A, which had been legally united with Parish Church B following the Fire of London, filed an information and bill seeking to have charity property that had been devised to Parish Church B applied to the repair of the church of the united parish. The Chancery Court upheld the information, opining that the trust required the court's administration, but dismissed the related bill on the basis that Parish Church A had no right or interest in the bequest.[63] In the aforementioned *A-G v East India Company* the court concluded that members of the governing body of a company that was alleged to have misapplied charity property were not entitled to bring a bill, for they were not seeking individual relief. And in *Lang v Purves* the Privy Council held that members of the Australian Synod of the Church of Scotland had no standing to bring a bill relating to the alleged misuse of church property by one of its ministers, since they had no 'private interest' in the suit.[64]

In contrast to the modern administrative law context, where the courts are consistently concerned to justify the limits they place on standing,[65] the Court of

[59] *Lang v Purves* (1862) XV Moore 389, 15 ER 541 (PC) 422.

[60] *Davis v Jenkins* (1814) 3 Ves & B 151, 35 ER 436 (Ch). See also *Ward v Hipwell* (1862) 3 Giff 547 (Ch).

[61] ibid 154.

[62] ibid 157.

[63] *A-G v Vivian* (n 40).

[64] *Lang v Purves* (n 59).

[65] These justifications include preserving scarce judicial resources, ensuring that courts benefit from the arguments of the persons most directly affected by the issue, and limiting the various branches of government to their appropriate, constitutional role. For a discussion, see Cromwell (n 22) ch 4.

Chancery was rarely explicit about its rationale for excluding an individual who could establish a misapplication of charity property from seeking relief for that wrong. The court at times expressed concern over the unnecessary expenditure of charity resources on litigation, warning that charity proceedings might cause the 'destruction of charity … by costs'.[66] The court also occasionally expressed a concern to exercise its charities jurisdiction in a way that would not 'deter all prudent persons' from serving as charity trustees,[67] suggesting that it might have factored the protection of the autonomy interests of those trustees into its standing decisions. Most commonly, however, the court simply proceeded by reaffirming the tradition whereby the Attorney General protected rights in charity property on behalf of the Crown.[68]

In sum, then, we can say the following about the standing rules that applied to charity proceedings in England and Wales prior to the creation of the Charity Commission. Trustees could sue co-trustees, and charitable corporations could sue corporate officers and directors, alleging the abuse or misadministration of charity property. In the rare case where the beneficiaries of a charitable trust were capable of exact ascertainment, the court sometimes recognized that they were entitled to sue to enforce its administration, in the same way as the beneficiaries of a private trust. Persons other than beneficiaries were also occasionally permitted to sue a charity, if they had a cognizable ownership interest involving the charity property. However, persons with less direct interest in having a charity properly administered had no standing to sue. In practice, there appear to have been a very limited number of situations where persons had both the requisite legal interest to bring a bill to remedy the misapplication of charity property, and the means to do so.[69] In most cases, the only way in which persons could bring their concerns about charity abuses before the court was to convince the Attorney General that the subject matter of the action was such as to justify the use of the officer's name.

III. Standing Under the Charities Act 2011

Ending the Attorney General's 'effective monopoly'[70] over the enforcement of charitable trusts was always a major goal of England and Wales's charity law reformers.[71] One of the nation's earliest charity law statutes, the Charities Procedure Act 1812, sought to simplify the common law relator procedure by

[66] *A-G v St Cross Hospital* (n 46).

[67] *A-G v Corporation of Exeter* (1826) 2 Russ 45, 38 ER 252 (Ch).

[68] See, for example, *Wallis v Solicitor-General for New Zealand* [1903] AC 173, 181–82.

[69] See Jones (n 33) 20, citing the Charity Commissioners' statement in 1857 that persons with a beneficial interest in charitable trusts were 'seldom in a position to originate measures affecting their government'.

[70] J Barratt, 'Public Trusts' (2006) 69 *MLR* 514, 542.

[71] See the discussion in Ch 2 and in Jones (n 33) 165.

allowing 'any two persons' to petition for a hearing into an abuse of a charitable trust, with the Attorney General's approval.[72] The Court of Chancery reportedly limited the availability of this statutory procedure, restricting its application to 'plain' breaches of trust, and refusing to apply it where jurisdiction could not be exercised with justice to all parties.[73] However, the Charitable Trusts Act 1853 definitively ended the Attorney General's effective monopoly over the enforcement of charities by providing that charity proceedings could be started, with the Commissioners' permission, by anyone with an interest in a charity, including any two inhabitants of the place where the charity applied.[74]

With the gradual extension to the Charity Commissioners of concurrent jurisdiction over the administration of charities, the question of who had standing to seek relief for the misadministration of charity property in England and Wales became more complex. The Charities Act 2011, we have already seen, establishes several separate procedures through which such misadministration can be addressed. First, the Charity Commission may institute an inquiry into a charity, and, where it finds evidence of misconduct or mismanagement in the charity's administration in the course of that inquiry, address such misconduct through a variety of remedial measures.[75] Second, even where no statutory inquiry has been commenced, the Commission may in certain circumstances exercise the same judicial powers as the High Court for the purposes of establishing a scheme for the administration of a charity, appointing or removing charity officers or trustees, and vesting or transferring charity property.[76] Third, an authorized party may bring 'charity proceedings' in any court in England and Wales.[77] Different rules of standing apply to each procedure; we will examine each in turn.

With regard to the statutory inquiry process and the exercise of the Commission's post-inquiry remedial powers, the rules regarding entitlement to seek relief are simple. The Commission exercises all of these powers of its own motion; no third party has anything akin to 'standing' to invoke this remedial route. Of course, a person who believes that a charity is administering its funds improperly may draw this to the attention of the Commission and ask that it commence an inquiry. If the Commission decides not to act in response to the complaint, however, its decision is not subject to appeal.[78]

More nuanced rules of standing apply to exercises of the Commission's concurrent judicial powers under section 69. As a general rule, the persons who are entitled to apply for an exercise of the Commission's jurisdiction to establish an

[72] An Act to provide a summary remedy in cases of Abuses of Trusts created for charitable Purposes (52 Geo 3 c 101) ss 1, 2.

[73] Jones (n 33) 166.

[74] CTA 1853, s 43.

[75] CA 2011, ss 46, 76, 78, 79, 84.

[76] CA 2011, s 69.

[77] CA 2011, s 115.

[78] S Lloyd, *Charities—The New Law 2006: A Practical Guide to the Charities Acts* (London, Jordans Publishing, 2007) 79.

administrative scheme or remove charity trustees are the Attorney General and the charity in whose respect the exercise is being sought.[79] An application by the charity means an application by all or a majority of the charity trustees.[80] The general rule of standing applicable to exercises of the Commission's section 69 powers is thus narrower than that applicable to common law charity proceedings, since a single charity trustee is not entitled to seek this form of relief.

The Charities Act 2011 does establish a number of exceptions to this general rule of standing. In the case of charities whose gross annual income does not exceed 500 pounds, an application for an exercise of the Commission's judicial powers may be made by one or more of the charity's trustees, 'any person interested in the charity', or any two or more inhabitants of the area of the charity if it is a local charity.[81] Additionally, where the Commission is satisfied that the trustees ought in the interests of the charity to apply for a scheme, and have 'unreasonably refused or neglected to do so', and the trustees have been given an opportunity to make representations, it may proceed as if an application for a scheme has been made.[82] Effectively, this entitles the Commission to exercise its concurrent judicial powers of its own motion in cases where charity property is being improperly administered and neither the trustees nor any other party is inclined to seek relief.

The third way in which a party may seek to remedy the misadministration of charity property under the Charities Act 2011 is to initiate proceedings in any court in England and Wales, invoking the inherent charities jurisdiction of the superior courts.[83] Sections 114 and 115 of the Act identify four classes of persons with standing to bring such 'charity proceedings': the Attorney General or Charity Commission, the charity or any of its trustees, 'any person interested in the charity', and any two or more inhabitants of an area served by a local charity.[84] Other than the Attorney General and the Charity Commission, however, no person is entitled to bring charity proceedings without the authorization of the Commission or the leave of the High Court.[85] The purpose of this authorization requirement, according to the case law, is to prevent charities from 'frittering away money subject to charitable trusts in pursuing litigation relating to internal disputes',[86] and to protect them from frivolous and ill-founded claims.[87] The

[79] CA 2011, s 70(2). A court that directs a scheme for the administration of a charity may also hand the matter over to the Commission for preparation and putting into effect: s 69(3).

[80] Picarda (n 37) 529.

[81] CA 2011, s 70(3). This income threshold has increased from its original amount of 50 pounds: see CTA 1853, s 43.

[82] CA 2011, ss 70(4), (5). The Commission may not generally alter a charity's purposes when it acts pursuant to this section.

[83] Pursuant to CA 2011, s 115(8), 'charity proceedings' means proceedings in any court in England and Wales brought under the court's jurisdiction with respect to charities, or brought under the court's jurisdiction with respect to trusts in relation to the administration of a trust for charitable purposes.

[84] CA 2011, ss 114(1), 115(1).

[85] CA 2011, s 115(2), (5). The Commission may not, without special reasons, authorize charity proceedings where it believes it can deal with the matter itself: s 115(3).

[86] *Muman v Nagasena* [1999] 4 All ER 178 (CA) 183.

[87] *Re Hampton Fuel Allotment Charity* [1989] Ch 484 (CA) 494.

focus of the inquiry is on the interests of the charity, and a court may deny permission to would-be litigants even where they have standing and a legally sustainable claim.[88]

With regard to the first two classes of persons listed in section 114, the Act's position on standing is broadly reflective of the common law position. The major innovation of the statutory regime has been to give the Charity Commission shared responsibility for the Attorney General's historical enforcement function, while retaining a supervisory role for the chief law officer of the Crown. Pursuant to section 114 of the Act, the Commission has the same powers to take 'legal proceedings with reference to charities or the property or affairs of charities' as the Attorney General acting *ex officio*, and the same practices and procedures apply. The Commission may exercise these powers of its own motion, but only with the agreement of the Attorney General on each occasion.[89] Where it appears desirable to the Commission for charity proceedings to be taken by the Attorney General himself or herself, the Commission has a duty to so inform the Attorney General and to provide relevant particulars.[90]

If the extension of standing rights to the Charity Commission represents only a partial devolution of the Attorney General's traditional enforcement role, the extension of standing to 'any person interested in the charity' and 'any two or more inhabitants of an area served by a local charity' represents a more significant departure from the common law position. The Charity Commission does not have an official policy on 'local charities', nor does it categorize charities as such on the register.[91] However, the Act defines a 'local charity' broadly, as a charity that is 'in relation to any area … established for purposes which are by their nature or by the trusts of the charity directed wholly or mainly to the benefit of that area or of part of it'.[92] While the scope of this provision has never been tested in court, it would appear, on its face, to allow any two persons to sue an English charity whose benefits are directed towards the region in which they live.

The meaning of a 'person interested' in a charity has more often been the subject of judicial consideration. The leading case is *Re Hampton Fuel Allotment Charity*, a 1989 decision of the English Court of Appeal that began when two charity trustees and a local city council sued to prevent the sale of the charity's land at what was alleged to be a grossly undervalued price.[93] A preliminary point was taken as to whether the council was a 'person interested' within the meaning of the Charities Act 1960.[94] Speaking for the court, Nicholls LJ began by noting the

[88] *Rai and others v Charity Commission for England and Wales* [2012] EWHC 111 (Ch) [27] and [28].

[89] CA 2011, s 114(5).

[90] CA 2011, s 115(7).

[91] Email from Charity Commission (First Contact Email Team) to author (31 November 2012).

[92] CA 2011, s 293.

[93] *Hampton Fuel* (n 87).

[94] The provision at issue was s 28(1) of the Charities Act 1960, but the language of the provision was the same.

'dearth of authority' on the statutory expression, and by choosing, by implication, not to incorporate the pre-statute common law on the interested persons entitled to bring a Chancery bill to remedy a charity's misadministration. Overturning in part the two existing authorities on the statutory provision, the court held that to qualify as an interested person, it was not necessary that a person either be capable of benefiting from the charity or be entitled to participate in its management. While a person would not qualify as interested in a charity 'simply because he [had] a sentimental or altruistic interest in it or provided modest financial support for it', a person who founded and financed a charity might well have the requisite interest.[95]

The *Hampton* court considered a variety of contextual factors in devising a 'person interested' test for the purposes of (now) section 115. On the one hand, the Court of Appeal noted that the requirement that a litigant obtain the authorization of the Commission or the High Court before proceeding already provided a 'protective filter' for charity proceedings under the statute, so that the court did not need to narrow the meaning of a 'person interested' in order to prevent frivolous or ill-founded claims.[96] On the other hand, the court accorded great significance to the fact that the Charities Act preserved the Attorney General's historical enforcement role:

> Thus the interest which ordinary members of the public … have in seeing that a charity is properly administered is a matter in respect of which the Attorney General remains charged with responsibilities … This suggests, therefore, that to qualify as a plaintiff in his own right a person generally needs to have an interest *materially greater than or different from that possessed by ordinary members of the public*.[97]

In the result, the court concluded that while a local authority did not *ipso facto* have standing with regard to a local charity in its area, the circumstances in the case before it—including the close nexus between the services the council and charity provided—placed the plaintiff council within the 'person interested' test.

In the years since the *Hampton Fuel* decision, the English courts have treated the 'person interested' test not as a 'technical' rule of law, but as 'a practical rule of justice affording a degree of flexibility responding to the facts of each particular case'.[98] The decisions on standing to bring charity proceedings evidence this flexibility, confirming that a wide range of interests may be 'materially greater than or different from' the public's interest in the proper administration of a charity. In *Gunning v Buckfast Abbey Trustees Registered* fee-paying parents of children attending a preparatory school run as a charitable trust were held to have a materially greater interest in the due administration of the school than ordinary

[95] *Hampton Fuel* (n 87) 493.

[96] ibid 494.

[97] ibid (italics added).

[98] *Royal Society for the Prevention of Cruelty to Animals v A-G* [2002] 1 WLR 44 (Ch D) [21] (noting how this is similar to the 'parallel rule requiring the applicant for judicial review to have a sufficient interest'). See also *Rai* (n 88) [23].

members of the public, despite being neither subscribers nor beneficiaries.[99] In *Scott v National Trust* the members of staghound hunting clubs and tenant farmers who opposed the Trust's decision to end deer hunting with hounds on its land were found to be 'persons interested' in the charity on the basis that they were, 'in a real sense, partners with the charity in its management of the land and its preservation of the deer population'.[100] However, a person who has only the interest of 'an ordinary member of the public' in the proper administration of a charity remains excluded from seeking relief in charity proceedings under the Charities Act 2011. The effect of this exclusion is that the test for obtaining standing in charity proceedings in England and Wales is substantially narrower than the parallel test for obtaining standing to seek judicial review.[101] The Charities Act standard 'is laid down as a form of protection of charity trustees', and a litigant will not be allowed to circumvent it by instead commencing judicial review proceedings against those trustees.[102]

In conclusion, then, the standing rules that govern access to relief for the misadministration of charity property under the Charities Act 2011 may be summarized as follows. While the Charity Commission has the statutory authority to inquire into the administration of any English charity and to remedy any misconduct or mismanagement that it finds through its inquiry, no other individual is entitled to invoke these remedial powers. Except in the case of small charities, only the Attorney General, the majority of a charity's trustees, and (in specified cases) the Commission itself, have standing to request that the Commission exercise its concurrent judicial powers to remedy misapplications of charity property by replacing trustees, transferring charity property or establishing an administrative scheme. However, a broader range of parties, including any person interested in a charity, have standing to bring charity proceedings under section 115 of the Act, provided that they obtain the authorization of the Commission or the leave of the High Court. Only persons with a 'merely public' interest in the proper administration of a charity are excluded from seeking relief.

IV. Conclusion

We are now in a position to articulate some conclusions about the standing rules that limit access to relief for misapplications of charity property in England and Wales, and the manner in which these rules may be said to partake of public law and private law. We may begin by reiterating the claim that the quintessential

[99] *Gunning v Buckfast Abbey Trustees Registered* (Times, 9 June 1994) (Ch D).
[100] *Scott v National Trust* [1998] 2 All ER 705 (Ch).
[101] Woolf and others (n 14) [2-010].
[102] *Royal Society for the Prevention of Cruelty to Animals* (n 98) [22].

'private law' and 'public law' approaches to the question of who can sue can be distinguished on two grounds: private law integrates the question into its causes of action and grants standing as a matter of right on the basis of the plaintiff's personal rights and interests, while public law considers the question separately and grants standing as a matter of discretion on the basis of a variety of factors. In respect of the first prong of this distinction, we may quite confidently situate the law of charities at the 'public' end of the procedural public law–private law divide. For as in a paradigmatic public law action, the common law and the modern Charity Commission regime both address the question of a person's entitlement to bring charity proceedings separately from the substantive merits of the claim.

The relationship between charity law's standing rules and the second prong of our posited distinction is more complex. The common law standing rules exhibit both public law-leaning and private law-leaning tendencies. First, we have seen that the Court of Chancery did on occasion grant persons standing to sue charity trustees on the basis of their ownership interests in charity property, whether as identifiable beneficiaries or otherwise. This must be regarded as a *private law-leaning* tendency: the court sometimes treated charitable projects as private projects in the sense that they could be the subject of cognizable ownership interests, and was prepared to grant 'personal' or 'associational' standing rights on this basis. Second, irrespective of whether there were any cognizable ownership interests in a charity, the Attorney General was entitled and expected to bring proceedings to remedy misapplications of charity property on the public's behalf. This must be regarded as an even stronger *public law-leaning* tendency: the court treated charitable projects as public projects in the sense that they were *always* a matter of general concern, and (as in the historical public law context) granted automatic and exclusive 'public interest standing' to the Crown's chief law officer on that basis. Taken together, these tendencies allow us to conclude that the standing rules applicable to charity proceedings at common law were of a somewhat hybrid character, but that their public component was dominant.

As I suggested in the first part, this 'procedural' material offers a number of interesting insights into the substantive dimension of the common law charities tradition. First, because the law of *locus standi* effectively acts as a limitation on a court's jurisdiction to adjudicate disputes, we may conclude that the notionally 'unlimited' inherent jurisdiction of the superior courts to regulate the administration of a charity at common law has always been limited in its practical scope. In the Chancery context, it was limited *de jure* by the small number of individuals who were entitled to bring a bill to enforce a charity, and *de facto* by the reality that many of the individuals that had a strong argument for entitlement were generally poor or otherwise unable to initiate a claim. The court's jurisdiction was also limited by the Attorney General's control over the initiation of relator proceedings, and the fact that exercises of that control were not subject to judicial review.

A second substantive insight is that historically the common law perceived charity property as *public* property in the sense that it was a matter of general concern. This conclusion is implicit in the House of Lords' description of the relator action for the protection of charity property as 'an action to assert a public right'.[103] However, the nuances of the position were articulated most eloquently by the great Chancery lawyer Sir Samuel Romilly while appearing as counsel in a nineteenth-century relator action concerning property devoted to protecting coastal residents from the encroachment of the sea:

> All property in this kingdom belongs either to private individuals, including bodies corporate, or to the public; for injuries to the former the ordinary remedy is an action; for injuries to the latter, an information by the Attorney General. To one species of private property, however, the policy of the law extends a particular protection, and injuries to it are redressed neither by action nor by mere information, but information at the relation of individuals, upon whom the assumption of that character imposes a liability to costs. *Property of this description, to a certain degree private, partakes the character of public property, as devoted to purposes in which, though more peculiarly beneficial to certain individuals, every subject is interested.*[104]

The full consequences of characterizing charity property as property 'partaking the character of public property' are not immediately evident. However, Sir Samuel's speech supports the view that the common law regards the proper administration of charity property first and foremost as a matter of *general concern*, and only secondarily as a matter of *individual concern* to charity founders, beneficiaries or trustees. It suggests, in other words, that where the property of a hospital or even a house of worship is improperly administered, it is the public, rather than merely patients or worshippers, whose interest is engaged.

The third insight our procedural study provides into charity law's substantive dimension is that the common law traditionally attributed great *value* to the public rights in charity property. This value is evidenced by the Crown's historical and deeply symbolic role as the constitutional defender of charity property, and the court's role as its constitutional trustee.[105] It is supported by the English Attorney General's consistent practice of acceding to requests to bring relator proceedings for the protection of charity property in cases where there was an arguable question to be submitted to the court. And despite the major delay and expense associated with charity proceedings in Chancery, the importance attributed to public rights in charity property is attested to by the substantial number of charity law decisions that were rendered by eighteenth- and nineteenth-century courts at the behest of the Crown.

Based on this analysis of the common law position, what may we conclude about the standing rules that today regulate access to relief for misapplications of charity property in England and Wales? While the Charities Act 2011 encompasses a range of judicial and administrative remedies with distinct standing rules, several features of the procedural regime bear mention. First, the Charity Commission is authorized to act of its own motion in a large variety of circumstances, in

[103] *Gouriet* (n 12) 477.
[104] *A-G v Brown* (1818) 1 Swanston 265, 36 ER 384.
[105] *Moggridge v Thackwell* (1803) 7 Ves 36, 32 ER 15 (Ch). See also Ch 1, text at nn 71–72.

order to remedy misapplications of charity property that it is informed of or otherwise perceives. While the range of the Commission's remedial powers may not be as extensive as the charities jurisdiction of the superior courts, therefore, the practical scope of the modern regulator's jurisdiction is far broader. For unlike the courts, the Charity Commission can address misapplications of charity property without the intervention of an interested party.

Second, sections 114 and 115 of the Charities Act 2011 have effected both 'public law-leaning' and 'private law-leaning' adjustments to the common law rules governing charity proceedings, which allow us to conclude that the standing rules governing charity proceedings in England and Wales continue to be marked by a public–private hybridity. The question of who can seek relief for a misadministration of charity property continues to be considered apart from the substantive merits of the claim. Further, the English courts have interpreted the statutory 'person interested' test not as a rigid rule of law, but as 'a practical rule of justice' that affords the courts a measure of flexibility and discretion in responding to particular charity law disputes. This approach is consistent with the broader public law trend towards viewing the determination of *locus standi* as a discretionary judicial task involving the balancing of a variety of factors and concerns.

However, other aspects of the statutory standing rules that limit access to charity proceedings under the Charities Act 2011 seem to represent *private law-leaning* adjustments to the common law approach. In particular, English law has greatly expanded the range of persons who may be awarded standing to bring charity proceedings on the basis of a 'greater-than-public' interest in the administration of a charity, while declining to extend public interest standing to any private individual. Two features of this position are worthy of note. First, to the extent that the expansion of personal and associational standing has increased the opportunities for persons to remedy misuses of English charity property, it is likely to benefit the public at large. Nevertheless, the expansion of personal and associational standing takes English charity law some way away from the historical common law view that the protection of charity property is primarily a matter of *general concern*, and towards the view that it is a matter of *individual concern* to interested persons or groups. For it suggests that where the property of a hospital or a house of worship is improperly administered, it is the patients and worshippers (rather than individual members of the public) who should be sufficiently interested to bring a claim in their own name.

Second, in continuing to deny standing to individuals with a merely public interest in a charity, the Charity Commission regime has diverged from the contemporary public law trend towards granting individuals standing to represent the public interest where illegalities are alleged. The courts have noted this *private law-leaning* divergence, and defended it on the basis that the stricter charity law standard provides a form of protection of the autonomy of charity trustees. The justifiability of charity law's continued non-recognition of public interest standing to bring charity proceedings is debatable, particularly in circumstances where charities play a government-like role in providing welfare services or distributing overseas aid.[106] In the English context, however, the effects of this private law-leaning tendency are attenuated by the continued interest and involvement of the Attorney General and the Charity Commission in the proper administration of charity property, and by their responsibilities under the Act. In other words, while the non-recognition of public interest standing may represent an outdated view of the Attorney General as the only proper representative of the public interest, it does not necessarily suggest that England and Wales's civil regime of charity regulation assigns less value to the public rights in charity property than did the common law. This may not be the case in a tax-based regulatory regime such as the one we shall turn to in the next chapter, where the effects of refusing to recognize public interest standing for misapplications of charity property may be rather more extreme.

[106] See *World Development Movement* (n 19).

5

Alternative Equilibriums: Tax-based Charity Regulation and the Public Law–Private Law Divide

I. Introduction

This work has so far focused on the public–private hybridity of the English law of charities. We have examined notable institutional, substantive and procedural features of English charity law, exploring the manner in which they partake of the respective spheres of public and private law, and how their public–private equilibrium has shifted over time. In the course of this exploration, I have proposed a 'general' or 'categorical' sense in which we can regard the law of charities as a hybrid legal tradition. However, I have deliberately described the public-private character of the modern Charity Commission regime not in this general hybrid sense, but rather as a context-specific hybridity.

The reason for this careful use of language is that there are today many regimes of charity regulation that share links to the common law tradition, but vary widely in their orientation and scope. The British colonial empire carried the common law of charities far afield in the nineteenth and twentieth centuries, where it settled in such jurisdictions as Canada, the United States, Australia, New Zealand, Singapore and Hong Kong. When the British withdrew from the colonies, elements of their charity law remained, only to be variously transformed in their interactions with other legal processes and norms. As a result, there exists today a clearly recognized and ever-growing cluster of 'international charity regulators' in the common law world, which can be characterized both by their diversity and by their 'common', common law roots.[1] Mapping the entire cluster is a task beyond the scope of this book. However, I have suggested an initial principle of division, which would classify these charity law regimes according to whether they are of a 'civil' or 'tax-based' character. A civil regime of charity regulation, as I explained in Chapter 2, is one in which decisions about the status and regulation of charities are

[1] In 2014, the Australian Charities and Not-for-profits Commission hosted the seventh 'International Charity Regulators meeting' in Melbourne: www.acnc.gov.au/ACNC/Pblctns/Rpts/IntReg/ACNC/Publications/Reports/InternationalReg.aspx?noleft=1.

made independently of the tax consequences that attach to that status. A tax-based regime of charity regulation is one in which decisions about the status and regulation of charities are embedded within a general framework of tax administration.

The Charity Commission regime that we have explored over the last three chapters is a civil charity law regime. Its regulator is a non-ministerial government department that was created to more efficiently carry out many of the traditional charity law functions of the Crown and the Court of Chancery. It regulates charities independently of the tax consequences of charitable status, and relies on procedures and remedies that are broadly in line with the common law charities tradition. We have seen that the modern Charity Commission has tended to regulate English charities increasingly as public-leaning projects, in part because emerging public interests like the non-discrimination norm have borne down upon the field. However, the primary public–private axis of the contemporary English regime of charity regulation continues to run between the (private) autonomy interests of benevolent property owners, and the public interest in properly and effectively administered charity property.

What does charity regulation look like when this primary axis is changed? This chapter addresses itself to that question, exploring the nature of the public–private hybridity that inheres in a tax-based charity law regime with significant common law roots. Principally, I will argue that although civil and tax-based charity regulators share a common vocabulary and fulfil many of the same functions, they pursue very different goals. A civil regulator limits the autonomy interests of benevolent property owners primarily in order to protect a public interest in charity property, while a tax-based regulator limits those autonomy interests primarily in order to protect a public interest in the integrity of the tax base. Organizing a regime of charity regulation around the latter tax interest will clearly affect the nature and orientation of the jurisdiction's charity regulator. It will also, I argue, reverberate throughout the substantive and procedural dimensions of that jurisdiction's charity law. The result is that even where a tax-based regime relies upon concepts and vocabulary from the common law charities tradition, its relationship with that tradition may be tenuous.

This chapter explores these claims by reference to a particular tax-based charity regulator, the Canada Revenue Agency's 'Charities Directorate'. In Section II, I describe the origins of the Charities Directorate, paying particular attention to the constitutional context in which charity regulation came to rest with the federal revenue authority in Canada, and the nature of the public interest the regime was designed to protect. I outline the nature of the Directorate's mandate, and its supervisory and remedial powers. In Sections III and IV, I reflect upon the ways in which the general tax orientation of the Charities Directorate permeates the substantive and procedural dimensions of Canadian charity law. Building on the content of the previous chapters, Section III examines the status and regulatory operation of the public benefit criterion in Canada. Section IV takes up the question of who can seek relief for the misadministration of charity property in Canada. I summarize the chapter's conclusions in Section V.

II. Canada's Tax-based Charity Regulator

A. Origins

In 1853, when the centuries-old UK Parliament decided to create a regulatory body to address long-standing issues relating to the abuse of charitable trusts, the federation that was to form the basis of the Canadian state did not even exist. While the lands on Canada's eastern shores were settled English colonies and the future provinces of Quebec and Ontario existed as a (temporarily) united political entity, much of the massive territory to the west was still unsettled and without colonial government.[2] The English law of equity had been received in the settled colonies, along with such statute law as existed in England at the date of reception.[3] Nevertheless, the nineteenth-century English project of protecting property held in trust for charity was not mirrored in these massive, sparsely populated lands.

In 1867, seven years after the Charity Commissioners for England and Wales had been granted concurrent jurisdiction with the Chancery Court, the constitutional structure for the Dominion of Canada was finally put into place.[4] Section 129 of the Constitution Act 1867 left the received English law in place, continuing in force the laws existing in the uniting colonies at the date of confederation. In dividing legislative authority between the Dominion of Canada and the provinces, however, the Constitution Act 1867 assigned to the provinces the exclusive authority to make laws regarding the 'establishment, maintenance and management of … charities and eleemosynary institutions', and over property and civil rights in the province.[5] For its part, the federal government was accorded residual authority to make laws in relation to matters not falling under provincial jurisdiction, and specific authority over 'the raising of money by any mode or system of taxation'.[6] The rights of the Crown were similarly distributed, with 'the Crown in each right receiving the prerogatives and duties appropriate to its property and legislative competence'.[7]

This division of legislative authority had special repercussions in Quebec, a province whose private law was not based on the common law, but on the civil law tradition established by the French Crown in the colony of New France.[8]

[2] See JE Cote, 'The Reception of English Law' (1977) 15 *Alberta Law Review* 29, 87–92. The territory was, of course, inhabited by indigenous peoples with their own laws and government: see eg, B Slattery, 'The Hidden Constitution: Aboriginal Rights in Canada' (1984) 32 *American Journal of Comparative Law* 361.

[3] ibid.

[4] This was accomplished by the British North America Act 1867 (30 & 31 Vict c 3), subsequently renamed the Constitution Act 1867.

[5] Constitution Act 1867, s 92(7), (13).

[6] Constitution Act 1867, s 91, 91(3). The residual authority has not been construed as expansively as it might have been: P Hogg, *Constitutional Law of Canada*, vol 2, 5th edn (Scarborough, Thomson Carswell, 2007) ch 17.

[7] Cote (n 2) 61.

[8] See generally JEC Brierley and RA Macdonald (eds), *Quebec Civil Law: An introduction to Quebec Private Law* (Toronto, Emond Montgomery, 1993) ch 1.

Following the military conquest of the English and the change of sovereignty to the English Crown in 1763, Quebec became subject to all relevant and applicable English law.[9] However, the Quebec Act 1774 provided that matters of 'property and civil rights' in Quebec would henceforth be determined according to the French civil law tradition.[10] The phrase, which made its way into the Constitution Act 1867, was understood as a 'compendious description of the entire body of private law which governs the relationships between subject and subject'.[11] As a result, it is generally understood that the law of Quebec consists of the pre-1760 French civil law as subsequently altered by Quebec in regard to anything affecting the private law, and 'the common law as it existed in England at the same time with its subsequent alterations in Quebec and in Canada in regard to anything affecting the public law'.[12]

This colonial history has a number of implications relevant to the present work. A first is that the Crown in right of Canada did not inherit the English Crown's prerogative powers with respect to charities, and that the federal government has no authority to regulate the administration of charities *per se*. A second is that the provincial superior courts and the Crowns in right of the common law provinces *did* receive the prerogative powers associated with the law of charitable trusts,[13] and that the provinces are fully authorized to regulate the charitable sector. A final implication of Canada's colonial history is that, according to the prevailing authority, the common law of charities has no application in Quebec.[14] This means that the superior courts of Quebec have no inherent jurisdiction to administer charitable resources, and that the Crown in right of Quebec does not enjoy the English Crown's prerogative powers over charities. The common law of charities does exert an influence in the province, as it is relied upon as providing the suppletive law for the interpretation of the federal registered charity provisions in Quebec, and for Quebec's own tax code.[15] In general, however, the registered charity regime operates in Quebec against the background of a distinctive private law tradition of devoting property to social purposes, which is rooted in the unenacted civil law and the Civil Code of Québec.[16]

Given Canada's constitutional structure, one might have expected the provinces to drive the development of a paradigm of Canadian charity regulation. However,

[9] Cote (n 2) 42 and footnotes 61–67; *Donegani v Donegani* (1835) 3 Knapp 62, 12 ER 571.

[10] Quebec Act 1774 (14 Geo 3 c 83) s 8.

[11] Hogg (n 6) 21–22.

[12] *St-Hilaire v Canada* [2001] 4 FC 289 (CA) [40]. See also *Prud'homme v Prud'homme*, 2002 SCC 85, [2002] 4 SCR 663 [46].

[13] *Bonanza Creek Gold Mining Co Ltd v R* [1916] 1 AC 566 (HL) 579.

[14] *Ross v Ross* (1894) 25 SCR 307. However, if it is indeed the case that certain elements of the common law of charities are 'public' in nature, Canada's constitutional framework would suggest that those rules could form part of Quebec law. A determination of this interesting issue falls outside the scope of this book.

[15] K Chan, 'Taxing Charities/Imposer les Organismes de Bienfaisance: Harmonization and Dissonance in Canadian Charity Law' (2007) 55 *Canadian Tax Journal* 481, 520.

[16] Civil Code of Québec, LRQ c C-1991, arts 1270, 1277, 1287, 1294 and 1298.

only Ontario took significant steps in this direction, establishing a statutory regime of charity regulation based loosely on the Charity Commission model in 1915.[17] The Charities Accounting Act established a basic regime of supervision applicable to every gift made under a written instrument for any 'religious, educational, charitable or public purpose'.[18] It also gave the Attorney General powers to inquire into the use of charity property, which have since been delegated to the province's Public Guardian and Trustee.[19] Ontario's 'charity regulator' has a far narrower jurisdiction than the Charity Commission for England and Wales: while the Public Guardian and Trustee carries out some of the historic functions of the English Attorney General, the officer enjoys none of the judicial powers of the superior courts. Nevertheless, the existence of a public officer with a mandate to oversee the administration of charitable trusts and corporations distinguishes Ontario from the rest of the Canadian provinces. It also explains the disproportionate number of Canadian charity law cases decided by the Ontario courts.

The nine remaining Canadian provinces have made very little use of their extensive jurisdiction over charities. The provincial legislatures do exercise their authority over matters that intersect with charity law, including corporate law and human rights law, aspects of which will be considered later in this chapter. Apart from Ontario, however, the provinces have enacted very few statutes directly concerning the maintenance and management of charities.[20] Moreover, as we shall see in Section IV, the provincial Crowns have almost never invoked their prerogative powers to institute charity proceedings, and often take no position where such proceedings are brought by others. One may speculate that in the Canadian context of abundant land and sparse populations, the English project of protecting property held in trust for charity has simply never been considered a priority. But whatever the reason for the provincial inactivity, it has fallen to the federal government to regulate the charitable sector within its constitutional constraints.

In constitutional terms, the federal government's regulation of the Canadian charitable sector is today understood as an adjunct of its legislative authority over the raising of money by taxation. However, the first federal scheme for the regulation of charities in Canada was not tied to the administration of tax revenues. Rather, it arose during the First World War in response to a perceived need to 'control fraudulent "war charity" appeals and to encourage the efficient operation of legitimate war charities'.[21] Based closely on a UK statute enacted the previous year, the War Charities Act 1917 prohibited any fund or association whose objects were 'connected with the present European war' from raising money unless it was

[17] OLRC Report, 536.

[18] CAA (Ont) s 1(1). The Act brings charitable corporations within its scope by deeming them to be trustees: CAA (Ont), s 1(2).

[19] CAA (Ont) s 2.

[20] Some have legislated regarding charitable fundraising or specific types of charity property: see, eg, Charitable Fundraising Act, RSA 2000, c C-9; Trustee (Church Property) Act, RSBC 1996, c 465.

[21] OLRC Report, 258. See also Canada HC Debates (1 February 1917) 377–78.

registered under the Act.[22] A registration authority considered written applications, and could reject them where the authority believed the war charity was not established in good faith for charitable purposes, would not comply with the Act, or would not be properly administered.[23] The regulatory regime put into place by the War Charities Act 1917 was not a permanent regime, nor did it apply to all of the country's charitable institutions.[24] Nevertheless, as the only piece of federal legislation that ever 'aimed at preserving and promoting the integrity and efficiency of the sector for its own sake',[25] it forms an important part of the history of federal charities regulation in Canada. It also serves as a reminder that the constitutional possibilities for federal involvement in the charitable sphere are broader than is often thought.[26]

The emergence of Canada's revenue agency as the primary regulator of charities was a more gradual process, which was tied to the development of substantive rules on charitable donations in Canada's federal tax statutes. The first of these statutes, the Income War Tax Act 1917, exempted from taxation the income of 'religious, charitable, agricultural and educational institutions' and provided for the deduction, without limit, of amounts paid to the Patriotic and Canadian Red Cross Funds, and other approved patriotic and war funds.[27] It was initially administered by the federal Minister of Finance, who was given specific authority over 'the control and management of the collection of the taxation levied... and of all matters incident thereto'.[28] In 1927, however, Parliament created a Department of National Revenue with its own responsible Minister, who assumed the administrative duties of the Minister of Finance.[29] This arrangement has stayed in place, with tax administration being carried out by the Canada Revenue Agency and tax policy being developed by the Department of Finance.

The involvement of the Department of National Revenue in the administration of charities grew as the tax rules pertaining to charities and charitable gifts multiplied. An amendment to the Income War Tax Act in 1922 made it mandatory for charities and other tax-exempt entities to file annual income returns.[30] Another in 1930 allowed taxpayers to deduct up to 10 per cent of their net income for donations paid and *receipted by* any charitable organization.[31] In 1948 the

[22] War Charities Act 1917, 7 & 8 Geo 5, c 38 (Canada). The UK predecessor was the War Charities Act 1916 (6 & 7 Geo 5) c 43 (UK).

[23] War Charities Act 1917, s 4(4).

[24] The War Charities Act was in effect from 1917 until 1927, and again from 1939 to 1947: see R Watson, 'Charity and the Canadian Income Tax: An Erratic History' (1985) 5 *The Philanthropist* 3.

[25] OLRC Report 262.

[26] Presumably, the federal government enacted The War Charities Act 1917 pursuant to its emergency power during wartime: see Hogg (n 6) ch 17.

[27] Income War Tax Act 1917, SC 1917, c 28, ss 3(1)(c) and 5(d). The war fund deduction was repealed in 1920: see An Act to amend the Income War Tax Act 1917, 10–11 Geo 5, c 49 (Can) s 5.

[28] Income War Tax Act 1917 (n 27) s 22.

[29] Department of National Revenue Act, SC 1927, c 34, ss 3, 5.

[30] See Watson (n 24) 7 for this history.

[31] An Act to amend the Income War Tax Act, SC 1930, c 24, s 3.

Department issued a policy directive that required charitable organizations wanting to issue receipts to apply for recognition at the district level and provided a prescribed form for that purpose.[32] Prior to 1967, however, there was no body or unit dedicated specifically to the supervision of charities or charitable gifts, and the Department of National Revenue's administration of charities was considered 'quite unsophisticated'.[33]

When the Canadian Parliament finally created a dedicated body to supervise charities and charitable gifts, it was, like the nineteenth-century UK Parliament, reacting to a specific problem that was garnering increasing public attention. However, the issue was not that charitable resources were being subject to abuse and neglect at the hand of individuals, as had been the case in England and Wales. Rather, the identified mischief was that *government* resources were being subject to abuse and neglect at the hand of *charities*, primarily through the issuance of tax receipts for amounts that had not been received.[34] The government was also concerned that organizations not qualified as charities were improperly issuing donation receipts.

In 1966 then-Minister of National Revenue Edgar Benson introduced a series of amendments to the Income Tax Act to address these perceived abuses. The amendments required all charitable organizations issuing donation tax receipts to be registered with the Minister of National Revenue, to keep records and books of accounts for the purpose of verifying donations, and to report annually to the revenue agency on their finances and operations.[35] Speaking in Parliament, Minister Benson described the proposed registration system in the following terms:

> [T]his is a move toward a system of control whereby people may not abuse the right of being a charitable organization to the detriment of all other taxpayers in Canada, and thus force those taxpayers to pay more tax to make up for the advantage taken of this system by people who should not do so.[36]

While the government was acting in a perceived public interest in creating Canada's federal charity regulator, therefore, the public interest that was identified was *not* an interest in the proper administration of charity property. Instead, it was a public interest in the integrity of the federal tax base.[37] In 1967 the National Revenue Minister created a new unit of the Department's assessments branch, the Charitable and Non-Profit Organizations Section, to administer the new registered charity regime.[38] Its successor, the 'Charities Directorate' of the Canada Revenue Agency (CRA), remains the primary regulator of Canadian charities today.

32 OLRC Report, 259.
33 OLRC Report, 261.
34 Canada, House of Common Debates (7 June 1966) 6114; see also Watson (n 24) 11.
35 An Act to amend the Income Tax Act, SC 1966–67, c 47, s 3.
36 Canada, HC Deb 7 June 1966, 6115.
37 See P Monahan and E Roth, *Federal Regulation of Charities: A Critical Assessment of Recent Proposals for Legislative and Regulatory Reform* (Toronto, York University, 2000) 13, describing this as the 'main rationale' for involving the federal government in charities regulation.
38 ibid 12 and OLRC Report, 264.

B. Nature and Orientation

In seeking to compare the nature and orientation of the Canadian Charities Directorate with that of the Charity Commission for England and Wales, we immediately confront a number of difficulties. Apart from the fundamentally different nature of each regulatory body, one comparative challenge relates to the *amount* of law that is encompassed by each regime. The Charities Act 2011 (UK) is a long statute, with 358 sections and 11 schedules, which articulate in great detail the legal definition of charity, the functions and powers of the Commission, and the ongoing role of the Crown and the courts.[39] The rules of the Canadian registered charity regime, on the other hand, are set out in a dozen sections of the Income Tax Act,[40] which are often noted for what they do *not* say.[41] The sector is heavily reliant on extra-statutory guidance issued by the Charities Directorate to fill in these legislative gaps. The Directorate has no constituting statute specific to that body, and the Income Tax Act contains no explicit statement of the Directorate's objectives, functions or duties. Despite the challenges posed by this sparer legal landscape, this section will seek to identify the principal functions and powers of the tax-based Charities Directorate, and to contrast its orientation with that of the civil Charity Commission for England and Wales.

As an internal government unit, the Charities Directorate has a mandate and authority that are identical to those of the broader revenue agency within which it is housed. This mandate is to support and assist the Minister of National Revenue, the elected Cabinet member charged with administering and enforcing the federal Income Tax Act.[42] Pursuant to section 220 (2.01) of that Act, the Minister has delegated responsibility for exercising powers and performing functions arising from the registered charity provisions to the Director General of the Charities Directorate.[43] The Director General carries out these functions with a staff of approximately 270 employees spread throughout six divisions. There are also approximately 40 field auditors who carry out charity audits across the country.[44]

[39] It has been said that the Charities Act 2006, the predecessor to the Charities Act 2011, was subject to 'more consideration and more parliamentary scrutiny than any other piece of legislation in the UK': L Driscoll, 'England and Wales: *Pemsel* Plus' in M McGregor-Lowndes and K O'Halloran (eds), *Modernising Charity Law: Recent Developments and Future Directions* (Cheltenham, Edward Elgar Publishing, 2010) 48.

[40] The core provisions of the registered charity regime are set out in ss 149(1), 149.1, 168, 172, 188, 188.1, 189, 230 and 248(1) of the ITA.

[41] *AYSA Amateur Youth Soccer Association v Canada (Revenue Agency)* 2007 SCC 42, [2007] 3 SCR 217 [8], [15].

[42] Canada Revenue Agency Act, SC 1999, c 17, s 5(1)(a); ITA, s 220(1). The Agency is for all purposes an agent of Her Majesty in right of Canada: Canada Revenue Agency Act, s 4(2).

[43] ITA, s 220 (2.01). An administrative consolidation of this delegation is posted on the Government of Canada website: see www.cra-arc.gc.ca/tx/tchncl/dlgtnfpwrs/mnstr/ita-eng.html.

[44] Office of the Auditor General for Canada, *Report of the Auditor General of Canada to the House of Commons* (autumn 2010) ch 7, para 7.5.

Based on the CRA's constituting statute and the substance of the registered charity provisions, it is possible to identify three primary functions of the Charities Directorate. The first function is to determine whether applicant institutions qualify as registered charities under the Income Tax Act, and to register those institutions that do qualify.[45] The second is to identify and investigate apparent violations of the Act by registered charities, and to take remedial action in connection with such violations.[46] The third, ancillary function of the Charities Directorate is to provide to registered charities such support, advice and services as are consistent with the Directorate's objective of administering and enforcing the Income Tax Act.[47] Unlike the Charities Act 2011, the legislation contains no explicit statement of how or to what end the Charities Directorate must carry out these functions.

Like the Charity Commission, the Charities Directorate has broad powers to institute inquiries (called audits) into registered charities of its own motion, in order to identify cases of abuse. Section 231.1 of the Income Tax Act authorizes the CRA to inspect the books and records of any registered charity, as well as any document that may relate to the information contained in those records. The CRA is authorized to issue search warrants, and to require a registered charity to provide any additional information that is relevant to its compliance with the Act.[48] A registered charity that is the subject of a CRA audit is required to provide 'all reasonable assistance' to the auditor, and hindering or interfering with the work of an auditor is a specific offence under the Act.[49]

Consistently with Canada's federal structure and the Directorate's status as an internal unit of a revenue agency, Canada's primary charity regulator has no jurisdiction to address the misadministration of charity property unless that misadministration also constitutes a violation of the Income Tax Act. However, there is a significant degree of functional overlap between the acts that the registered charity regime prohibits, and the 'misconduct or mismanagement' that the Charity Commission for England and Wales is tasked to address. It is a violation of the Income Tax Act, for example, for a registered charity to confer an 'undue' personal benefit on any of its settlors, members or trustees.[50] It is a violation of the Income Tax Act for a registered charity to appoint as director a person who has been convicted of an offence that is relevant to the operation of the charity, or to keep incomplete

[45] This function, which flows from the statutory definition of a registered charity, will be explored in further detail in Ch 6: see ITA, s 248(1) ('registered charity/*organisme de bienfaisance*').

[46] The Charities Directorate also regulates non-charitable entities such as registered Canadian amateur athletic associations: see, eg, ITA, ss 149.1(1) ('qualified donee/*donataire reconnu*'), 149.1(4.2).

[47] Canada Revenue Agency Act, s 5(2). This list is broadly consistent with the CRA's own identification of the Directorate's responsibilities: *Report of the Auditor General* (n 44) para 7.3.

[48] ITA, ss 231.2, 231.3.

[49] ITA, ss 231.1(1)(d) and s 231.5(2). Charities audits are discussed further in AB Drache, RB Hayhoe and DP Stevens, *Charities Taxation, Policy and Practice. Taxation* (Toronto, Thomson Carswell, 2007) ch 10.

[50] ITA, s 188.1(4)–(5).

or inaccurate records.[51] Most importantly, it is a violation of the Income Tax Act for a registered charity to cease operating exclusively for charitable purposes or to cease devoting all of its resources to charitable activities.[52] Effectively, these provisions authorize the Charities Directorate to address many of the same instances of misconduct and neglect in the administration of charity property as the Charity Commission and the superior courts.

Where the Charity Commission and the Charities Directorate part ways significantly is in the context of their remedial powers. The Commission, as we have seen, has at its disposal most of the remedies that inhered in the charities jurisdiction of the Court of Chancery. Where the Commission identifies an institution that is not properly applying its resources to charitable purposes, therefore, the Commission's approach is not to remove that charity from the register, but to replace or give directions to charity trustees.[53] The Charities Directorate, by contrast, has very limited tools to remedy cases of charity 'abuse'. Where a registered charity engages in certain prohibited behaviours listed in section 188.1 of the Income Tax Act, the Directorate may impose associated monetary penalties, or suspend the registered charity's authority to issue charitable tax receipts. Where a registered charity engages in prohibited behaviours listed other than in section 188.1, however, the Directorate's only formal remedial option is to revoke the entity's charitable registration.[54] Once a charity's registration is revoked, the charity becomes liable for a revocation tax equivalent to the fair market value of all its property, minus amounts expended during a one-year 'winding-up period' on charitable activities and gifts to arm's-length charities.[55] At the end of the one-year period, the charity must turn over any property that has not been so expended to the federal Crown, which may use it for the general purposes of the government.[56] The registered charity regime thus departs from a key common law principle: namely, that property that has once been devoted to charity must stay forever in the charitable sphere.[57]

What, then, may we say about the nature and regulatory disposition of the Charities Directorate, based on its admittedly sparse statutory foundations? Despite the Directorate's efforts to portray itself as a regulator that aims to improve the 'integrity of the charitable sector and the social well-being of Canadians',[58]

[51] ITA, ss 149.1(4.1)(e) and 230(2).

[52] ITA, ss 168(1) and 149.1(1).

[53] Charity Commission, *Maintenance of an Accurate Register of Charities* (RR6, Dec 2012), [14]–[16].

[54] ITA, s 168(1). The Directorate sometimes relies on informal remedial tools, such as an education letter or compliance agreement: see Drache, Hayhoe and Stevens (n 49) [10.2.11].

[55] ITA, s 188(1), (1.1), (1.2), (1.3).

[56] ITA, s 189(6.1)(c). The monetary penalties imposed under s 188.1 are also payable to the federal Crown.

[57] For a fuller discussion, see K Chan, 'The Role of the Attorney General in Charity Proceedings in Canada and in England and Wales' (2010) 89 *Canadian Bar Review* 373, 398–99.

[58] Canada Revenue Agency, 'About the Charities Directorate', www.cra-arc.gc.ca/chrts-gvng/chrts/bt/mssn_vsn-eng.html.

it has neither the statutory mandate nor any clear constitutional authority to further a public interest in the proper and effective administration of charitable resources. The registered charity provisions adopt some of the vocabulary of the common law charities tradition, and address many similar instances of misconduct. Nevertheless, the Charities Directorate is neither in fact nor in spirit a regulatory heir of the charities jurisdiction of the Chancery Court. It lacks the remedial flexibility to effectively address instances of trustee misconduct, and exercises of its regulatory authority may ultimately lead to charitable resources ceasing to be charitable at all.

However, despite the Directorate's limited remedial powers and its lack of authority to further a public interest in the proper administration of charity property, there is little in the registered charity regime to suggest that the Charities Directorate is a 'light-touch' regulator that is committed to protecting the autonomy interests of charities and their trustees. The Directorate's remedial toolkit may be limited, but the procedures and sanctions that it applies to registered charities under audit are heavy regulatory tools. Together with substantive rules like the undue benefit rule, which effectively targets charity mismanagement, they manifest the federal government's intention to push to the constitutional limits of its regulatory authority in the field.[59] Like the Charity Commission, then, the Charities Directorate is best understood as a regulator that is oriented towards intervening in the affairs of charities in a perceived public interest. However, the public interest that the Directorate aims to protect is not a public interest in properly and effectively administered charity property, but a public interest in the integrity of the tax base.

III. Public Benefit in Canada

How do charity law's substantive doctrines fare in a regulatory regime whose primary axis extends between the (private) autonomy interests of benevolent property owners and a public interest in the integrity of the tax base? This section addresses this question by considering the status and regulatory operation of the public benefit criterion under the Canadian registered charity regime. It offers two principal reflections. First, in a context where the regulator's primary public concern is to protect the integrity of the tax base, we witness public benefit playing a subsidiary role, and legal tools with more direct fiscal consequences being used to monitor the placement of charities on the continuum between altruistic and self-regarding projects. Second, in a context where the regulator is oriented towards tax considerations and the agent of an elected Cabinet Minister, a regulatory effort emerges to align the projects of registered charities more closely with the public welfare goals of the state.

[59] Drache, Hayhoe and Stevens (n 49) [10.3.2].

A. Status

In Chapter 3 we examined the public benefit criterion in relation to two important public–private continuums that have life in the law of charities. I suggested that while the common law doctrine requires charitable projects to be largely altruistic (rather than self-regarding) projects, private law thinking dominates on the continuum between public-welfare compliance and public-welfare deviance. The effect of this private law thinking is that charity founders and trustees retain substantial autonomy to define what type of benefit their charity will provide and who will receive that benefit. I then examined how the Charity Commission's 2008 Public Benefit Guidance appeared to alter the traditional equilibrium between public benefit's public and private elements, and described the strong responses that those equilibrium shifts provoked.

It was implicit in this discussion that public benefit is a central doctrine of the law of charities in England and Wales, which has catalysed debates about charity law's proper objects and scope. In this regard, the first point of note in the Canadian context is that public benefit has played only a minor role in Canadian charity law's operation and development. The Parliament of Canada has never articulated the public benefit concept within the Income Tax Act, nor entered into a substantive debate about its meaning or application.[60] The Supreme Court of Canada has confirmed that public benefit is an implicit condition of charitable registration under the Income Tax Act. In the leading case on the registered charity regime, the majority described the incorporated common law doctrine as a reflection of the general concern that charitable activity should seek the welfare of the public,[61] while the minority cast public benefit as a requirement that charities confer an 'objectively measurable and socially useful benefit'.[62] However, apart from being cited as the justification for the political purposes rule, public benefit has almost never formed the basis of a judicial ruling on registered charity status in Canada.[63] In cases where public benefit has been raised, Canadian courts have tended to invoke the leading English authorities, without engaging in any substantial analysis of their own on the principles of public benefit.[64]

There are a number of possible explanations for this dearth of Canadian law on the public benefit doctrine. Some of these are linked to the constitutional

[60] This despite the fact that the court and members of the charitable sector have periodically suggested that it do so: see, for example, *Vancouver Society of Immigrant & Visible Minority Women v MNR* [1999] 1 SCR 10, 169 DLR (4th) 34 [197].

[61] ibid [147] and [177].

[62] ibid [41].

[63] Public benefit figured only 'obliquely' in the court's analysis of charitable purposes in *Vancouver Society*: ibid [41]. For a rare instance where public benefit was central to the court's analysis, see *Seventh Division, Pacific Northwest Region, National Model Railroad Association v MNR* [1989] FCJ No 63 (CA).

[64] See, for example, *Vancouver Society* (n 60) [41], [147]; *Everywoman's Health Centre Society (1988) v Canada (MNR)* [1992] 2 FC 52 (FCA) [22].

issues discussed earlier, and the general failure of the Canadian provinces to either exercise their legislative authority over charities, or carry out the Crown's historical role in enforcing charitable trusts.[65] One might also argue that Canadian courts have rarely had occasion to address public benefit, since the overwhelming majority of decisions on the meaning of charity under the Income Tax Act have been decided on the basis of non-conformity with the Statute of Elizabeth. However, the minimal role of public benefit doctrine in Canadian case law is also a function of the regulatory context in which that doctrine operates. When we compare this to the English context, we see that the Charities Directorate has neither a strong statutory basis nor a strong fiscal incentive to monitor the public benefit of registered charities on an ongoing basis.

We saw in Chapter 3 that the Charity Commission for England and Wales relies on the public benefit criterion to police the altruism, and to a certain extent the public-welfare compliance, of charitable projects. If an aspiring charity is constituted so as to benefit persons with whom the founder has a familial connection, the Commission may refuse to register that charity. If an *existing* charity operates in a discriminatory way, the Commission has a number of tools with which to remedy that 'dis-benefit', including removing a charity trustee or ordering him or her to apply the charity property in a specified manner.[66] The Commission's statutory functions, which include facilitating the better administration of charities and taking remedial or protective action in connection with charity mismanagement, support the Commission's exercise of these powers to ensure that charities operate for the public benefit.

The regulatory paradigm in Canada is fundamentally different. Because the Income Tax Act requires registered charities to devote all of their income to exclusively charitable purposes and charitable activities, the Directorate may, like the Charity Commission, refuse to register an applicant organization on the basis that it is not for the public benefit. If an *existing* registered charity operates in a way that is not for the public benefit, however, the Commission cannot remove, replace or give directions to that charity's trustees. The Directorate may, and does, use the threat of revocation to persuade charity trustees to operate their charity exclusively for charitable purposes. However, the Directorate's imprecise tax administration mandate does not orient the Canadian regulator towards exercising its powers to ensure that charities operate for the public benefit. Anecdotally, Canadian charity lawyers recount that public benefit audits are very rare.

The Charities Directorate also has less fiscal incentive than the UK tax authority to monitor whether charities are expending all of their resources for the public benefit. While most significant sources of charity revenue are eligible for UK

[65] Even in the provincial law sphere, only a handful of Canadian cases have considered the common law doctrine in any depth. A review of the Canadian case law on public benefit is available in DWM Waters, MR Gillen and LD Smith, *Waters' Law of Trusts in Canada*, 4th edn (Toronto, Thomson Reuters Publishing, 2012) 730–35, 743–45, 760–63.

[66] CA 2011, ss 79, 85.

income tax exemptions, the exemptions may only be claimed so far as a charity *applies* the income 'to charitable purposes only'.[67] If HMRC finds that a charity has spent money in ways that are not for the public benefit, therefore, it may restrict the charity's exemptions from income, corporation and capital gains tax by an amount equal to those expenditures.[68] Under the Canadian Income Tax Act, by contrast, registered charities enjoy a blanket exemption from most categories of income tax.[69] They are required to devote all of their income to charitable purposes and activities, and if they fail to do so, the Charities Directorate is authorized to revoke their charitable registration.[70] Since 2004, as we have seen, the Directorate has also been authorized to impose monetary penalties on registered charities that confer 'undue benefits' upon non-arm's-length persons. However, the Income Tax Act concept of an undue benefit proscribes a narrower range of behaviour than the public benefit doctrine.[71] Further, the Act does not authorize the Charities Directorate to impose monetary penalties on registered charities on the sole basis that they have incurred non-charitable expenditures. Unlike UK tax law, in other words, Canadian tax law does not create a regularized context within which the Directorate may tax registered charities on the basis that some of their income is not being applied for the public benefit.

Given the subsidiary role of public benefit in the registered charity regime, it would be tempting to conclude that benevolent property owners in Canada have more autonomy than their English counterparts to locate their charitable projects further along the continuum towards self-regarding projects. If the CRA is not oriented toward monitoring the altruism of charitable *institutions*, however, it does monitor the altruism of charitable *donations*. Pursuant to sections 110.1 and 118.1 of the Income Tax Act, the entitlement of a donor to tax relief depends largely on whether his or her charitable donation qualifies as a 'gift/*don*'. In the absence of a statutory definition of the term, the federal courts have held that a gift means a voluntary transfer of property owned by a donor to a donee, in return for which *no benefit or consideration flows back to the donor*, either directly or indirectly, or anticipatorily.[72] The CRA regularly relies on the Income Tax Act gift concept to reassess taxpayers who are alleged to have received a direct or indirect benefit

[67] See, for example, Income Tax Act 2007 (UK) ss 521(4), 522(5), 531(3); Taxation of Chargeable Gains Act 1992 (UK) s 256(1) ('applicable and applied for charitable purposes'). For a more complete list of the tax exemptions enjoyed by charities and charitable donors, see H Picarda, *The Law and Practice Relating to Charities*, 4th edn (Hayward's Heath, Bloomsbury Professional, 2010) 1006–39.

[68] Picarda (n 67) 1032. See also HMRC, *Tax and Charitable or Non-charitable Expenditure*, www.hmrc.gov.uk/charities/tax/expenditure.htm.

[69] ITA, s 149(1)(f).

[70] This authority is the combined effect of ITA, s 149.1(1) 'charitable organization' (*oeuvre de bienfaisance*), s 149.1(1) 'charitable foundation' (*fondation de bienfaisance*), and s 168(1)(b).

[71] For example, the ITA definition of an 'undue benefit' specifically excludes benefits conferred in the course of a charity's ordinary charitable activities, unless the beneficiary's eligibility for the benefit 'relates *solely* to the relationship of the beneficiary to the charity': ITA, s 188.1(5)(b).

[72] See *Friedberg v Canada* [1989] FCJ No 23 (FCA), leave to appeal to SCC refused; *Woolner v Canada* [2000] 1 CTC 35 (FCA); *Webb v The Queen* [2004] TCC 619 [16].

in return for their charitable donation. The effect of such a reassessment is to require the taxpayer to repay to the CRA (with interest) any tax benefit received on account of the donation. The CRA's gift audits have produced a substantial number of judicial decisions, which, like the public benefit decisions, tend to focus on donors that are alleged to have an emotional or obligational connection to the charity's beneficiary class.[73]

The Charities Directorate's tendency to police the altruism of donors rather than charities, and the fiscal incentives associated with that tendency, are illustrated by the series of events that led to *Coleman v Canada (MNR)*.[74] *Coleman* had its genesis in the grant-making practices of an educational institution with admittedly charitable purposes. Pursuant to its 'Christian Higher Education Assistance Fund' programme, the charity, the National Foundation for Christian Leadership (NFCL), encouraged students to solicit donations to NFCL, and provided bursaries and scholarships to the soliciting students in accordance with an established set of eligibility criteria. Donations to NFCL could not be designated to a specific student, and the charity testified that it regarded itself as having the discretion to award whatever amounts it saw fit to any worthy individual.[75] In practice, however, the court found that NFCL informed students of the amount of the bursary for which they were eligible, issued tax receipts to their relatives for corresponding donations to NFCL, and then provided bursaries to students that correlated closely to the amounts that they had raised.[76]

The scheme carried out by NFCL raised a predictable objection on the part of the revenue authority: namely, that the vast majority of the beneficiaries of the charity's educational grants were distinguishable from other members of the public on the basis of their relationship to a person or employer that financed the charity.[77] The scheme was simply not sufficiently *altruistic*. Less predictable, on the other hand, was the course of action chosen by the CRA. Under the terms of the Income Tax Act, the CRA could have sanctioned NFCL for its grant-making practices, on the ground that the scheme was not for the public benefit and the foundation was therefore not operating for 'exclusively charitable purposes'.[78] As we have seen, however, this would likely have entailed revoking NFCL's registration, a penalty that would have been harsh and, perhaps more importantly, unlikely to produce any tax revenue. Consistent with this lack of incentive, a tax audit of NFCL's bursary scheme did not result in the charity's revocation,[79] and the case

[73] See, for example, *The Queen v McBurney* [1985] 2 CTC 2124 (FCA); *Friedberg* (n 72); *Woolner* (n 72).

[74] *Coleman v Canada* 2010 TCC 109, [2010] TCJ No 63; *Coleman v Canada* 2011 FCA 82, [2011] FCJ No 264.

[75] *Coleman* (TCC) [3].

[76] ibid [14], [50].

[77] See ibid [49].

[78] Much as HMRC has done in a similar context: see *IRC v Educational Grants Association Ltd* [1967] Ch 993 (CA).

[79] This audit is referred to in *Coleman* (TCC) [3].

came to court after the CRA rejected the *donors*' tax exemption claims on the basis that the donations to NFCL were not 'gifts'.[80] This approach to regulating the altruism of charitable projects raises a number of important policy questions, which are beyond the scope of the present work.[81] For present purposes, we may simply point to *Coleman* as an illustration of the reflection that where a charity regulator's primary concern is to protect the integrity of the tax base, legal tools with more direct fiscal consequences than public benefit may be used to monitor the altruistic quality of charitable projects.

B. Regulatory Alignment with Public Welfare Goals

While the Charities Directorate does not rely heavily on public benefit to regulate charities on an ongoing basis, it does use the criterion to deny organizations charitable status at the registration stage. In this regard, the second phenomenon that is observable in Canada is that of a charity regulator using public benefit to align charitable projects in an unprecedented way with the public welfare goals of the state. In March 2006, responding in part to the considerable attention being devoted to public benefit in England and Wales, the Charities Directorate released new guidelines that articulate how the CRA understands and applies the public benefit criterion when making determinations of registered charity status (the Guidelines).[82] The Guidelines rely heavily on the English common law authorities and early regulatory decisions of the Charity Commission.[83] They are structured around the traditional pillars of the public benefit doctrine, and set out all of the major principles associated with pre-Charities Act 2006 cases such as *Anti-Vivisection* and *Gilmour v Coats*. To this extent, the Guidelines are broadly consistent with the common law position on public benefit.

However, a number of further statements in the Guidelines evince the Charities Directorate seeking to adjust the equilibrium that the common law public benefit doctrine has traditionally set between individual and collective project pursuit. As in the English context, this can be understood as a regulatory effort to align Canadian charities more closely with various public welfare goals. Although the Guidelines pre-date the Charity Commission's 2008 Public Benefit Guidance, two of these adjustments restrain the autonomy of charity founders and trustees in ways broadly consistent with the English adjustments discussed in Chapter 3. The final adjustment is uniquely Canadian, and reflects a more radical effort to align

[80] *Coleman* (FCA) [2].

[81] For example, who should bear the burden of ensuring that charitable programmes are carried out in accordance with charity law? In *Coleman* the court found that at least one of the donors had 'relied on NFCL to properly implement the program': *Coleman* (TCC) [49].

[82] CRA, *Guidelines for Registering a Charity: Meeting the Public Benefit Test* (CPS-024, March 2006) (*CRA Public Benefit Guidelines*) [1.0].

[83] See, for example, ibid [3.1.3].

charitable projects in Canada with the substantive welfare agenda of the Canadian state.

The first public law-oriented position that the CRA takes in the Guidelines is broadly consistent with the English position that an organization that defines its benefiting 'public' in a discriminatory way will not meet the public benefit test. Institutions that restrict their benefits to a 'specific group of beneficiaries', the Guidelines declare, 'must always ensure that the restrictions proposed are not illegal or contrary to public policy. *Any such restrictions are incapable of providing a public benefit*'.[84] Canada faces unique challenges in enforcing this principle, as the Guidelines recognize.[85] In England and Wales, as we have seen, there is now a single statutory provision that specifies the conditions under which an English charity may restrict the provision of benefits to persons who share a protected characteristic under human rights law. Canada, on the other hand, has over a dozen human rights instruments, which all set out different conditions under which a discriminatory distribution of benefits may be allowed.[86] It also has a constitutionally entrenched Charter of Rights and Freedoms, which is almost certainly applicable to some Canadian charities as well as the human rights instruments themselves.[87] The effect of this diversity is to make it nearly impossible to analyse the relationship between public benefit and Canadian non-discrimination law in the abstract. In broad terms, however, the CRA's regulatory position is consistent with the regulatory position in England and Wales.

The second significant position articulated in the CRA's Public Benefit Guidelines is that a charity 'cannot charge fees for its services where the effect of the charge would be to unduly exclude members of the public'.[88] The Guidelines state that any fees charged by a charity 'should be reasonable in the circumstances and … typically aim at cost recovery', and that a charity's services 'should not in practice cater only to those who are financially well-off'.[89] The CRA has cited *Independent Schools Council* in more recently drafted policy documents,[90] suggesting that it would likely accede to the Upper Tribunal's views on the common law authorities regarding the exclusion of the poor. As we have seen, however, the hybrid character of the *Independent Schools Council* decision leaves it open to competing interpretations. The only certain conclusion is that like the Charity Commission, the CRA has tended to view the public benefit doctrine to some

[84] ibid [3.2.2] (emphasis added).

[85] ibid (stating that organizations with discriminatory purposes *may* offend the Canadian Charter of Rights and Freedoms or the various provincial and federal human rights regimes).

[86] cf Ontario Human Rights Code, RSO 1990, c H19, s 18; Human Rights Code, RSBC 1996, c 210, s 41.

[87] The Supreme Court of Canada has denied that human rights legislation has to 'mirror' the Charter. However, it has also struck down human rights legislation that omitted a ground of discrimination identified in the Charter: see Hogg (n 6) 37-31, fn 151. The Charter's application to Canadian charities will be discussed in Ch 6.

[88] *CRA Public Benefit Guidelines* (n 82) [2.0].

[89] ibid [3.2.5].

[90] CRA, *Charitable Purposes and Activities that Benefit Youth* (CG-020, June 2013) fn 5.

extent as a means of limiting the autonomy of benevolent property owners in order to further a competing public interest in a society where charitable benefits are distributed equitably, and are accessible to the poor.

If the first two public law-oriented positions articulated in the Guidelines accord generally with the English regulatory position, the third reflects a more radical effort to align charitable projects with the government's policy agenda. Essentially, the Guidelines indicate that in assessing the public benefit of an applicant for registered charity status, the CRA does not only consider the relevant case law, but also takes into account how closely the applicant's purposes and activities align with government policy and existing government programmes. Noting that the existence of public benefit 'must be demonstrated through evidence', the Guidelines advise applicant institutions to support their applications for registered charity status with some of the following information:

- Identification of government programs addressing the community need in question along with details on how the [applicant's] program complements or supplements the government program;
- Identification of explicit statements of government policy that may be consistent with the goals and objects of their organization;
- Demonstration of existing public sources of financial support for the organization;
- Identification of new or recent legislative initiatives consistent with the proposed purpose; and
- Any other types of objective material that supports the proposal.[91]

The implication of this 'advice', which is inconsistent with the common law position but consistent with the co-optative regulatory trends that we will examine in the next chapter, is that the public benefit of a charity can be measured by its alignment with the contemporary government's policy agenda, as well as the level of public support for its aims.

IV. Charity Law Standing Rules in Canada

If the tax orientation of Canada's registered charity regime affects the status and operation of the public benefit criterion, it seems likely that its effects would also be felt in the procedural dimensions of Canadian charity law. This hypothesis can be tested by examining who has standing to seek relief for legally recognized wrongs that involve the misadministration of charity property in Canada. This examination offers two principal observations. First, in a context where the charity regulator's primary public concern is to protect the integrity of the tax base, no private individual has standing to seek relief for the misadministration of charity property within that regime. Second, in a context where the tax-based charity

[91] *CRA Public Benefit Guidelines* (n 82) [3.3].

regulator is effectively the *primary* charity regulator, the standing rules in the subsidiary provincial regimes are relatively undeveloped, and boast limited opportunities to seek relief for the misadministration of charity property.

A. Standing Under the Registered Charity Regime

We have seen in Section II that while the CRA is not vested with any of the prerogative powers of the English Crown, and has no authority to address the misadministration of charity property per se, the CRA's Charities Directorate does address certain instances of charity misconduct in the course of administering the registered charity regime. Where a registered charity fails to devote all of its funds to charitable purposes and activities as required by the Income Tax Act, the Charities Directorate may revoke its registration.[92] Where a registered charity confers an undue benefit on its directors or trustees, a range of sanctions may apply.[93] Effectively, as noted in Section II, these provisions confer on the CRA a remedial authority that parallels, to a certain extent, the charities jurisdiction of the Charity Commission and the superior courts.

Despite vesting the CRA with these 'parallel' remedial powers, however, the Income Tax Act contains no procedures akin to those set out in the Charities Act 2011, which would entitle a person other than the CRA to seek relief for the misadministration of charity property. Unlike the Charity Commission, the CRA acts in all instances of its own motion when it addresses violations of the registered charity regime. A member of the public is free to contact the regulator to make a complaint about a registered charity; indeed, such complaints have been known to trigger charity audits.[94] However, there is no ordinary context in which a person has a legal entitlement to request that the CRA address the misadministration of a registered charity's funds.

In Chapter 4, we saw that the main rationales for limiting standing rights in matters involving charity property in England and Wales are to prevent the unnecessary expenditure of charity resources, and to protect charity trustees from ill-founded claims. Very different considerations are at play in a regulatory regime whose primary axis extends between the autonomy interests of benevolent property owners and the public interest in the integrity of the tax base. Several rationales help to explain. First, the CRA's function of identifying and remedying instances of charity misconduct is carried out against the general regime of privacy protection that is associated with tax statutes.[95] The Income Tax Act generally protects the confidentiality of taxpayer information, prohibiting government officials

[92] ITA, ss 168(1) and 149.1(1).

[93] ITA, s 188.1(4)–(5).

[94] Drache, Hayhoe and Stevens (n 49) [10.2.4].

[95] See C Campbell, *Administration of Income Tax 2012* (Toronto, Thomson Carswell, 2012), citing *Slattery (Trustee of) v Slattery* [1993] CTC 243, 247 (SCC).

from knowingly disclosing such information to any person except as specifically authorized by the Act.[96] Registered charities have been the subject of an increasing number of exceptions to the general rule, such that CRA officials are now authorized to provide to any person a registered charity's governing documents, its filed financial statements or a list of its directors.[97] Nevertheless, the confidentiality of taxpayer information, as the prevailing norm, supports the position that the CRA is the only appropriate party to initiate procedures concerning an alleged violation of the registered charity provisions.

A second rationale for the registered charity regime's exclusionary approach to standing relates once again to the division of powers established by the Constitution Act 1867. Given that both legislative authority over charities and the Crown's prerogative powers over charities have been allocated to the provinces, it seems appropriate that persons seeking relief for the misadministration of charity property in Canada would proceed under provincial rather than federal law. We will see that provincial law does provide some remedial options to persons seeking to remedy a misuse of charity property, with distinctive standing rules applying to each. Overall, however, the law of *locus standi* relating to charities is patchy and relatively undeveloped in Canada, and opportunities to seek relief for the misadministration of charity property are limited.

B. Standing in the Provinces

Given what we have seen of the absence of standing rights under the registered charity regime, it is evident that persons who wish to seek relief for the misadministration of charity property in Canada must do so through an alternative route. The remedial options that are available to a potential complainant depend on the organizational form of the charity and the jurisdiction in which it is located. The Ontario Charities Accounting Act establishes several procedures for initiating proceedings against a charity trustee or charitable corporation. In Saskatchewan, a specialized charitable oppression remedy may be available. However, in most of the common law provinces, a person seeking to remedy a misapplication of charity property must rely upon the inherent charities jurisdiction of the superior courts. Different rules of standing apply to each of these procedures.

Consistent with its relative attentiveness to the administration of charities within the province, Ontario law permits a wide range of people to seek various forms of relief for the misapplication of charity property. The relevant procedures are set out in the Charities Accounting Act, which, as we saw in Section II, delegated some of the *parens patriae* powers of the provincial attorney general to the Public Guardian and Trustee (PGT). Like the Charities Act 2011, the Ontario legislation

[96] ITA, s 241(1).
[97] ITA, s 241(3.2).

establishes three procedures for addressing misuses of charity property, which are each subject to separate standing rules. First, like the Charity Commission, the PGT is authorized to investigate alleged misapplications of charity property.[98] There is a well-publicized procedure for members of the public to complain to the PGT about such misapplications,[99] but there is no statutory entitlement to do so and the PGT's decision as to whether it shall investigate is not subject to review. Second, where it is alleged that funds collected from the public for a charitable purpose have been misused, 'any person' is entitled to make a written complaint to a judge of the Superior Court of Justice, who may then order the PGT to investigate the complaint.[100] Finally, 'any two or more persons' who allege a breach of a charitable trust or seek the court's direction for its administration may apply to the Superior Court of Justice, and the court may make such order as it considers just for the carrying out of the trust under the law.[101] The combined effect of these provisions is to allow almost any person to seek relief for the misadministration of charity property in Ontario.

In the province of Saskatchewan, a person may also be able to seek relief for the misadministration of charity property by suing under a specialized 'charitable oppression' remedy. While most of Canada's not-for-profit corporation statutes either lack an oppression remedy or model their oppression remedy directly on that of their for-profit counterpart,[102] the Saskatchewan Non-Profit Corporations Act expressly extends its oppression remedy to charitable corporations.[103] Section 225 provides that a wide range of judicial relief may be available where a charitable corporation exercises its powers in a manner which is oppressive or unfairly prejudicial to or unfairly disregards the interests of a member, director, officer or 'the public generally'. The persons with standing to apply to the court for an oppression order against a charitable corporation in Saskatchewan include the charity's members, directors and officers, as well as 'any other person who, in the discretion of the court, is a proper person to make an application'.[104] While the question of who is a 'proper person' in regard to a charitable corporation has not yet come before a court, the statute would seem to provide a basis for an oppression claim by any person who believes a charitable corporation has misused charity property in a manner that is prejudicial or oppressive to the general public.

The statutory procedures that Ontario and Saskatchewan have adopted to address misuses of charity property, while important for the residents of those

[98] CAA (Ont), s 2. Unlike the Commission, however, the PGT lacks the power to remedy any misapplications that it identifies: CAA (Ont), s 4.

[99] See Ontario Ministry of the Attorney General, 'Complaining About Charities', www.attorneygeneral.jus.gov.on.ca/english/family/pgt/charbullet/bullet4.asp.

[100] CAA (Ont), s 6(1)–(3).

[101] CAA (Ont), s 10(1).

[102] Compare, for example, Canada Business Corporations Act, RSC 1985, c C-44, s 241 and Canada Not-for-Profit Corporations Act, SC 2009, c C-23, s 253.

[103] The Non-Profit Corporations Act 1995 (Sask), SS 1995, c N-4.2, s 225.

[104] ibid s 222 ('complainant'). For an application by the director of a charitable foundation, see *Thiessen v Borden Hospital Foundation*, 2011 SKQB 232, (2011) 378 Sask R 238.

provinces, remain anomalies within the Canadian landscape. Most of Canada's provincial statute books contain no mention of 'charity proceedings' or their associated standing rules. Given this legislative silence, and the common law background against which it operates in most of Canada, one would expect to find a common practice of provincial attorneys general initiating charity proceedings in the provincial superior courts. However, this has not been the case: the Canadian jurisprudence contains relatively few cases addressing allegations of misadministered charity property, and within those that exist, the presence of the chief law officers of the provinces can only sporadically be ascertained.[105]

The British Columbia Supreme Court recently sought to address this lacuna in the Canadian law of charities by granting standing rights to an individual along the lines of the English statutory approach. In *Lee v North Vancouver School District No 44* the co-founder of a charitable trust fund established in honour of her mother brought a petition alleging that the fund had been improperly invested and disbursed by the charity's trustees.[106] The trustees objected to Lee's petition for an accounting, claiming that standing to enforce a charitable trust resided exclusively in the attorney general for British Columbia. Lee disputed this claim, relying on the English Court of Appeal decision in *Re Hampton Fuel* to argue that she also had the requisite interest to enforce the trust.[107] Neither party, the trial judge noted, was able to cite any Canadian authority on the subject of 'standing to bring an action in relation to charitable trusts'.[108]

With no Canadian authority to rely on, the court chose to resolve the issue of the petitioner's entitlement to sue on the basis of the English decision, and the 'basic rules of standing' articulated in Thomas Cromwell's leading (though by that time dated) text on *locus standi*. The court cited the following passage from the textbook's introduction:

> The law of standing to sue in Canada can be put in a nutshell. There are two fundamental rules. The first is that apart from certain cases in which standing is in the discretion of the Court, the plaintiff must possess an interest in the issues raised in the proceeding. The second is that where the private plaintiff relies on an interest in the enforcement of a public right and not of a private right, standing will be denied unless the Attorney General consents to a relator action, or the plaintiff can establish some special interest beyond that possessed by the public generally.[109]

'Assuming without deciding' that what was at stake in the petition was the enforcement of a private right, and relying on the reasoning in *Re Hampton Fuel*, the court concluded that as a person who founded and financed the charity, the petitioner had an interest in the issues raised.[110] The court went on to say, however, that if

[105] Chan (n 57) 389–91.
[106] *Lee v North Vancouver School District No 44*, 2008 BCSC 896, 42 ETR (3d) 249.
[107] ibid [16]–[19]. *Re Hampton Fuel* is discussed in Ch 3, text at nn 93–97.
[108] ibid [23].
[109] ibid [24], citing TA Cromwell, *Locus Standi: A Commentary on the Law of Standing in Canada* (Toronto, Carswell Publishing, 1986).
[110] ibid [26].

what was at issue was the enforcement of a *public* right, then either the attorney general had consented to the petitioner's action, or the petitioner had established a 'special interest beyond that possessed by the public generally': the petitioner's involvement in the establishment and financing of the trust, her previous efforts to rectify its wayward administration, and her entitlement to receipt of audited financial statements all combined to distinguish her interest from that of the general public.[111]

In the wake of *Lee v North Vancouver School District No 44*, it will certainly be open to litigants to argue that the common law rules of standing applicable to charity proceedings in Canada recognize the same spectrum of interests in the proper administration of a charity as section 115 of the Charities Act 2011. The decision in *Lee* is nonetheless vulnerable to several criticisms, which may weaken the argument that it should apply in every common law province. First, the 'nutshell' statement of the law of standing that the *Lee* court relied on was portrayed by Cromwell himself as a descriptive summary of the general principles underlying the 'particular and specialized standing rules' applicable to the four substantive legal areas he explored in his book.[112] Since Cromwell's text does not examine the law of charities, however, and since not all substantive legal areas have the same standing rules, the court's use of his nutshell description to *prescribe* the content of charity law's standing rules may be regarded as somewhat suspect. Second, the English case law that the court relied upon to recognize the standing of the petitioner is based on a provision of the Charities Act 2011 that has no equivalent in British Columbia. As we saw in Chapter 4, that provision (section 115) requires potential litigants to obtain the authorization of the Commission or the High Court before initiating charity proceedings, an additional protective filter for charities that justifies wider standing rights. Finally, as we saw in Chapter 4, the law of standing has evolved significantly since the publication of Cromwell's book, particularly with regard to claims involving public rights.[113] It is therefore difficult to predict whether other provincial courts will rely on *Lee* as having modified the common law position on standing in Canadian charity proceedings.

The upshot of this patchwork of federal and provincial law is that there are limited opportunities for an individual to seek relief for the misadministration of charity property in Canada. Canada's primary, tax-based regime of charity regulation contains no procedure for any person other than the Minister of National Revenue to seek relief for the misapplication of property by a registered charity. Ontario has established broad standing rules in its Charities Accounting Act, and Saskatchewan offers the possibility of discretionary standing under its charitable

[111] ibid [27].

[112] Cromwell (n 109) 165.

[113] As a member of the Supreme Court of Canada, Cromwell J has himself been involved in the movement away from an insistence on 'special interests' and 'private rights', and towards a more flexible exercise of judicial discretion: see *Canada (AG) v Downtown Eastside Sex Workers United against Violence Society* [2012] 2 SCR 524 [1].

oppression remedy. However, the standing rules governing charity proceedings in the rest of the country are undeveloped and unclear. Common law relator proceedings are virtually unknown, and the provincial attorneys general have not generally exercised their inherited role of bringing judicial proceedings where misapplications of charity property are alleged. And while the *Lee* decision opens the door for individuals to seek personal or associational standing to sue for a breach of charitable trust outside of Ontario, its reliance on judicial interpretations of an English statute weakens the decision. Combined, these factors mean that in many parts of Canada the public is effectively excluded from participating in the collective project of overseeing the proper administration of charity property and that the notionally 'unlimited' charities jurisdiction of the superior courts is of very little effect. The substantive message that emerges from this patchwork of procedural rules and practices is that Canadian law assigns considerably less value to the public's rights in charity property than did the English common law tradition it received.

V. Conclusion

In order to illuminate the dichotomy between civil and tax-based charity regulators, this chapter has explored the nature of the public–private hybridity that inheres in the Canadian registered charity regime, a tax-based regulatory regime with significant common law roots. I have argued that, like the Charity Commission, the CRA's Charities Directorate is oriented towards intervening in the affairs of charities in a perceived public interest. However, the public interest that the Directorate aims to protect is not a public interest in properly and effectively administered charity property, but a public interest in the integrity of the tax base.

The Directorate's regulatory orientation towards protecting the fisc reverberates throughout the substantive and procedural dimensions of Canadian charity law. Substantively, it contributes to public benefit playing a comparatively minor role in the ongoing regulation of registered charities. Procedurally, it means that no private individual has standing to seek relief for the misadministration of charity property within the primary Canadian regime of charity regulation, while opportunities to seek relief outside that regime are limited. Finally, we have seen that in a context where the regulator is oriented towards the proper administration of tax resources and is the agent of an elected Cabinet Minister, there is evidence of a regulatory effort to use the public benefit criterion at the registration stage to align the projects of registered charities more closely with the public welfare goals of the state. This unique stance on the alignment between public benefit and existing government policy hints at the existence of a more substantial divergence between the English and Canadian charity law regimes, which will be the focus of the next chapter.

6

Challenges to the Hybrid Equilibrium: The Co-optation of Charitable Resources by Threatened Welfare States*

I. Introduction

The hypothesis that has been pursued up to this point in the work is that the law of charities may properly be regarded as a *hybrid* of public law and private law. I have claimed that charity law is a public law–private law hybrid in a *general* or *categorical* sense. I have also argued that charity law is a hybrid in the *context-specific* or *functional* sense that within different regulatory regimes, both the conditions for obtaining charitable status and the regulation of charities' conduct are continually being adjusted so as to maintain a broad equilibrium between individual project pursuit and collective project pursuit in the charitable sphere. These adjustments occur along a number of notional 'public–private' continuums, including a continuum between wholly altruistic and wholly self-regarding projects, and a continuum between projects that are a matter of general concern and projects that are a matter of individual concern.

We have seen that in several respects, charity law has tended to drift towards the 'public' end of the identified continuums: the Charity Commission's 2008 Public Benefit Guidance illustrates this tendency, as does the 'discretionary' judicial approach to determining standing under the Charities Act 2011. However, we have also witnessed these 'publicizing' tendencies being offset by legal developments that reassert the importance of protecting the autonomy of donors and trustees. The *Independent Schools Council* decision falls generally into this latter camp, as do the continuing limits on public interest standing to seek relief for the misadministration of a charity. Nothing we have seen to this point, in other words, poses a serious challenge to the claim that charity law has achieved a long-term, functional equilibrium between the protection of the autonomy of benevolent

* Much of the material in this chapter has previously been published in K Chan, 'The Co-optation of Charities by Threatened Welfare States' (2015) 40 *Queen's Law Journal* 34.

property owners to control and direct their own wealth, and the furtherance of competing public interests or visions of the good.

Any conclusion as to the ongoing hybridity of the charity law tradition must be reassessed, however, in light of an increasing consensus about the contemporary use (or misuse) of charitable resources by 'threatened welfare' states. There is a growing chorus of voices, centred in England and Wales but audible across the Anglo-Commonwealth world, expressing concern that charities are increasingly being treated as instruments of government welfare policy rather than as independent institutions.[1] These concerns raise the spectre of a more radical form of 'publicization' in the charitable sphere, suggesting that in certain economic and political contexts, charities may experience regulatory or other government activity that so greatly tends towards compelling them to conform to or carry out the government's welfare objects that charities may be said to be *co-opted* to the policy agenda of the state. Such co-optation, to the extent it exists, represents a greater challenge to charity autonomy than anything this work has heretofore described, and has the potential to significantly destabilize charity law's hybrid equilibrium.

The English have long been committed to the principle that charities are independent from government. Despite (or perhaps because of) this political commitment, they have also harboured fears about the threats that might be posed to this independence by an 'overbearing State'.[2] The level of angst increased markedly when the government of Margaret Thatcher embarked on its neoliberal agenda of 'slimming down the welfare state'.[3] It has intensified again since 2010, when the government of David Cameron embarked on its 'Big Society' agenda of further decentralizing government functions, and involving charities even more heavily in the delivery of public services.[4] Today, in a climate of significant economic austerity, increasing numbers of charities deliver social welfare services that were previously delivered directly by government on the basis of performance-based contracts. In this climate, there is a growing perception that the UK government views charities and other voluntary sector organizations as 'instruments of government policy rather than independent agents'.[5] Prominent public figures have

[1] See especially: M Smerdon (ed), *The First Principle of Voluntary Action: Essays on the Independence of the Voluntary Sector from Government in Canada, England, Germany, Northern Ireland, Scotland, United States of America and Wales* (London, The Baring Foundation, 2009). See also D Morris, 'Paying the Piper: The "'Contract Culture" 'as Dependency Culture for Charities?' in Alison Dunn (ed), *The Voluntary Sector, the State and the Law* (Oxford, Hart Publishing, 2000); A Dunn, 'Demanding Service or Servicing Demand? Charities, Regulation and the Policy Process' (2008) 71 *MLR* 247; D Morris, 'Charities and the Big Society: a Doomed Coalition?' (2012) 32 *Legal Studies* 132, 144.

[2] N Deakin, 'Voluntary Action and the Future of Civil Society' in Dunn (ed), *The Voluntary Sector* (n 1) 241.

[3] For a short review of this history, see H Woolf and others, *De Smith's Judicial Review*, 7th edn (London, Sweet & Maxwell, 2013) [3-057]. See also Deakin (n 2) 246–47; Dunn, 'Demanding Service' (n 1) 249–50.

[4] Morris (n 1) 133.

[5] B Cairns, 'The Independence of the Voluntary Sector from Government in England' in Smerdon (n 1) 37.

begun to comment on the issue, and the Baring Foundation has set up a special panel to study and monitor the situation. The 2013 report of this Panel on the Independence of the Voluntary Sector found that the conditions for sectoral independence had continued to deteriorate during the 12 months leading up to the report, such that 'the very identity of the sector is in question'.[6]

In Canada, where there is no equivalent political commitment to the charitable sector's independence, the trend towards using charities as instruments of government policy is arguably even stronger. Certain categories of Canadian charities have historically worked in 'interdependent partnership' with their federal and provincial governments, delivering government-funded services such as health care and education within the context of a 'mixed social economy of social service delivery'.[7] The Canadian charitable sector came of age at a time when there was arguably already a welfare state in place, and never achieved the representational capacity or the political clout of its English counterpart. Thus, when the Canadian government began cutting block funding for charities as part of its own welfare retrenchment programme in the 1980s, the charitable sector mustered little opposition. Instead, Canadian charities gradually decreased their role in policy advocacy and increased their role in service delivery under performance-based contracts with government.[8]

In 2001 then-Prime Minister Jean Chrétien's Liberal government made a rare political commitment to the principle of charity independence, describing the voluntary sector as 'autonomous', and affirming its right to advocate for change.[9] Today, however, many people working in the Canadian charitable sector consider the 2001 Accord a dead letter. Charities complain not only of onerous reporting requirements and of unpredictable project-based funding, but also of 'witch hunts' against charities that are opposed to the government's policies.[10] A growing number of Canadian voluntary organizations claim to have lost their charitable status or their government funding because of their dissenting views.[11]

What are we to make of these perceived threats to the 'independence' of the charitable sector? Looking back at the history of charities in the Anglo-Commonwealth world, it is arguable that government has *always* been inclined to direct charitable resources towards its own political agenda. Charities provided health care, education, and other 'core welfare services' long before the birth of the welfare state, occasionally doing so in return for some form of government

[6] Panel on the Independence of the Voluntary Sector, *Independence under Threat: The Voluntary Sector in 2013* (London, Baring Foundation, 2013). See also Hodgson Review [3.15], [4.21]–[4.23].

[7] P Elson, 'Independence in a Cold Climate: a Profile of the Nonprofit and Voluntary Sector in Canada' in Smerdon (n 1) 17.

[8] For an overview of this process, see SD Phillips, 'Dual Restructuring: Civil Society and the Welfare State in Canada, 1985–2005' (2012) 25(2) *British Journal of Canadian Studies* 161.

[9] Government of Canada, *Accord between the Government of Canada and the Voluntary Sector* (Ottawa, Voluntary Sector Task Force, Privy Council Office, 2001).

[10] S McCarthy, 'Group's Charitable Status Being Audited', *The Globe and Mail* (8 May 2012).

[11] Many of these claims are documented at the website of the Voices/voix coalition. See Voices-Voix, 'Voices-Voix: Defending Advocacy and Dissent in Canada', http://voices-voix.ca/en/hit-list.

payment.[12] Moreover, as we shall see in Section III, the UK Parliament's most famous legislative initiative to align the resources of the charitable sector with its own policy agenda occurred not in the twenty-first century, but at the turn of the sixteenth. If instances of definitional and contractual co-optation can be identified throughout charity law's history, however, the phenomenon undoubtedly intensifies in a 'threatened welfare' state, where the government has made extensive public service commitments that are increasingly difficult to sustain. While there is a sense in which today's charities are 'reassuming' historical responsibilities in taking up the delivery of core welfare services, they are far less likely than in the past to do so on their own terms. For in a retreating or threatened welfare state, charities often deliver welfare services bearing the pressures and constraints of the government bodies that have the statutory duty to provide them.

There is room for reasonable disagreement on what degree of alignment between charitable projects and the government's social welfare priorities is desirable in times of economic austerity. The tax subsidization of charitable projects is a major consideration, as is the growing concern about just how far charities have strayed from the core needs of their communities in some parts of the world.[13] However, I suggest that there are good reasons to guard against regulatory or other institutional mechanisms that tend towards compelling charities to conform to or carry out the government's substantive goals. First, the very notion of co-optation—of the government assuming charitable resources for its own use—is antithetical to the spirit of 'voluntariness' that typically characterizes charitable activity and that has historically been understood to be its greatest strength.[14] Charities whose resources have been co-opted by the state are also unlikely to have the capacity to play their historic role in 'pioneering' new and innovative educational, social and cultural projects.[15] If voluntariness and a capacity to innovate are among the greatest strengths of the charitable sector, we should be wary of phenomena that work against those strengths.

A second reason to be concerned about mechanisms that erode the independence of the charitable sector, as we shall see in the next section, is that co-opted charities may find themselves subject to onerous public law standards that are designed to address the special powers and responsibilities of the state. While the trend is not yet notable in Canada, English claimants have begun relying on the 'public' character of charities to argue that charities, like governmental bodies, must give a fair hearing to those affected by their decisions, or respect their human rights.[16]

[12] Morris provides nineteenth-century examples of charities providing services in return for payment by the state: Morris (n 1) 124. See also Deakin (n 2) 241.

[13] S Strom, 'Donors Weigh the Ideals of Meaningful Giving', *The New York Times* (1 November 2011).

[14] The classic statement of this view is generally attributed to Lord Beveridge. See WH Beveridge, *Voluntary Action: A Report on Methods of Social Advance* (London, G Allen & Unwin, 1948).

[15] For a description of this pioneering role, see Nathan Report 162, 166.

[16] *Scott v National Trust* [1998] 2 All ER 705 (Ch) 719; *R v Charity Commissioners for England and Wales* (2001), 33 HLR 48 (QB) [55]. See also J Garton, 'The Judicial Review of the Decisions of Charity Trustees' (2006) 20 *Tolley's Trust Law International* 160, 178–79.

From the perspective of the consumers of health, education or other public welfare services, the extension of public law liabilities to charities that carry out 'public functions' or 'government activities' may be perfectly appropriate. However, such an extension is likely to unduly burden small charities that are effectively compelled to carry out a governmental agenda against their better judgement, and that are ill-equipped to meet or even understand the requirements of public law.

This chapter aims to shed some light on these emerging debates over co-optation by advancing a theoretical contrast between 'independent' and 'co-opted' charities, and identifying certain legal and institutional mechanisms that may either encourage or limit the co-optation of charitable resources by governments in a given jurisdiction. I begin in Section II by articulating two indicia of a 'co-opted' charity, relating these indicia to an important body of Anglo-Commonwealth law on the functional public law–private law divide and associated debates over what types of entities should bear human rights obligations and the other special responsibilities of the state. In Section III, I distinguish three broad categories of co-optation that are applicable to charities: definitional (or existential) co-optation, managerial co-optation and contractual (or fiscal) co-optation. I then examine several modern phenomena that tend towards the co-optation of charitable resources by government: the exertion of government influence over the legal definition of charity, the creation of statutory charities that are controlled by government or directed towards its purposes and the exertion of influence over the administration of charitable resources through the negotiation of funding agreements or the appointment of government authority trustees. I consider how, in their response to each of these phenomena, English and Canadian laws and institutions either assist or obstruct government efforts to make charities comply with particular public welfare goals. I conclude in Section IV with some comments on the relative threat that processes of co-optation present to the hybrid nature of the law of charities in England and Wales and in Canada.

II. Co-optation and the Functional Public Law–Private Law Divide

The balance of this chapter is devoted to identifying certain modern mechanisms that tend to result in the co-optation of charitable resources by government, and to considering how English and Canadian law either promote or limit these mechanisms. In order to embark upon this task, however, we need a more robust account of what co-optation means, and how it relates to the spectrum we have put forward between 'public-welfare-compliant' projects, and projects that are deviant from the public welfare policy of the state. I argued in Chapter 3 that, as a starting point, we might regard public-welfare compliance as requiring that a charity's benefits be accessible and useful to the entire political community.[17] Co-optation, I would now suggest, may be regarded as a more radical form of public-welfare compliance, which envisages a charity's benefits being aligned with, and directly supportive of, the government's policy agenda. Co-optation represents one end of a continuum that extends, at the opposite pole, to full independence from the public welfare goals of the state. Without purporting to articulate an exhaustive list, we may identify two key indicia of a co-opted charity. The first is that a co-opted charity furthers a specific government policy or programme in carrying out its purposes and activities. The second is that a co-opted charity is subject to governmental influence and control in carrying out its purposes and activities.

These indicia of a co-opted charity have not been plucked from thin air. Rather, they reflect a growing body of Anglo-Commonwealth law that is focused on controlling the exercise of public (or government) functions by non-governmental institutions.[18] During the last 30 years, the widespread effects of neoliberalism have led jurists to acknowledge the existence of a range of institutions that are neither self-evidently public bodies nor private persons.[19] Jurists have also recognized that these 'hybrid institutions' may perpetrate the types of abuses of power historically associated with government.[20] One response to these developments has been the expansion of the 'province' of public law,[21] which has been achieved by shifting public law's focus 'from controlling the *institutions of … government* to controlling the exercise of the *functions of governance* … whether performed by government or non-government entities'.[22] In practice, the courts continue to also take into account the *institutional* character of the body whose functions are being judged, and the *relationships* that body may have with a core governmental authority.[23] However, in England and Wales at least, modern statutes tend to require that the 'ultimate focus … be upon the nature of the functions undertaken'.[24]

[17] See Ch 3, text at n 53.

[18] For a short summary of the evolution of this body of law, see P Cane, 'Accountability and the Public/Private Distinction' in N Bamforth and P Leyland (eds), *Public Law in a Multi-Layered Constitution* (Oxford, Hart Publishing, 2003) 247, 249.

[19] ibid.

[20] See, eg, G Borrie, 'The Regulation of Public and Private Power' [1989] *PL* 552.

[21] See M Taggart, 'The Province of Administrative Law Determined?' in M Taggart (ed), *The Province of Administrative Law* (Oxford, Hart Publishing, 1997). Another significant development has been the reassertion of the court's private supervisory jurisdiction in contexts such as a restraint of trade: see *Bradley v Jockey Club* [2005] EWCA Civ 1056.

[22] P Cane, *Administrative Law*, 4th edn (Oxford, Clarendon Press, 2004) 5.

[23] D Oliver, 'Functions of a Public Nature under the Human Rights Act' [2004] *PL* 329, 331; see also *YL v Birmingham City Council* [2008] 1 AC 95 (HL) [103], per Lord Mance (the 'hallmarks of a core public authority throw light on the nature of a person's functions'). Woolf and others make a similar observation of the judicial review cases: Woolf and others (n 3) [3-045].

[24] *YL* (n 23) [105] (Lord Mance) and [61] (Baroness Hale). The statutory terms 'public function' and 'function of a public nature' are increasingly common in the UK: Woolf and others (n 3) [3-075]. This work will not address the debate over whether there is any difference between the two terms.

The criteria of a 'public function' vary between jurisdictions and between legislative contexts—in the context of the Canadian Charter of Rights and Freedoms, as we shall see, the terms 'public' and 'function' are not used at all. In all of these contexts, however, the fundamental normative question that courts are being asked to address is whether an entity that is not strictly governmental should nonetheless, in relation to a particular function or act it carries out, be considered sufficiently of or like government to 'bear the special responsibilities of the state'.[25] The issue arises in judicial review, and under a variety of statutory instruments. For our purposes, however, a brief review of the chief human rights instruments in England and Wales and Canada will suffice to illustrate how the answer to this normative question has come to depend on whether, in carrying out these functions or acts, the entity furthers a specific government policy or programme, or is subject to governmental influence and control.

Human rights law is an important area in which the application of public law standards to a charity will depend on whether the charity is characterized as exercising public (or governmental) functions (or acts).[26] In the UK this determination is carried out under the Human Rights Act 1998, which makes it unlawful for a 'public authority' to act in a way which is incompatible with the rights set out therein. The term 'public authority' is not comprehensively defined in the Act, but section 6(3)(b) states that it includes 'any person certain of whose functions are functions of a public nature'. While there is no single test of universal application to determine whether a body exercises functions of a public nature within the meaning of the Act, the relevant factors include whether the function is 'intrinsically an activity of government',[27] whether government has assumed responsibility for seeing the function performed[28] and whether those appointed to carry out the function are subject to government influence and control.[29] Such 'hybrid public authorities', as they have come to be known, assume human rights obligations in respect of their public acts.[30]

In the Canadian constitutional context, where the relevance of the public law–private law distinction is sometimes questioned,[31] and the courts have officially rejected a 'public function' test,[32] the substance of the test for the imposition of human rights liability is nonetheless similar. Pursuant to section 32(1) of

[25] N Bamforth, 'The Public Law-Private Law Distinction: A Comparative and Philosophical Approach' in P Leyland and T Woods (eds), *Administrative Law Facing the Future: Old Constraints and New Horizons* (London, Blackstone Publishing, 1997) 137, 151.

[26] In the context of judicial review and human rights law, 'public' is understood to mean 'governmental': see *R (Mullins) v Jockey Club* [2005] EWHC (Admin) 2197 [15]; *Aston Cantlow and Wilmcote with Billesley Parochial Church Council v Wallbank* [2003] UKHL 37 [163].

[27] *Cameron v Network Rail Infrastructure Ltd* [2006] EWHC 1133 (QB) [29].

[28] *YL* (n 23) [66].

[29] *Cameron* (n 27) [29].

[30] Human Rights Act 1998, s 6(5) (clarifying that a person will not be considered a public authority in relation to a particular act if the nature of the act is private).

[31] P Hogg, *Constitutional Law of Canada*, vol 2, 5th edn (Scarborough, Thomson Carswell, 2007) 337–30.1.

[32] *McKinney v University of Guelph* [1990] 3 SCR 229 (LaForest J).

the Canadian Charter of Rights and Freedoms, the application of Canada's constitutional human rights instrument is limited to 'the Parliament and government of Canada' and to 'the legislature and government of each province'. However, case law has established at least two situations where the Charter may be found to apply to an entity that is not, by its very nature, 'government'. First, an entity may be characterized as 'government' within the meaning of section 32(1) by virtue of the degree of governmental control exercised over it. Second, a non-governmental entity may be found to attract Charter scrutiny to the extent that it 'performs governmental activities'.[33] The fact that an entity performs a 'public service' will not be sufficient to make it subject to the Charter, even if it is subject to government regulation and receives funding from the public purse.[34] However, if an institution performs an act that is truly 'governmental' in nature—for example, by implementing a specific statutory scheme or a government programme—the institution will be required to carry out that act in accordance with Charter values.[35]

In sum, the tests that are emerging to determine when an entity is sufficiently of or like government to bear the special responsibilities of the state have many parallels with the indicia of a co-opted charity that I put forward in this part. These parallels suggest that where charities are co-opted in the ways outlined in this chapter, they are more likely to be subject to human rights liability, judicial review and other public law standards. The question of how far Canadian and English charities *in fact* further government policies or are subject to government influence and control is a complex and multifaceted question, which is beyond the scope of this doctrinal work. However, by examining specific modern phenomena that tend towards the co-optation of charitable resources by government, and comparing the ways in which they are addressed by English and Canadian law, we may reach some conclusions about the extent to which English and Canadian law either enable government to, or prevent government from, compelling charities to conform to or carry out particular public welfare goals.

III. Mechanisms of Co-optation

The co-optation of charitable resources by government can take a variety of different forms. For example, a legislative body with authority to regulate charities may at any time enact a definition of 'charity' that reflects (to its chosen degree of specificity)

[33] See *Eldridge v British Columbia (AG)* [1997] 3 SCR 624; *Greater Vancouver Transportation Authority v Canadian Federation of Students—British Columbia Component* [2009] 2 SCR 295 [16].

[34] *McKinney* (n 32) [35].

[35] *Eldridge* (n 33). Note that this standard is apparently higher than that set by the HRA 1998; in the UK, an entity may be amenable to human rights liability if it performs functions that government 'typically' performs: *Aston Cantlow* (n 26) [12] as interpreted by *R (Weaver) v London and Quadrant Housing Trust* [2010] 1 WLR 363 (CA) [70] (the provision of subsidised housing is 'typically, although not necessarily, a function which government provides' and can properly be described as a public service within the meaning of *Aston Cantlow*).

the policy agenda of the incumbent government. Government may put in place tax laws that assign greater or lesser fiscal advantages to different categories of charities, depending on how closely their objects align with the objects of the state. It may require that government representatives be placed on the boards of charities that it wishes to influence or control. Alternatively, government may provide funding to charities on terms that prohibit them from criticizing government policy, or that ensure that the government's own welfare priorities are carried out.

If the specific mechanisms and manifestations of government co-optation in the charitable sphere are potentially infinite, they may nonetheless generally be understood to fall within one of three broad categories of co-optation: definitional (or existential) co-optation, managerial co-optation and contractual co-optation. Definitional co-optation stems from the government's ultimate power to define (or redefine) the concept of charity, and to make the acquisition or retention of charitable status dependent upon compliance with the government's laws and administrative policies. Managerial co-optation occurs where the government is able to affect the administration of a charity through its influence over members of the board. Finally, contractual or fiscal co-optation stems from the ability of government to enter into contractual or other funding arrangements with charities, and to negotiate the terms upon which charities will be paid for the services they provide.[36] We will examine some common instances of each of these categories of co-optation below.

A. The Legal Definition of Charity

A first modern phenomenon that tends towards the co-optation of charitable resources by government involves the exertion of government influence over the legal definition of charity. The legal definition of charity plays the crucial function of setting the outer bounds of the purposes and activities which charities are authorized to pursue. Thus, a government that exercises a high degree of control over that definition has a greater capacity to align the resources of the charitable sector with its own policies and programmes.

i. Historical Roots

The exertion of government influence over the formation, interpretation and application of the legal definition of charity is a modern phenomenon with distinct historical roots. The Preamble to the Statute of Elizabeth, the statutory list of 'good, godly and charitable uses' that became the 'judicial lodestar'[37] as to

[36] While I concentrate on contractual funding agreements in this chapter, the financial pressures that may cause charity trustees to agree to terms put forward by government may equally affect charities seeking grants or other non-contractual funding.

[37] *Vancouver Society of Immigrant & Visible Minority Women v Minister of National Revenue* [1999] 1 SCR 10 [144], citing DWM Waters, *Law of Trusts in Canada*, 2nd edn (Toronto, Carswell, 1984) 550.

the objects the common law would recognize as charitable, was itself a manifestation of the legislature's ultimate authority to give legal meaning to the term 'charity', and to align the legal concept with a specific welfare agenda. While there is debate about the precise provenance of the Preamble,[38] there is significant consensus that the charitable uses set out therein were designed to reinforce a broader Tudor policy agenda involving the construction of public works, local taxation, forced labour and the criminalization of vagrancy.[39] By articulating the charitable objects within the jurisdiction of the statute's commissioners, the Elizabethan Parliament explicitly sought to draw philanthropic resources towards the governmental agenda of the day.[40]

From 1601 until the middle of the twentieth century, however, the task of articulating the legal meaning of charity fell mostly to the independent courts. In both England and Wales and Canada, the courts developed and refined the common law concept of a charitable purpose in judgments concerning the validity of charitable trusts, the application of mortmain legislation and, eventually, the application of tax legislation. Over the course of several centuries, the judicial practice of drawing analogies to the Preamble list, and further analogies to those analogies, produced a legal concept of charity that would have been within neither the intention nor the imagination of the Elizabethan Parliament. In 1891, Lord MacNaghten's four-fold classification of charitable purposes—the relief of poverty, the advancement of education, the advancement of religion and 'other purposes beneficial to the community'—effectively replaced the Preamble as the starting point of the law.[41]

The courts also developed a new charity law doctrine in the twentieth century, which placed some distance between the legal definition of charitable purposes and the government policy realm. According to the political purposes doctrine, charities cannot have a principal purpose of furthering the interests of a particular political party, procuring changes in domestic or foreign law or procuring reversals of government policy or of particular government decisions.[42] It is less well known, but also generally accepted, that an institution whose purpose is to *promote* the maintenance of an existing law or government policy falls within the scope of the prohibition.[43] Thus, in *Re Hopkinson* the English Chancery Division held that a gift to four members of the ruling Labour Party, to be applied for the

[38] See H Picarda, *The Law and Practice Relating to Charities*, 4th edn (Haywards Heath, Bloomsbury Professional, 2010) 496, suggesting that the Preamble took its inspiration from a fourteenth-century poem.

[39] B Bromley, '1601 Preamble: The State's Agenda for Charity' (2002) 7(3.4) *Charity Law & Practice Review* 144. See also M Chesterman, *Charities, Trusts and Social Welfare* (London, Weidenfeld & Nicolson, 1979) 18.

[40] See Nathan Report, 18; MR Fremont-Smith, *Foundations and Government: State and Federal Law and Supervision* (New York, Russell Sage Foundation, 1965) 26.

[41] *Vancouver Society* (n 37) [144].

[42] *McGovern v Attorney General* [1981] 3 All ER 493 (Ch) 509.

[43] See Picarda (n 38) 240.

advancement of adult education with reference to a Labour Party memorandum, was intended to secure a certain political policy and thus was not charitable.[44] Similarly, in *Re Co-operative College of Canada* the Saskatchewan Court of Appeal concluded that a college that (like the incumbent government) encouraged the 'specific economic principles' of co-operatives and credit unions was not charitable, holding that any effort to change existing laws, enact new laws or to 'resist any such change or enactment' would fall outside the concept of charity.[45]

While the political purposes doctrine prevents charities from explicitly furthering government policy as a principal purpose, it does not prevent charities from furthering the *same* policies as government, nor from assisting government in its own policy implementation. As the Nathan Committee noted in 1960, the theory of 'mutual exclusiveness' between charitable and government functions held favour with the Court of Chancery for a period during which it sought to prevent charitable endowments from being applied in relief of rates to a greater extent than necessary.[46] However, the theory was at odds with the fact that some of the charitable uses listed in the Preamble, such as the repair of bridges, had been provided by local authorities for centuries, and that others, such as assisting the poor in the payment of their taxes, were directly in aid of the National Revenue.[47] The theory was (and is) also at odds with the endlessly shifting scope of the government's welfare role; some functions that are, at one time, understood to be charitable may, at another time, come to be understood as the responsibility of the state. The theory of mutual exclusiveness between charitable and government functions never gained much ground and thus a charitable purpose may coincide with an existing government policy if it otherwise meets the common law test.[48] However, the courts (and later the Charity Commissioners) maintained a preference for applying charitable resources to purposes that fell outside the government's mandatory functions when they settled *cy-près* schemes.[49]

By the mid-twentieth century, then, the courts had assumed most of the responsibility for the legal definition of charity, and had placed some degree of distance between that definition and the government policy realm. The trend that has characterized the last half-century, however, has been the shifting of control over the legal definition of charity to *outside* the judicial domain. A number of factors have contributed to this shift, including the rise of charitable registration systems and

[44] *Re Hopkinson* [1949] 1 All ER 346 (Ch) 350.

[45] *Re Co-operative College of Canada and Turnbull v Saskatchewan Human Rights Commission* (1975) 64 DLR (3d) 531; [1976] 2 WWR 84 (Sask CA) [21]. *Re Hopkinson* was also referred to with apparent approval.

[46] Nathan Report, 157–58.

[47] Picarda (n 38) at 201–02.

[48] J Garton, 'Charities and the State' (2000) 14(2) *Trust Law International* 93. Since the motive of the settlor or founder is irrelevant to the charitable nature of a gift, it will be irrelevant that such settlor desires to further government policy through their charity. See also Picarda (n 38) 24.

[49] Nathan Report, 157.

the role of charities regulators therein, the cost of appealing regulatory decisions[50] and, in Canada, the general failure of the provincial attorneys general to bring charity law matters before the courts. The shift may also reflect dissatisfaction with the analogical reasoning used by the courts to develop the common law definition of charity, and dissatisfaction with the substantive law this methodology has produced.[51] Canada and England have both experienced this shift away from judicial control over the legal definition of charity, but each has filled the resultant gap in a different way. While the UK Parliament has explicitly adjusted the parameters of the English charitable sector, following an extended political debate, the Canadian Parliament has remained silent, leaving the Canadian government with a broad ability to use the legal concept of charity to align charitable resources with its own programmes and goals.

ii. Government Influence over the Definition of Charity in England and Wales

Until quite recently, the Preamble to the Statute of Elizabeth remained the most up-to-date statutory articulation of charitable purposes in the UK. The Charitable Trusts Act 1853, which established the jurisdiction of the Charity Commissioners, defined the term 'charity' by reference to 'the meaning, purview or interpretation' of the seventeenth-century Act.[52] The Preamble was formally repealed by the Charities Act 1960.[53] However, both the 1960 and 1993 versions of the Charities Act defined charitable purposes as 'purposes which are exclusively charitable according to the law of England and Wales',[54] leaving the common law requirement that a charitable object be within the 'spirit and intendment' of the Preamble in place.

Once the Charity Commission for England and Wales became responsible for maintaining the official register of charities in 1960, however, it effectively replaced the judiciary as the body with operational responsibility for determining questions of charitable status within its jurisdiction.[55] Over time, the Commission came to the position that it had 'the same powers as the court' to recognize new purposes as charitable in carrying out its registration function.[56] The Commission exercised these powers actively during the years prior to 2006, adding purposes

[50] See C Mitchell, 'Redefining Charity in English Law' (1999) 13 *Tolley's Trust Law International* 21, 30–31.

[51] For an exploration of the particular disjuncture that exists in Quebec between the objects that are legally charitable and those that are of special importance to society, see K Chan, 'Charitable According to Whom? The Clash Between Québec's Societal Values and the Law Governing the Registration of Charities' (2008) 49(2) *Les Cahiers de Droit* 277.

[52] CTA 1853, s 66.

[53] CA 1960, s 48(2), sch 7.

[54] CA 1960, s 46; CA 1993, s 97(1).

[55] CA 1960, s 5(1); CA 1993 s 4(1); CA 2011 s 37. See also Ch 2, s II.

[56] Charity Commission, *RR1a—Recognising New Charitable Purposes* (October 2001) [8].

such as the relief of unemployment, the promotion of community capacity building and the promotion of human rights to the 'fourth head' of the *Pemsel* test.[57] It also determined in the 2004 *Trafford and Wigan* decision that if an organization was otherwise exclusively charitable and independent, it could have as its purpose 'a function or service that a governmental authority had a responsibility to provide'.[58] The recognition that public service delivery was a valid charitable objective marked 'a new juncture in state/charity relations'[59] and extinguished any embers of the theory of mutual exclusiveness between charitable and government functions.

The Charity Commission's role in developing the English concept of charity changed somewhat with the enactment of the Charities Act 2006. Parliament seized upon its political opportunity to redraw the outer boundaries of the charitable sector, making England and Wales only the third Commonwealth jurisdiction to adopt a statutory definition of charitable purposes since the time of Elizabeth I.[60] Pursuant to section 2 of what is now the Charities Act 2011, a purpose may be charitable if it falls within one of 13 'descriptions of purposes' set out in section 3.[61] The list in section 3 begins with a slightly modified version of the first three *Pemsel* heads: the relief and prevention of poverty, the advancement of education and the advancement of religion.[62] It continues with nine other descriptions of purposes, which largely restate the purposes that courts and the Commission had already recognized as charitable under the 'fourth head' of the *Pemsel* test.[63] The list concludes with a 'catch-all' provision, which specifies that the definition of charitable purposes includes any purpose that was recognized as charitable prior to the Charities Act 2006 coming into force, and any purpose that may 'reasonably be regarded as analogous to' an existing charitable purpose.[64]

At one level, the definition of charitable purposes in the Charities Act 2011 can be seen as a reassertion of the perennial power of the legislature to direct the charitable sector towards the ends of its choosing. While the list in section 3 largely restates purposes that had previously been recognized as charitable by the courts and the Commission, it is nonetheless a *statutory* list, which emerged from

[57] Dunn, 'Demanding Service' (n 1) 252. See also L Driscoll, 'England and Wales: *Pemsel* Plus' in M McGregor-Lowndes and K O'Halloran (eds), *Modernising Charity Law: Recent Developments and Future Directions* (Cheltenham, Edward Elgar, 2010) 48, 53–54.

[58] *Decisions of the Charity Commissioners for England and Wales made on 21 April 2004: Applications for Registration of (i) Trafford Community Leisure Trust and (ii) Wigan Leisure and Culture Trust (Trafford and Wigan)* [6.1.5].

[59] Dunn, 'Demanding Service' (n 1) 253.

[60] Prior to 2003, only Barbados had enacted a statutory definition. See Lloyd, *Charities: The New Law 2006—A Practical Guide to the Charities Acts* (London, Jordan Publishing, 2007) 3. In 2005 Scotland passed its own Act: *Charities and Trustee Investment (Scotland) Act 2005*.

[61] CA 2011, s 2(1)(a). The purpose must also be for the public benefit within the meaning of s 4: see s 2(1)(b).

[62] CA 2011, s 3(1)(a)–(c). The 'prevention' of poverty is a new addition: see Driscoll (n 57) 56–58.

[63] Driscoll (n 57) 55.

[64] CA 2011, s 3(1)(m).

a long and contentious process of democratic deliberation.[65] Moreover, the statutory definition alters the common law status quo in several material respects. For example, it provides that the 'religions' that a charity may properly advance include multi-deity and non-deity faiths. This position had little support in the common law jurisprudence, and was the subject of extensive legislative debate.[66] The Act also makes the advancement of amateur sport (and of health-promoting mental games such as chess) charitable, an extension the Supreme Court of Canada has been unwilling to carry out by judicial analogy.[67] Finally, the Act undoes the link drawn by the common law between the definition of charitable purposes and the Statute of Elizabeth, and instead makes its own section 3 list of purposes the starting point for any extension of the definition by analogy.

While the Charities Act 2011 reasserts Parliament's ultimate sovereignty over the legal definition of charity, it does little to enable the English government to shift the boundaries of the charitable sector on an ongoing basis, in accordance with the government's own shifts in policy. The Act's preservation of the common law method of analogical reasoning has admittedly ensured that the Charity Commission will continue to enjoy substantial discretion in the exercise of its charitable registration function. However, because of its relative specificity, the new statutory definition of charity has *reduced*, not increased, the scope for the Commission to use personal assessments in applying the definition.[68] The enumeration of 13 descriptions of charitable purposes has bounded the Commission's discretion, and thus made the outer boundary of the English charitable sector less malleable than it was before 2006.

Perhaps more importantly, the Charities Act 2011 places a number of institutional barriers in the way of the Commission's discretion becoming subject to political influence. While the Charities Act 2011 does not make the Charity Commission a wholly independent body, it does establish the Commission as a non-ministerial government department, and specifically provides that in the exercise of its functions it shall 'not [be] subject to the direction or control of any Minister of the Crown or of another government department'.[69] The Act also goes a long way in ensuring that the Commission remains oriented towards the goal of promoting the public interest in charity property, providing, among other things, that the Commission must carry out its registration function in a manner consistent with its statutory objective of increasing public trust and confidence in

[65] See Lloyd (n 60) (noting that the statutory list of charitable purposes and public benefit test were the 'most high profile and hotly debated elements of the new legislation').

[66] CA 2011, s 3(2)(a). See also Driscoll (n 57) 59.

[67] CA 2011, ss 3(1)(g), 3(2)(d). Cf *AYSA Amateur Youth Soccer Association v Canada (Revenue Agency)*, 2007 SCC 42, [2007] 3 SCR 217.

[68] See DJ Galligan, *Discretionary Powers: A Legal Study of Official Discretion* (Oxford, Clarendon Press, 1986) 8–9 (arguing that the concept of discretion is based around two variables: the scope for personal assessments in the course of a decision, and the extent to which such assessments are accepted as final and conclusive by other officials).

[69] CA 2011, s 13(4).

charities.[70] Finally, the Commission's registration decisions are appealable in the first instance to the First-Tier Tribunal (Charities), an independent judicial body with the power to quash the Commission's registration decisions;[71] the Commission's policies on the interpretation of the statutory definition have also been subject to judicial review.[72] All of these measures serve to limit the Commission's discretion over the definition of charitable purposes, to direct the exercise of that discretion towards particular ends, and to reduce the risk of that exercise coming under the influence of the executive branch.

iii. Government Influence over the Definition of Charity in Canada

How does the definition of charity under the Canadian registered charity regime compare to English law in this regard? As we saw in Chapter 5, the Parliament of Canada has never exercised its power to determine the substantive purposes that registered charities may carry out. The ambit of the Canadian charitable sector is effectively set by subsections 248(1) and 149.1(1) of the Income Tax Act, which together define the three categories of charities that the Minister of National Revenue may register under the Act.[73] Subsection 149.1(1) defines charitable organizations and foundations by reference to the 'charitable purposes' for which they are constituted and the 'charitable activities' they carry out. However, the Income Tax Act does not specify the meaning of a 'charitable purpose', save to state that it includes the disbursement of funds to defined 'qualified donees' and does not include gifts that constitute 'political activities'.[74] Similarly, the Act does not define 'charitable activities', although it does clarify that certain business and investment activities fall within the term.[75] In this absence of substantive legislative content, the meaning of the terms 'charitable purpose' and 'charitable activity' in the Income Tax Act has always been determined exclusively by reference to the common law.[76]

The open-ended nature of the Income Tax Act provisions could be taken to suggest that the Canadian government is more 'hands-off' in shaping the charitable sector than its English counterpart. With no statutory definition of charity in Canada, the operative definition of charity is, in theory at least, almost surreally

[70] CA 2011, ss 14, 16(1).

[71] CA 2011, sch 6.

[72] See eg *Independent Schools Council v Charity Commission for England and Wales* [2011] UKUT 421 (TCC).

[73] ITA, ss 149.1(1) and 248(1), 'registered charity' (*organisme de bienfaisance enregistré*).

[74] ITA, s 149.1(1), 'charitable purpose' (*fin de bienfaisance*).

[75] The ITA specifies, for example, that the carrying on of a related business, the disbursement of income to an associated charity or qualified donee and the devotion of part of an organization's income to 'ancillary' non-partisan political activities are all charitable activities: ITA, ss 149.1(1), 149.1(6), 149.1(6.2).

[76] For a criticism of this position, see K Chan, 'Taxing Charities/Imposer les Organismes de Bienfaisance: Harmonization and Dissonance in Canadian Charity Law' (2007) 55(3) *Canadian Tax Journal* 481.

dislocated from the country's public policy goals; an institution is charitable in Canada if its purposes fall within the spirit and intendment of an ancient statute enacted in a far-off land. Furthermore, unlike the Charity Commission, the CRA's Charities Directorate has never claimed to have the same powers as the courts to recognize new charitable purposes, and anecdotally takes a conservative approach in applying the case law to applications before it. These factors would seem to suggest that the legal definition of charity in Canada is independent and insulated from the government's public welfare agenda.

However, while Parliament has exerted minimal influence over the legal definition of charity, and the CRA claims not to make new charity law, the operative definition of charity is constantly being adjusted and evolved by the CRA in a way that undermines its deferential claims. Like the Charity Commission for England and Wales, the CRA in Canada is the main source of decisions, policies and guidance documents on what the term 'charitable' means. Despite its purported lack of power to recognize new charitable purposes, there is little question that the CRA approaches its task broadly, and exercises a broad institutional discretion in determining the outer bounds of the charitable sphere.[77] The breadth of this discretion is evidenced by the fact that the CRA and Charity Commission often interpret the same common law authorities in a different way; a comparison of each regulator's political purposes policy, for example, reveals that the CRA takes a significantly stricter view of the advocacy that the common law prohibits.[78] The CRA has extensive policy documents on purposes whose charitable nature has never been addressed in any substance by the courts. It also periodically publishes bulletins with specific examples of 'charitable', and prohibited 'political' activities, which are often perceived by charities as reflecting the particular ideology of the incumbent government.[79]

Against this background, it is significant that the provisions of the Income Tax Act do far less than the Charities Act 2011 to protect the regulator's discretion from becoming subject to political influence. First, compared to the definition of a charitable purpose under the Charities Act 2011, the open-ended definitions in the Income Tax Act provide the CRA with significant autonomy in determining

[77] The Agency has developed an extensive collection of policy and guidance documents, which articulate its views on whether and in what circumstances specific purposes are charitable. See CRA, 'Alphabetic Index of All Policies and Guidance' (27 August 2014), www.cra-arc.gc.ca/chrts-gvng/chrts/plcy/csp/csp_mnn-eng.html.

[78] Some, but not all these differences, are attributable to the Canadian jurisprudence. Cf Charity Commission, *CC9—Speaking Out: Guidance on Campaigning and Political Activity by Charities* (March 2008) and CRA, Policy Statement *CPS-022, Political Activities* (September 2003).

[79] For example, a recent CRA publication about distinguishing between charitable and political activities illustrates impermissible 'political activity' with an example of a refugee settlement charity that calls for the government to make application forms for government social programmes available in various languages. The author has corresponded with members of the refugee community who interpreted this as evidence of the current government's anti-refugee ideology. CRA, 'Distinguishing Between Charitable and Political Activities' (12 March 2013), www.cra-arc.gc.ca/chrts-gvng/chrts/cmmnctn/pltcl-ctvts/chrtblpltcl-eng.html.

the boundaries of the charitable sphere. Second, as we have seen, the Income Tax Act does not lay out any charity-specific objectives or duties to guide the CRA's application of the statutory terms; the regulator's mandate is simply to support the administration and enforcement of the Income Tax Act.[80] Third, the Charities Directorate's registration decisions are appealed in the first instance to the Charities Redress Section of the Tax and Charities Appeals Directorate; like the Directorate itself, this is an internal division of the CRA whose decisions and policies are not generally available to the public.[81] Finally, unlike the Charity Commission, the CRA is a *ministerial* government department, which is subject to the direction and control of the Minister of National Revenue. All of these characteristics of the registered charity regime serve to expand the ambit of official discretion respecting the definition of charitable purposes in Canada, and to increase the risk of it coming under political influence.

B. The Creation of Statutory Charities

A second modern phenomenon that tends towards the co-optation of charitable resources by government is the proliferation of statutory charities. Statutory charities are constituted by the legislature, which also defines their purposes and domestic rules. As such, a government that establishes statutory charities increases its potential to align the resources of the charitable sector with its own policies, and to subject charities to its influence and control.

i. Historical Roots

It has long been settled that the constituting instrument created by a charity's settlor or founder is the primary source of rules for the administration of the charity's property.[82] A charity's constituting legal instrument (often called a charitable instrument) enshrines the particular charitable objects that the charity is bound to pursue. It also sets down the charity's fundamental rules of governance, and may include detailed directions about how charity property is to be held and managed, how the property's managers are to be selected, how disputes over the charity's governance are to be resolved and how the property should be distributed if the charity is wound up. Whether the charitable instrument takes the form of articles of association, a trust deed, a constitution, a Royal Charter or an Act of Parliament, the principle of the document's primacy remains the same. When we are considering the extent to which the law of charities enables government to

[80] Canada Revenue Agency Act, SC 1999, c 17, s 5(1).

[81] ITA, s 168(4). There is a further right of appeal to the Federal Court of Appeal under s 172(3). However, the Federal Court of Appeal has tended to defer to the decisions of the CRA. See eg *Canadian Magen David Adom for Israel v Canada (MNR)*, 2002 FCA 323, 293 NR 144.

[82] See, eg, P Luxton, *The Law of Charities* (Oxford, Oxford University Press, 2001) 256.

influence and control charitable institutions, therefore, it is important to consider the role that the executive and legislative branches of government play in the creation of these charitable instruments.

Looking back at the history of this matter, we must draw a distinction between the role that government played in the creation of charitable corporations and charitable trusts. FW Maitland points out that as unincorporated creatures, charitable trusts 'asked nothing and obtained nothing from the State'.[83] Their existence was the automatic consequence of a settlor communicating his intention that certain ascertainable property be held on trust for charitable purposes.[84] The common law required only that the courts be competent to control and reform the charitable trusts that were created.[85] While government was presumably able to create charitable trusts for its own purposes, provided they remained within the jurisdiction of the courts, this does not appear to have been a common practice in either England and Wales or in Canada. In general, therefore, it seems fair to say that *individuals* settled charitable trusts within the common law tradition, and that government had little scope for influencing the particular objects or rules of governance that settlors chose. It is perhaps for this reason that the Court of Chancery sometimes referred to charitable trusts as 'private charities' when comparing them to charitable corporations.[86]

Government historically played a far greater role in the creation of charitable *corporations*, which depended on the Crown for their very existence. As we saw in Chapter 2, granting corporate status was historically a royal prerogative in English law. Therefore, the incorporation of English corporations could technically only be achieved by the consent of the sovereign, and was in practice accomplished by a grant of letters patent, a Royal Charter or the enactment of a special Parliamentary Act.[87] A significant effect of this government involvement was to insulate charitable corporations from judicial supervision by replacing it with the supervision of an appointed visitor. The rule that every charitable trust must be subject to the controlling power of the court did not apply to charitable corporations at common law,[88] and the court could not alter or act inconsistently with any charitable instrument established by government.[89] By creating charitable corporations, in other words, the government could effectively control both the objects to which charitable resources were devoted, and the manner in which those resources were administered.

[83] FW Maitland, 'Trust and Corporation' in D Runciman and M Ryan (eds), *State, Trust and Corporation* (Cambridge, Cambridge University Press, 2003) 75, 118.

[84] DWM Waters, M Gillen and L Smith, *Waters' Law of Trusts in Canada*, 4th edn (Toronto, Thomson Reuters, 2012) 140.

[85] *National Anti-Vivisection Society v IRC* [1948] AC 31 (HL) 232, Lord Simonds ('One of the tests, and a crucial test, whether a trust is charitable lies in the competence of the court to control and reform it').

[86] *A-G v Smart* (1748) 1 Ves Sen 72 (Ch).

[87] Picarda (n 38) 267.

[88] *R v Hull University Visitor, ex parte Page* [1993] AC 682 (HL) 698–700. See further Ch 2, s II(C).

[89] Picarda (n 38) 523–24.

Today, the UK and Canadian governments only rarely establish charities by Royal Charter.[90] The practice of establishing charities by statute, however, has continued apace. Museums, libraries, art galleries, hospitals, universities and colleges are among the charitable institutions commonly established or continued by statutory instrument.[91] These statutory instruments vary widely, and a comprehensive study of their contents is far beyond the scope of this chapter.[92] It seems fair to assume, however, that as creatures of the legislature, statutory charities are particularly likely to act in furtherance of specific government policies and programmes, and to be subject to government control. The question addressed in this section is whether the modern law of charities in either England and Wales or in Canada does anything to limit this co-optative potential.

ii. Statutory Charities in England and Wales

There are two main ways in which English charity law limits the ability of government to constitute statutory charities as instruments of its own welfare policy; both are related to the definition of charity set out in the Charities Act 2011. First, the Act preserves the pre-enactment case law on the meaning of charity and thus implicitly incorporates *Re Hopkinson* and the related case law on 'pro-government' political purposes. While the modern reach of these decisions is not beyond debate, the Charity Commission has interpreted them broadly, stating in its publications that a charity must exist in order to carry out its charitable purposes, and not for the purpose of carrying out the policies or directions of a governmental authority.[93] If a body with a stated charitable purpose is constituted in terms that enable a government authority to make political determinations about what services the body will provide and who will benefit from those services, the Commission is likely to conclude that the body is not a charity at all.[94] Factors that may indicate an unstated, non-charitable purpose include restraints on the trustees' ability to reject funding on the terms proposed, restraints on the trustees' ability to discuss business in confidence, the existence of trustees with a conflict of interest and a lack of discretion on the part of the trustees to select beneficiaries for the services provided.[95]

[90] Privy Council Office, 'Applying for a Royal Charter', http://privycouncil.independent.gov.uk/royal-charters/applying-for-a-royal-charter.

[91] See, eg, the British Library Act 1972 and the Museums and Galleries Act 1992. In Canada, see An Act respecting the National Sanitarium Association, SC 1896, c 52; National Arts Centre Act, RSC 1985 c N-3. Some, although not all, of the more recent Canadian statutes 'deem' these institutions to be registered charities.

[92] Cliff Goldfarb has written a useful overview of statutory corporations in Canada. See C Goldfarb, 'Special Challenges of Special Act Corporations' (CBA National Charity Law Symposium, Toronto, 2013).

[93] Charity Commission, *RR 7: The Independence of Charities from the State* (Review of the Charities Register, 2009) [5].

[94] ibid [6]–[7].

[95] ibid [8].

The second way in which the Charities Act 2011 limits the ability of government to construct statutory charities as instruments of public welfare policy is by requiring that all charities be subject to the controlling power of the courts. At common law, as we have seen, charitable corporations could be constituted so as to avert this jurisdiction, and this remained the case under the Charitable Trusts Act 1853.[96] In 1960, however, the UK Parliament expressly extended the stricter trust law rule to charitable corporations that wanted to register, by incorporating the requirement of subjection to judicial control into the statutory definition of charity.[97] This extension continues in the Charities Act 2011, which provides in section 1 that in order to qualify as a charity, an institution must not only be established for purely charitable purposes, but must also 'be subject to the control of the High Court in the exercise of its jurisdiction with respect to charities'.[98]

The meaning and significance of this provision have only been closely considered in one case. In *Construction Industry Training Board v A-G*[99] a corporation that had been established by ministerial order under the Industrial Training Act 1964 for the purpose of providing training to persons in the construction industry applied to be entered on the register of charities. The regulator refused the Training Board's application on the ground that institutions set up under the Industrial Training Act 1964 were not subject to the High Court's control. On an appeal by the Attorney General, the Court of Appeal agreed that the effect of the Charities Act 1960 definitional provision was to exclude from the statutory definition of charity any institution that by its terms 'substantially ousted the jurisdiction of the court', for example by leaving control of the institution in the hands of the executive branch of government.[100] The court split in the result, however, with the majority holding that the relevant provisions of the Industrial Training Act 1964 did not oust the court's charitable jurisdiction over the Training Board.[101]

The *Construction Industry* decision arguably sets the bar fairly high for ousting the court's jurisdiction over charities by statutory instrument. As Russell LJ noted in dissent, the statute at issue in that case required the board to submit proposals as to the functions it would carry out for the approval of the Minister of Labour. It also empowered the Minister to appoint the board's directors, to approve the remuneration of its chairman and to remove directors in specified circumstances.[102] However, as the majority noted in concluding that the statute did not oust the court's jurisdiction, the Industrial Training Act 1964 did not give the Minister any means of controlling how the board *performed* its functions once they were approved.[103] *Construction Industry* may therefore be taken as authority for

[96] The CTA 1853 did not define charity, in other words, by reference to the supervisory jurisdiction of the courts: see CTA 1853, s 43.
[97] CA 1960, s 45(1).
[98] CA 2011, s 1(1)(b).
[99] *Construction Industry Training Board v A-G* [1973] Ch 173 (CA).
[100] ibid 176, 181–82, 188.
[101] ibid 187–88.
[102] ibid 182–83.
[103] ibid 188.

the proposition that where an institution's constituting statute gives the executive branch of government broad authority to control the institution's trustees or directors in the exercise of their functions, that institution will not qualify as a charity under the Charities Act 2011.[104] In this way, the statutory definition of charity acts as a limit on government influence and control.

iii. Statutory Charities Under the Canadian Registered Charity Regime

Turning to the Canadian context, it is arguable that the first definitional element that serves to limit government control of statutory charities in England and Wales is also observable under the Canadian registered charity regime. The Income Tax Act, as we have seen, defines registered charities primarily in terms of the 'charitable purposes' and 'charitable activities' they must carry out. The courts and the CRA interpret these terms by reference to the common law tradition in every Canadian province, and rely heavily on English law in doing so. If a Canadian court was faced with an argument that an applicant for registered charity status was *not* a charity because it was constituted to carry out the policies or directions of the government, therefore, it would need to address the effect of *Re Hopkinson* and *Re Co-operative College of Canada*. However, the only party that would generally be in a position to *make* such an argument would be the Charities Directorate itself,[105] and, rather unsurprisingly, this delegate of the Minister of National Revenue has never taken a public position on the independence of charities from the state.

With regard to the Charities Act 2011 requirement that all charities be subject to the controlling power of the courts, the parallels between the Canadian and English regimes cease. Neither section 149.1 nor any other provision of the Income Tax Act requires that registered charities be subject to the jurisdiction of the superior courts. It is of course arguable that to the extent the terms in the Income Tax Act are interpreted by reference to the common law, a trust will not be 'constituted and operated exclusively for charitable purposes' within the meaning of the statute unless the courts remain competent to control and reform it. As we have seen, however, the common law provides far less support for the argument that every corporation constituted for charitable purposes must be subject to the charities jurisdiction of the superior courts. In the absence of any statutory extension of the trust law rule, it must be concluded that the Canadian registered charity regime permits the creation of statutory charities that are substantially controlled in the exercise of their functions by the executive branch of government provided they do not have an unstated, non-charitable purpose.

[104] ibid 188 (the case also suggests that certain grants of visitatorial authority may also place an institution outside the statutory definition of charity).

[105] This is because the applicant for registered charity status would be arguing that it *was* a charity. It is possible that a third party could intervene to make such an argument, but such intervention is very rare in registered charity appeals.

What are the implications of this seldom-noted distinction between the English and Canadian regimes of charities regulation? To answer this question thoroughly, one would need to study the instruments constituting the statutory charities in each jurisdiction, and assess the level of governmental control built into each. For a taste of where such research might lead, however, let us consider the status of one Canadian educational institution that has been found to meet one of the tests of 'publicness' described in Section II. Douglas College is a post-secondary college in British Columbia falling within the purview of the province's College and Institute Act. In the early 1990s employees challenged the college's mandatory retirement policy, requiring the Supreme Court of Canada to consider whether the college was subject to the Canadian Charter of Rights and Freedoms. Having considered the college's constituting statute, a unanimous court held that this issue could be 'quickly disposed of':

> As its constituent Act makes clear, the college is a Crown agency established by the government to implement government policy. Though the government may choose to permit the college board to exercise a measure of discretion, the simple fact is that the board is not only appointed and removable at pleasure by the government; the government may at all times by law direct its operation. Briefly stated, it is simply part of the apparatus of government both in form and in fact.[106]

The important point for our purposes is that despite this high-profile ruling that Douglas College was established to implement government policy and was controlled by the government to the point of being its agent, the college at all times maintained its registered charity status under the Income Tax Act.[107] While a variety of explanations might be offered for this situation (including mere inadvertence on the part of the regulator) a perusal of the Canadian charities register suggests that Douglas College is not the only government-directed institution with registered charity status. The more likely explanation, therefore, is that already discussed: the only limitation that the Income Tax Act places on the creation of government-controlled statutory charities stems from the common law rule that charities may not carry out pro-government political purposes, and the registered charity regime gives this rule little force or effect.

C. Charities and the Contract Culture[108]

A final modern phenomenon that tends towards the co-optation of charitable resources by government is the exertion of government influence over the *administration* or *management* of charities through the negotiation and

[106] *Douglas/Kwantlen Faculty Assn v Douglas College* [1990] 3 SCR 570 at 584, 77 DLR (4th) 94.

[107] See CRA, 'Charities Listing: Douglas College', http://www.cra-arc.gc.ca/chrts-gvng/lstngs/menu-eng.html.

[108] Morris, 'Paying the Piper' (n 1) 123. This is the term used by Debra Morris. I arguably use it to describe a broader range of trends.

implementation of service delivery contracts, and through the appointment of government authority trustees. Working within the frameworks of their charitable instruments, trustees and other charity officers must continually make decisions about what activities their charity should carry out, who should benefit from those activities and how those activities should be organized and administered. A government that can influence these decisions through the imposition of contractual terms or through the influence of its officers has considerable potential to align charitable resources with its own policies, and to bring even non-statutory charities under its effective control.

We have already seen that in 'post-welfare' or 'threatened-welfare' states such as England and Wales and Canada, the practice of contracting out important welfare services to charities and other non-governmental organizations has become increasingly prevalent. The English charitable sector derives well over a third of its income from government sources, much of which is made up of payments for the delivery of welfare services that were formerly the responsibility of the state.[109] In Canada the number may be significantly higher.[110] Historically, much of this government income took the form of block funding grants with few strings attached. Today, however, it is more common for charities to deliver public services on the basis of legally binding service agreements, which often include detailed provisions about performance targets, financial and reporting requirements, and permissible and impermissible 'advocacy'.[111]

Within this evolving 'contract culture', the co-optation of charitable resources by government is increasingly a source of concern. In an early and important article, Debra Morris noted that the increasing reliance of charities on contracts has meant 'increased intrusion into [their] general management and goal-setting processes'.[112] The more dependent that charities are on contract funding, the more pressure they will feel to direct their charity's resources in ways that reflect the agenda and priorities of the purchaser of their services. Studies have found that charities routinely undervalue their services in order to win government contracts, 'topping up' the contractual payment with other charitable income, and thereby subsidizing core welfare services with charitable funds.[113] Some charities claim that government has bullied them into accepting unfair contract provisions.[114] Charities that carry out work under contract with government also complain of restrictive or inappropriate performance measures, limitations on their advocacy

[109] Dunn, 'Demanding Service' (n 1) 251.

[110] See generally B Emmett and G Emmett, *Charities in Canada as an Economic Sector* (Toronto, Imagine Canada, 2015).

[111] Morris, 'Paying the Piper' (n 1) 125. In Canada, see Imagine Canada, 'Investing in Citizens and Communities: a Submission on the Community Nonprofit Sector of Canada to the Blue Ribbon Panel on Grants and Contributions Under the Federal Accountability Action Plan, 2006' (4 August 2006).

[112] Morris, 'Paying the Piper' (n 1) 128.

[113] ibid 136.

[114] ibid 126.

ability, and excessive prescription of their organizational practices.[115] All of this suggests that the greatest threat to charity independence in the modern age may not be *imperium*, but *dominium*: the use of the government's economic power to achieve its aims.[116]

The pressures that have been placed on charities by the trend towards contract-based, limited-term funding have only been exacerbated by the practice of appointing government representatives as charity trustees. Appointing government representatives as charity trustees appears to be a relatively common practice, though it is rarely discussed in Canada.[117] In a statutory charity, where the legislature generally establishes the method of appointment, provision is often made for trustees to be appointed by government authorities. Individual charity founders may also choose to appoint a government authority (or the authority's nominee) as the sole trustee of their charity because the authority knows the local beneficiary population, has the power to rezone the charity's land or represents a potential source of additional funds for the charity's operations.[118]

While the appointment of government trustees may produce advantages for charities, it also increases the likelihood that those charities will become subject to government influence and control. Where a government authority acts as the trustee of a charity located in its area, the authority will face potential conflicts between its duties to the charity, and its general democratic duty to serve the interests of its constituents. Where a local authority is authorized to appoint one or more nominee trustees to a charity, similar conflicts will arise. A party that appoints a nominee trustee to the board of a charity generally expects that trustee to act as its voice on the board,[119] particularly if it is also the nominee's employer. This expectation creates the risk that trustees nominated by a government authority will act in the interests of the officer or body that appointed them, rather than in the interests of the charity.[120]

i. *Historical Roots*

The common law of charities does not specifically address the issue of government influence in the administration of charity property. The issue has emerged as a modern issue, which reflects the ways in which the roles of government and

[115] Cairns (n 5) 38–41.

[116] For a classic discussion on the government's use of *dominium*, see T Daintith, 'Regulation by Contract: The New Prerogative' (1979) 32(1) *CLP* 41.

[117] Charity Commission, *OG 56 A1—Local Authorities and Trustees: an Overview* (2012) [2]; Goldfarb (n 92) 5–6.

[118] Charity Commission for England and Wales, *OG 56 C1—Local Authorities and Trustees: Advantages and Disadvantages of a Local Authority Acting as Sole Trustee* (2012) [2].

[119] PD Finn, *Fiduciary Obligations* (Sydney, The Law Book Company Limited, 1977) 54.

[120] P Luxton, 'Conflicts of Interest in Charity Law' in Dunn (ed), *The Voluntary Sector* (n 1). For an illustration of the conflicts that may arise where a government council is the sole trustee of charity land within its jurisdiction, see *Maidment v The Charity Commission for England and Wales* (16 November 2009), London, UK CA/2009/0001 and 0002.

charities have been increasingly intertwined. Nevertheless, the common law contains a number of rules that may serve to protect charities from third-party influence over the direction of their funds. First, charity trustees are obliged to adhere to the terms of their charitable instrument.[121] For example, where a trust instrument stipulates that the object of the charitable trust is to provide housing to the elderly it will be a breach of trust to use the fund to provide housing to youth, even if the latter project has government funding attached to it or is supported by the government nominee on the board.[122] Strict liability follows a trustee's failure to adhere to the trust instrument,[123] and the Attorney General may seek an injunction to restrain a trustee from carrying out an act that falls outside the terms of a charitable trust.[124] Where there is no trust, as in the case of some corporate charities, the common law's ultra vires doctrine may provide an alternative tool to require that directors adhere to the charity's original purposes.[125] Depending on the form of the charity and the specificity of the charitable instrument, therefore, the 'duty of adherence' may protect charities against the pressures that mark the contract culture.

The second way in which the common law protects charities from becoming subject to outside influences in the administration of their property is by imposing a duty of loyalty on trustees and other fiduciary officers. The precise scope and function of the so-called duty of loyalty have long been a matter of debate in Anglo-Commonwealth law, with jurists on either side of the Atlantic taking somewhat different views of the duty's parameters.[126] It is agreed, however, that the trustees and directors of charities are required to act (or not act) in what they perceive to be the 'best interests' of the charity they serve, and to avoid various situations that might prevent them from acting in that best interest.[127] This general duty is bolstered by a variety of more particularized rules. The best known of these rules are the 'no-conflict' rule, which requires fiduciaries to avoid all conflicts of interest and duty or conflicts of duty and duty, and the 'no-profit' rule, which requires fiduciaries to avoid profiting from the fiduciary relationship.[128]

In principle, there are at least three offshoots of the fiduciary duty of loyalty that should function to protect charities from experiencing government influence over the actions of their trustees. First, a fiduciary generally may not delegate his

[121] J Warburton and others, *Tudor on Charities*, 9th edn (London, Sweet & Maxwell, 2003) 263.

[122] *A-G v The Earl of Mansfield* (1827), 38 ER 423 (Ch). Morris gives a similar example in 'Paying the Piper' (n 1) 129.

[123] L Smith, 'The Motive, Not the Deed' in J Getzler (ed), *Rationalizing Property, Equity and Trusts: Essays in Honour of Edward Burn* (London, LexisNexis Publishing, 2003) 53, 65.

[124] See *A-G v Ross* [1985] 3 All ER 334 (Ch).

[125] Modern corporate statutes in Canada and the UK have largely abandoned ultra vires, but the doctrine still applies to some companies that are charities. See eg Companies Act 2006 (UK), ss 39, 42.

[126] For an overview of this debate and an argument about the true function of the fiduciary duty of loyalty, see M Conaglen, *Fiduciary Loyalty: Protecting the Due Performance of Non-Fiduciary Duties* (Portland, OR, Hart Publishing, 2010).

[127] Smith (n 123) 73.

[128] ibid 55.

discretion to determine how the interests of his beneficiaries (or charity) will be best served, nor can he exercise that discretion under the dictation of another person.[129] As the House of Lords stated in *White v Baugh*, equity does not permit a fiduciary to '[relieve] himself from the fetters imposed upon his own custody and management of the fund, by sharing that management with another, and giving that other as much power over it as himself'.[130] In *Re Partanen* an Ontario court applied this 'no-delegation principle' to a charity, refusing an application by the charity's trustees to delegate their discretion to establish certain scholarships.[131] While the courts have not yet had occasion to address the no-delegation principle in a circumstance where government was seeking to influence the expenditure of a charity fund, the strict limitations placed on the delegation of a fiduciary's authority seem to provide a bulwark against such influence.

A second equitable principle that is potentially relevant to contractual agreements between charities and government is that a fiduciary cannot fetter his discretion by binding himself 'as to the manner in which he will exercise discretion in the future'.[132] Such a fetter does mischief, the Court of Chancery has explained, because it prevents a trustee or other fiduciary from exercising his discretion solely according to 'his own conscientious judgment *at the time* as to what is best in the interests of those for whom he is trustee'.[133] Based on this rule, the courts have refused to enforce lease agreements entered into by trustees that gave the lessee the exclusive option to purchase the trust property at a fixed price within a set number of years.[134] While the precise parameters of the principle are unclear, the general prohibition on the fettering of a trustee's discretion might well render unenforceable a contract entered into by charity trustees which committed the charity to carrying out various government programmes for an extended future time.

A final equitable principle, this one highly relevant to the appointment of government authority trustees, is that a fiduciary must avoid situations where his duty to one person conflicts with his duty to another. This 'duty-duty principle' is of more recent provenance than the classic rule regarding conflicts of duty and interest, but it developed by analogy with the earlier doctrine, and thus relies on similar reasoning.[135] In *Bristol & West Building Society v Mothew* the English Court of Appeal clarified that the duty has three constituent parts. First, the principle prevents a fiduciary from acting for two principals with *potentially* conflicting interests without the informed consent of both, whether or not there is an actual conflict.[136] Second, the principle requires a fiduciary to avoid situations

[129] Finn (n 119) 21.
[130] *White v Baugh* (1835), 6 ER 1354 at 1361 (HL).
[131] *Re Partanen Estate* [1944] 2 DLR 473, OWN 130 (CA).
[132] Finn (n 119) 25. See also J McGhee (ed), *Snell's Equity*, 32nd edn (London, Sweet & Maxwell, 2010) 10–16.
[133] Finn (n 119) 25, citing *Osborne v Amalgamated Society of Railway Servants* [1909] 1 Ch 163, 187.
[134] *Clay v Rufford* (1852), 64 ER 1337 (QBD).
[135] Conaglen (n 126) 143.
[136] *Bristol & West Building Society v Mothew* [1998] Ch 1 (CA) 18.

where there is an *actual conflict* of duty so that he cannot fulfil his obligations to one principal without failing in his obligations to the other.[137] Finally, according to *Mothew*, the duty-duty principle encompasses a 'no inhibition principle', which requires a fiduciary to 'not allow the performance of his obligations to one principal to be influenced by his relationship with the other'.[138] By prohibiting charity trustees from seeking to serve both a government and a charity master where such duties conflict, the duty-duty principle would seem to provide charities with a strong protection against having their trustees become subject to government influence and control.

However, the seeming robustness of these fiduciary protections is significantly undermined by difficulties related to their enforcement. In practice, there are major obstacles to the application of the no-delegation, no-fettering and duty-duty principles. These include the evidentiary difficulties of proving that a fiduciary did not exercise independent discretion for the no-delegation principle,[139] and the 'weak and unclear' nature of the remedies available for breaches of the duty-duty rule.[140] The general difficulties involved in enforcing fiduciary principles are exacerbated in the charitable sector, as there is generally no ascertainable beneficiary to enforce them, and the attorneys general are not prone to act.[141] These factors help to explain why, despite the increasing use of government authority trustees and the economic pressure on charity trustees to submit to contractual terms put forward by government, there is very little case law in England and Wales or Canada considering the application of the duty of loyalty to charity trustees.[142] In what follows, I will consider whether contemporary English and Canadian law contain any additional tools to protect charities from these pressures.

ii. Charities and the Contract Culture in England and Wales

Before the rise and subsequent retrenchment of the English welfare state, charity law did not devote much attention to the potential difficulties associated with the contractual delivery of welfare services. However, the issues raised by the appointment of government authority trustees for charities were on the radar by the mid-nineteenth century. As a former head of the Charity Commission recounts, the

[137] ibid 19.

[138] ibid, noting also that 'the principle which is in play is that the fiduciary must not be inhibited by the existence of his other employment from serving the interests of his principal as faithfully and effectively as if he were the only employer'.

[139] Finn (n 119) 21.

[140] See Conaglen (n 126) 158.

[141] See generally K Chan, 'The Role of the Attorney General in Charity Proceedings in Canada and in England and Wales' (2011) 89 *Canadian Bar Review* 373.

[142] Luxton suggests that in EW, the dearth of case law on conflicts of interests involving charities is due to the fact that such issues are usually dealt with by the Charity Commission: Luxton (n 120) 228. However, there appears to be a similar dearth of case law in Canada. See C Goldfarb, 'Dual Loyalties on Non-Profit Boards: Serving Two Masters' (CBA-OBA National Symposium on Charity Law, Toronto, May 2011) 8.

policy of the UK Parliament during this period was 'to discourage the appointment of local authorities as trustees because of the risk of confusion between their duties as trustees and as organs of government'.[143] Thus, a series of nineteenth-century Acts removed municipal corporations from their existing positions as the trustees of charities vested in them, and empowered them to appoint individuals as trustees instead. The Local Government Acts of the period did not authorize local councils to accept charitable trusts.[144]

The current legislative position is significantly more permissive, but nonetheless evidences a policy to limit the use of local authority trustees. Pursuant to section 139 of the Local Government Act 1972, a local authority may accept, hold and administer gifts of property for the purpose of discharging any of its functions, or for the purpose of benefiting the inhabitants of its area or of some part of it. However, no local government can act as the trustee of an ecclesiastical charity or of a charity for the relief of poverty.[145] In respect of these trusts the conflict between the authority's duties to the charity and its democratic duties is considered to be particularly severe.[146] Special provision is made under the Open Spaces Act 1906 and the Charities Act 2011 for transferring land held under certain charitable trusts to local authorities.[147] However, the legislation specifies that such transfers can only be made on terms consented to by the Charity Commission, and the policy of the Commission is to consent only where it is satisfied that the transfer is 'the most beneficial arrangement for the charity having regard to the need to avoid conflicts of interest to safeguard the charity's property and the beneficiaries' interests'.[148]

Indeed, the Charity Commission seeks, in the exercise of its regulatory authority, to serve as an additional barrier against the threats posed to charities by the trusteeship of local authorities and their nominees. The Commission cannot rightly refuse to register a charity on the basis that it names a local authority or local authority nominee to its board, unless the evidence indicates that the true purpose of the institution is some 'ulterior non-charitable purpose of the local authority'.[149] Where the Commission exercises its own statutory power to appoint charity trustees, however, it will not appoint a local authority unless there is some compelling reason for doing so.[150] Charity Commission schemes sometimes

[143] CP Hill, *A Guide for Charity Trustees*, revised edn (London, Faber and Faber Publishing, 1974) 32.
[144] ibid 33.
[145] Local Government Act 1972, s 139.
[146] F Quint, 'Local Authorities and Charities I: Trusteeship' (1991) 155 *Local Government Review* 922, 922. See also Charity Commission, *OG 56 A1—Local Authorities and Trustees: An Overview* (March 2012).
[147] Open Spaces Act 1906, s 3; CA 2011, s 298.
[148] Charity Commission, *OG 56 C1—Local Authorities and Trustees: Advantages and Disadvantages of a Local Authority Acting as Sole Trustee* (March 2012) [4].
[149] Charity Commission, *OG 56 B1—Local Authorities and Trustees: Local Authorities as Trustee* (June 2012) [1].
[150] Charity Commission, *OG 56 A1* (n 146) [2]. In cases of concern the Commission may also ask a local authority trustee to voluntarily stand down: ibid.

provide that the boards of local charities shall include trustees appointed by local authorities. However, the Commission's stated preference in making schemes is 'not to confer a power on local authorities to nominate all or a majority of trustees'.[151]

The Charity Commission also provides significant online resources for local authority and nominee trustees. These resources aim to draw attention to, and ultimately prevent, situations where charity trustees may act in the interests of their government instead of their charity. Thus, the Commission's operational guidance, *Local Authorities as Trustees*, stipulates that unless charitable funds are held for charitable purposes that 'necessarily involve applying them for the statutory functions of the local authority', a local authority cannot, as charity trustee, use charity funds to pay for staff or services required for the discharge of its statutory functions.[152] Related guidance clarifies that where a local authority officer appoints a trustee to a charity, he or she 'must not expect its appointee to represent its interests. He or she must appoint the individual best fitted to carry out the trusteeship of the charity in question'.[153] And where a nominee trustee has a conflict in relation to any matter, including a conflict arising from his or her employment by or membership of a local authority',[154] the guidance confirms that 'he or she should consider withdrawing from any meetings in which the matter is discussed'.[155]

A final set of rules, which protect against breaches of loyalty in *corporate* English charities with local authority trustees, is set out in secondary legislation under the Companies Act 2006. The Local Authorities (Companies) Order 1995 imposes additional regulatory requirements on companies (including charitable companies) that are controlled or influenced by local authorities.[156] Where a local authority has the power to appoint or remove a majority of a corporate charity's board, or where 20 per cent or more of a charity's directors are persons associated with a local authority and more than half of the charity's income or capital is derived from that local authority, the charity will be considered a 'regulated company' under the Order. Among other things, regulated companies are required to give the public notice of the fact that they are controlled or influenced by a local authority.[157] They are not permitted to remunerate their directors in excess of local authority rates, and they must make all minutes of their general meetings available for public inspection.[158] All of these measures increase the accountability

[151] Charity Commission, *OG 56 B2—Local Authorities and Trustees: Issues Conected with the Independence of Trustees, particularly When the Trustees Are Nominated by Local Authorities* (March 2012) [2.2].

[152] Charity Commission, *OG 56 B1* (n 149) [7.1].

[153] Charity Commission, *OG 56 B2* (n 151) [2.1].

[154] Charity Commission, *OG 56 C2—Local Authorities and Trustees: Potential Conflicts of Interest Which Trustees Nominated by the Local Authority May Face* (July 2000) [1].

[155] ibid [2].

[156] Local Authorities (Companies) Order 1995, SI 1995/849.

[157] ibid, Art 4.

[158] ibid, Arts 5, 10.

and transparency of corporate charities with local authority trustees, and thus reduce the temptation for their boards to act in the interests of government rather than the charity itself.

In terms of the growing potential for the contractual co-optation of charitable resources by government, the Charity Commission has been attentive to this issue for over 15 years. In 1998 the Charity Commission published its first guidance on 'charities and contracts', taking the position that while charities could use their resources to supplement government activities, they could not pay for services that the government was legally required to provide at the public expense.[159] The Commission reversed its position on this issue in the *Trafford and Wigan* decision, and held that there was 'no rule of law which prevented trustees entering into a contract with a government authority to carry out a function or service of that authority', whether the authority had a mandatory duty or a discretionary power to provide that service.[160] However, the Commission also stated that in entering into such a contract, the trustees had to consider certain 'guiding principles', including whether the service fell within the objects and powers of the charity, whether the undertaking of the function served the needs of the charity's beneficiaries, and whether the trustees were able to secure proper consideration for the service from the government.[161] Where the service to be subsidized was a legal responsibility of the government authority, the Commission suggested that the trustees should question 'why such responsibilities are not being carried out', and carefully consider whether the expenditure of the charity's funds to provide the service was the most effective use of the charity's resources.[162]

In March 2012, the principles articulated in *Trafford and Wigan* were confirmed and expanded upon in the Charity Commission's new guidance document, *Charities and Public Service Delivery.* In the foreword to the guidance, the Chair of the Commission wrote that it was 'not for the Commission either to encourage or discourage the delivery of public services by charities'.[163] Nevertheless, the guidance positions the Commission as a public defender of the independence of charities from government within the prevailing contract culture. *Charities and Public Service Delivery* makes it very clear that charity trustees must not enter into any contract or funding agreement with government unless they are satisfied that its terms are in their charity's best interests. It also addresses the contentious issue of contractual restrictions on advocacy, stating that charities that deliver public services should not feel inhibited from engaging in political activity or campaigning.[164]

159 Charity Commission, *CC 37—Charities and Contracts* (1998). See also Dunn, 'Demanding Service' (n 1) 253.

160 *Trafford and Wigan* (n 58) [6.1.7].

161 ibid [6.1.7].

162 ibid [6.1.10].

163 Charity Commission, *Charities and Public Service Delivery—An Introduction and Overview* (March 2012) 2.

164 ibid 21.

The 38-page document closes with a long list of sources of further information and advice, suggesting that the Commission views the 'contract culture' issue as one that is here to stay.

iii. Charities and the Contract Culture in Canada

Unlike in England and Wales, it is difficult in Canada to identify any coherent policy on either the negotiation of contracts between charities and government, or on the appointment of government authority trustees. At the federal level, the negotiation of service delivery agreements between charities and government falls within the scope of the far broader Treasury Board Policy on Transfer Payments. In 2006 a federally appointed 'Blue Ribbon Panel on Grants and Contributions' made a variety of recommendations on how the government could reduce 'the current morass of rules and general red tape' enveloping grants and contributions programmes, and the federal government amended its Treasury Board Policy in response. However, neither the report nor the policy distinguishes charities from other recipient organizations, nor does either document place any limit on the substantive 'performance conditions' that the government is entitled to impose.[165] Neither the CRA nor the Ontario Public Guardian and Trustee has any discernible policy on this issue.

With regard to the issue of local authority trustees, the regulation of municipal institutions is a matter of exclusive provincial jurisdiction in Canada.[166] Thus, the wide range of matters that English law addresses under the Local Government Acts are governed, in Canada, by a multiplicity of provincial statutory instruments. While many of these municipal statutes *do* require elected officials to declare any conflicts or divided loyalties that might arise as a result of their trusteeship of a charity when voting on matters in council,[167] the statutes *do not* place any limitations on the appointment of local authorities as charity trustees. Indeed, Nova Scotia's Municipal Government Act expressly provides that a local authority may acquire and own property granted or conveyed to the municipality in trust for a public or charitable purpose.[168] British Columbia's Local Government Act similarly allows the board of directors of a regional district to accept property in trust, and specifically authorizes the board to apply for judicial variation of such a trust if the board considers that the trust is 'no longer in the best interests of the regional district'.[169] These enabling provisions seem likely to exacerbate, rather than reduce, the natural conflicts between the democratic and fiduciary duties of government authority trustees.

[165] It is possible that there are provincial policies that address this issue in more detail.

[166] Constitution Act 1867, s 92(8).

[167] See especially the decision of the British Columbia Court of Appeal in *Schlenker v Torgrimson*, 2013 BCCA 9, [2013] 3 WWR 232.

[168] Municipal Government Act, SNS 1998, c 18, s 50(1).

[169] Local Government Act, RSBC 2015, c 1, s 282.

The registered charity provisions of the Income Tax Act also evidence no policy to protect charities from government influence and control, either by virtue of a service delivery contract or by virtue of the role of government authority trustees. It is, of course, arguable that any such policy would fall outside federal legislative authority over taxation. However, the federal Parliament has a long track record of 'federalizing' provincial law subjects for purposes of the registered charity regime where such federalization suits its aims. Recent amendments to the Income Tax Act, for example, have introduced several categories of 'ineligible directors', whose appointment to the board of a registered charity constitutes grounds for revocation of its charitable status.[170] Had Parliament so desired, it could presumably have extended the statutory definition of an 'ineligible director' to include local government authorities.

The argument that the registered charity regime evidences little concern to protect charities from government influence is further supported by recent amendments to the Income Tax Act definition of a charitable organization. Pursuant to these amendments, the definition of a charitable organization now excludes any organization that is 'controlled directly or indirectly in any manner whatever' by a person who has contributed over 50 per cent of the capital of the organization.[171] At first glance, this provision would appear to protect charities that receive most of their funding from government from also being controlled by that government, by contractual or administrative means. However, the amendment specifies that the prohibition on donor control does *not* apply to Her Majesty in right of Canada or a province, nor to any Canadian municipality. In light of this specific exemption, one might say that at best, the registered charity regime does nothing to discourage the appointment of government authority trustees for registered charities, nor to prevent other forms of government influence and control.

IV. Conclusion

I began this chapter by acknowledging that this book's claims about the hybridity of the charity law tradition—about its alleged ability to maintain a broad, functional equilibrium between individual project pursuit and collective project pursuit in the charitable sphere—face a major challenge in the present day. This challenge stems from a growing consensus that charities in the Anglo-Commonwealth world are experiencing regulatory and other government activity that orients them strongly towards conformity with the incumbent government's substantive agenda, and away from independent agency and dissent. These *co-optative* pressures and processes have always existed in the charitable sphere, but become

[170] ITA s 149.1 (1) 'ineligible individual' (*particulier non admissible*); s 149.1(4.1)(e).
[171] ITA, s 149.1(1) 'charitable organization' (*oeuvre de bienfaisance*).

particularly acute in times such as the present, when governments struggle with extensive welfare commitments that they no longer can or want to sustain. They are important to this work because a significant level of governmental co-optation has the potential to disrupt charity law's hybrid equilibrium and to tip charities decisively into the public law sphere.

In light of these concerns, I have sought to advance a theoretical contrast between independent and co-opted charities, to explore a number of phenomena that seem to be contributing to the co-optation of charitable resources in present day England and Wales and Canada, and to assess each jurisdiction's legal and institutional responses to these phenomena. Further work will be required to assess the extent to which Canadian and English charities *in fact* further government policies or are subject to government influence and control. We may nonetheless conclude from the present study that definitional, managerial and contractual co-optation pose a real threat to the public–private hybridity of charities in multiple jurisdictions. We may also conclude that England and Wales's civil regime of charity regulation does far more than Canada's tax-based regime to prevent charities from coming to function as agents of government policy.

With regard to the first identified co-optative phenomenon—the exertion of government influence over the legal definition of charity—the English and Canadian regimes have built upon the common law concept of charity in strikingly different ways. The Charities Act 2011 modifies the common law definition of a charitable purpose in several material respects, thereby reasserting the legislature's perennial power to direct charitable resources to the objects of its choosing. However, the UK legislation simultaneously limits the ambit of the discretion that may legitimately be exercised by the Charity Commission in applying this statutory definition, both through the definition's own specificity, and through the statute's articulation of the Commission's objects and functions. The Charities Act 2011 also protects the independence of the Commission itself, thereby reducing the risk of it coming under political influence. In Canada, by contrast, the boundaries of the charitable sector continue to be set by reference to the Statute of Elizabeth and court decisions. However, the tax-based regulator that applies these judicial decisions is a ministerial government agency with no articulated 'charity law' function, whose decisions are appealable at first instance to another division of the same agency. The effect of these structural characteristics is to expand the official discretion that is exercised in the interpretation of the legal definition of charity in Canada, to increase the potential for political influence and to make it more likely that the definition will be used as a tool to align charitable projects with the welfare agenda of the state.

If we turn to the second co-optative phenomenon—governments creating statutory charities—the contrast between the English and Canadian regimes is even starker. At common law, the sovereign's approval was required for the creation of charitable corporations, but such charities could be placed outside the controlling power of the courts. This meant that in respect of this limited but important class of charities, the legislative and executive branches of government could effectively mould the purposes to which charitable resources were directed, or craft governance rules that left control of the charity in the hands of the state. The Charities Act 2011 limits the government's ability to construct statutory charities in this way, by requiring that *all* charities be subject to the controlling power of the courts. The Charity Commission has also developed policies on identifying charities with an unstated, non-charitable purpose of carrying out government policies. The Canadian registered charity regime, by contrast, is silent on these matters, and has not extended the rule regarding the controlling power of the courts to charities that are not trusts. While it is conceivable that a Canadian court might prevent the co-optation of a statutory charity by reading the common law authorities on pro-government political purposes into the registered charity regime, it is difficult to imagine a judicial context in which such an argument might arise.

Finally, in respect of the third phenomenon—contractual co-optation and the appointment of government authority trustees—the approaches taken by English and Canadian law again evidence the different levels of public-welfare compliance towards which English and Canadian charities are oriented, and the different levels of government influence and control that each regime is willing to countenance. The common law tradition imposes a number of duties on charity officers, requiring them to adhere strictly to the terms of their charitable instrument and to always act in what they perceive to be the best interests of their charity. However, in light of the significant obstacles to enforcing these rules in the emerging contract culture, the UK Parliament and the Charity Commission have supplemented and operationalized these rules, increasing their impact by associating them with regulatory remedies and publicizing them in language that charity trustees can understand. In contrast, the Canadian registered charity regime is, again, largely silent and to the extent it does speak, it is to allow government bodies that contribute the majority of a registered charity's capital to also control them.

All of these trends are consistent with the CRA's position on the public benefit doctrine, which, as we saw in Chapter 5, is that the public benefit of an applicant for registered charity status is partly measurable by its consistency with the incumbent government's policy agenda. They allow us to conclude that while governmental co-optation poses a threat to charity law's hybrid equilibrium in both jurisdictions, Canadian law does far less than English law to prevent charitable resources from being co-opted by the state. While the degree of actual co-optation in each jurisdiction is a question for further empirical study, the legal landscape suggests that in Canada, in particular, the equilibrium between individual project pursuit and collective project pursuit in the charitable sphere is vulnerable to being upset.

7

New Equilibriums: Social Enterprise as a Post-charitable Legal Form

I. Introduction

The previous four chapters have been concerned with mapping some of the ways and dimensions in which the law of charities partakes of public law and private law. The thrust of the argument has been that the common law of charities was historically a true public–private hybrid, in the sense that it accorded comparable importance to the 'private law' goal of enabling property-owning individuals to improve the world according to their own particular vision, and the 'public law' goal of protecting the public interest in the proper and effective administration of charity property. The English Charity Commission regime continues to seek a balance between these competing legal objects, while the Canadian registered charity regime weighs the autonomy interests of benevolent property owners primarily against the public interest in the integrity of the tax base. However, this book has sought to demonstrate that in both jurisdictions, trends such as the development of human rights standards and especially the governmental co-optation of charitable resources are shifting the hybrid composition of charity law towards a significantly more 'public' composition, in which an individual's interest in pursuing his or her vision of the good through a charity is subject to an increasing number of public law constraints.

Modern charity law limits individual project pursuit in additional ways that this work has not addressed. In particular, the restrictions that Canadian and UK tax laws place on revenue generation by charities are increasingly seen as a major constraint on the autonomy of individuals to pursue benevolent projects in the charitable sphere. English charities are entitled to engage in 'non-primary purpose' trading activities to raise funds for their charity's objects, but are not permitted to do so where such trading would involve a 'significant risk' to their assets.[1] Canadian registered charities are significantly more restricted in their revenue-generating ability: charitable organizations and public foundations may

[1] Charity Commission, *CC 35—Trustees Trading and Tax: How Charities May Lawfully Trade* (February 2016) [3.2].

have their registration revoked for carrying on business activities that are not 'related' to their charitable purposes, and private foundations may not carry on any business activities at all.[2]

It is in the context of these accumulating constraints on individual project pursuit in the charitable sphere that the book turns, in its penultimate chapter, to the growing phenomenon of social enterprise.[3] If it is indeed true, as this book has posited, that the law of charities is increasingly edging out of the public law–private law border zone and towards the public law pole, one would expect the search to be on for *new* hybrid forms, which strike a finer balance between individual and collective project pursuit in the benevolent sphere. This search—from all appearances—is already in full swing. The United Kingdom, British Columbia, California and New York feature on a growing list of jurisdictions that have recently introduced new 'hybrid' vehicles in order to accommodate and encourage economic activity that is concerned, at some level, with improving human society or the welfare of human beings. Governments seem keen to harness a perceived swelling of goodwill within the business sector, at times casting their new corporate vehicles as adroit legislative responses to a growing demand for ethical entrepreneurship and 'socially focused' investment options.[4]

Whether or not it is plausible to argue that the present generation of business leaders is more altruistic than the last, the findings of this book suggest that it is at least equally plausible to characterize the new hybrids as legislative responses to a growing demand for greater individual autonomy in the benevolent sphere.[5] Viewed in this light, social enterprise vehicles may be characterized as a sort of 'post-charitable' legal form, the regulation of which emerges as a natural postscript to the descriptive focus of this work. In this chapter I claim that social enterprise vehicles, like charities, are legal hybrids. They are hybrids not only in the commonly understood sense that they occupy a place somewhere between the for-profit and not-for-profit worlds, but also in the sense that they, like charities, occupy a place between the public law and private law spheres. From the perspective of the law of charities, social enterprise vehicles represent alternative hybrid compositions of public law and private law elements. A study of these elements is useful both in its own right, and in bringing into sharper focus the particular mix of public law and private law that is embodied in the law of charities.

[2] ITA, ss 149.1(2)(a), 149.1(3)(a), 149.1(4)(a).

[3] There are many competing definitions of social enterprise: see, eg, the range of national definitions set out in M Doeringer, 'Fostering Social Enterprise: a Historical and International Analysis' (2010) 20 *Duke Journal of International & Comparative Law* 291, 294. For purposes of this chapter, it will suffice to define social enterprise as economic activity that is concerned with improving human society or the welfare of human beings.

[4] British Columbia, Official Report of Debates of the Legislative Assembly, *Hansard*, 39th Parl, 4th Sess, No 34:2 (16 April 2012) 10654–55.

[5] See the Explanatory Notes to the Companies (AICE) Act 2004 [190], describing the CIC as a suitable vehicle for 'those that wish to work for community benefit within the relative freedom of the non-charitable company form'.

In addition to the conceptual affinities between charities and social enterprise vehicles, there are a number of practical reasons for examining the early development of social enterprise law to round out this study of the law of charities. First, the proliferation of new social enterprise vehicles will almost certainly heighten the already substantial level of public confusion regarding the distinctions between charities, not-for-profits and other socially minded organizations. Such confusion is likely to disadvantage charities in particular, since they are the institutions that risk losing existing goodwill and other privileges if they become indistinguishable from other legal forms.[6] In June 2012 Dame Suzi Leather used her final official speech as chair of the Charity Commission to voice precisely this concern about the potential 'blurring of the boundaries' between charities and other legal vehicles with social objectives. If charities become indistinguishable from other types of organizations in the eyes of the public, she suggested, the trust placed by the public in charities and the privileges they enjoy might well disappear.[7]

The new social enterprise vehicles should also be of concern to charities and their managers because they threaten to divert resources away from the charitable sector. Governments are already devoting significant public resources to the development of these new legal forms. While non-charitable social enterprises do not presently benefit from the significant tax concessions granted to charities, some have access to special pools of capital, such as the UK government's social enterprise investment fund.[8] The dynamic social enterprise sector is pressing for further preferential measures, including social enterprise investment tax credits, and privileged status for social enterprises in government-sponsored business development.[9] The regulatory infrastructure supporting the new vehicles also creates a public expense.[10] The dedication of *private* resources to the social enterprise sector represents an even greater threat to the charitable sector. For if the new social enterprise vehicles succeed in attracting large amounts of capital to their projects, it will almost certainly be at the charitable sector's expense.

Given the conceptual similarities between charities and social enterprise vehicles, and the likelihood that public and private resources are to some degree being redirected from the former to the latter, it seems crucial that we better understand how these hybrid phenomena interrelate. This chapter embarks on

[6] This is arguably already occurring. In 2013, for example, the Parliament of Canada expanded the scope of a federal law that prohibits the bribery of foreign public officials by deleting the term 'for-profit' from the statute's definition of a business: Corruption of Foreign Public Officials Act, SC 1998, c 34, s 2 (as amended). I thank Peter Broder, General Counsel of the Muttart Foundation, for bringing this statute to my attention.

[7] D Ainsworth, 'Suzi Leather asks in final speech if charities will remain special' *Third Sector Online* (13 June 2012) www.thirdsector.co.uk/news/1136346/Suzi-Leather-asks-final-speech-charities-will-remain-special/.

[8] Doeringer (n 3) 313.

[9] BC Social Innovation Council, *Action Plan Recommendations to Maximize Social Innovation in British Columbia* (March 2012) 6–9.

[10] The annual budget of the CIC Regulator is approximately 300,000 pounds sterling: CIC Regulator, Annual Report 2014/15, 14.

that endeavour by examining the regulatory regimes associated with two presumptively *non-charitable* vehicles[11] that have been developed specifically for social enterprise purposes: the UK community interest company (or 'CIC') and the British Columbia community contribution company (or 'C3'). Each of these regulatory regimes, I claim, represents an alternative vision of how to balance the protection of the autonomy of property-owning individuals to direct and control their own wealth, and the furtherance of competing public interests. This chapter aims to draw attention to these competing visions, and to consider how they compare to charity law's vision of the proper balance between individual and collective project pursuit.

The chapter proceeds in the following way. In Section II, I review the legislative history of the CIC and the C3, and summarize the key features of each corporate vehicle. Following this general review, I examine how specific features of these post-charitable legal regimes compare to the law of charities in terms of their balancing of public law and private law elements. The examination is structured to reflect the inquiries undertaken of charity law in Chapters 3 and 4. Accordingly, Section III compares the 'community benefit' standards that are built into the CIC and the C3 regimes with charity law's public benefit criterion. Section IV considers who is entitled to seek what sort of relief for the misapplication of property held by a CIC or C3. The chapter closes by drawing some initial conclusions about the various hybrid compositions that have been created for social enterprise activity in England and Wales and in Canada, and by considering how each of these compositions reflects a competing vision of the 'public' or 'private' nature of benevolent projects.

II. New Social Enterprise Vehicles in England and Wales and Canada

A. The Community Interest Company (UK)

The creation of a new legal form for social enterprise in the UK took place within the broader context of not-for-profit law reform that was described in Chapter 2. *Private Action, Public Benefit*, the Strategy Unit report that paved the way for the enactment of the Charities Act 2006, also recommended a series of corporate law reforms to 'enable not-for-profit organizations to thrive'.[12] Social enterprises, the report claimed, were a diverse and growing group: some were registered as charities, others were societies with non-distribution constraints, while still others took

[11] Social enterprise *activity* may take place within both charitable and non-charitable vehicles, but purpose-built social enterprise vehicles are generally not charities.

[12] *Private Action, Public Benefit*, 49.

the form of mainstream businesses.[13] What they shared was a desire to trade in order to build long-term sustainability, and a commitment to 'operate for a social purpose and use their profits to this end'.[14] What they lacked were legal forms of incorporation that would reflect their distinctive ethos, and ensure that their assets were devoted to a public use.[15] *Private Action, Public Benefit* recommended a number of changes to the regulatory regime governing charitable social enterprises, including the relaxation of charity law's trading rules and the introduction of a new corporate vehicle, the Charitable Incorporated Organisation.[16] For *non-charitable* social enterprises, however, the report recommended the establishment of a distinct corporate vehicle which would both 'protect assets against distribution to members or shareholders', and create a strong new not-for-profit brand for small-scale, community-based social entrepreneurs.[17] Less than two years later, the government followed through on the Strategy Unit's recommendation by establishing the CIC in the Companies (Audit, Investigations and Community Enterprise) Act 2004.[18]

The CIC is a special breed of limited liability company. Subject to the general regime of English company law,[19] the CIC is additionally governed by provisions that are designed to ensure that the company will serve a social purpose.[20] Most of these provisions relate in one way or another to the two key features of the CIC form: its mandate to carry out activities that are in the 'community interest', and the restrictions on the distribution of its corporate assets.

A CIC may take the form of a company limited by guarantee or a company limited by shares.[21] CIC status is sought upon incorporation; an existing company may also apply to convert to a CIC, provided it makes the required alterations to its name and articles by special resolution.[22] Applications for registration of a company as a CIC are made to the Registrar of Companies, but eligibility for CIC status is determined by the Regulator of Community Interest Companies (the 'CIC Regulator'), an official appointed under the Companies (AICE) Act 2004 by the Secretary of State.[23] In order to be eligible for registration as a CIC, a company must be able to satisfy the CIC Regulator that it meets the community interest test, in that 'a reasonable person might consider that its activities are being carried on for the benefit of the community'.[24] It must not be owned or controlled by a

[13] ibid 50–51.
[14] ibid 50.
[15] ibid 52.
[16] ibid 44.
[17] ibid 49, 53.
[18] Companies (AICE) Act 2004, pt 2.
[19] Companies Act 2006 (UK), ss 1(1), 6(2).
[20] *Private Action, Public Benefit*, 50.
[21] Companies (AICE) Act 2004, s 26(2)(a). An existing company limited by guarantee with a share capital may also apply for CIC status: s 26(2)(b).
[22] Companies (AICE) Act 2004, s 37(1).
[23] ibid ss 27(2), 36A(1), 38(1).
[24] ibid s 35(2).

political party or campaigning organization, and its corporate name must include a designation indicating its CIC status.[25] Finally, the company's articles must comply with a number of regulations restricting the distribution of corporate assets.[26]

Despite the fact that many English charities would meet the stipulated requirements for CIC status, a charity cannot simultaneously be a CIC. The Companies (AICE) Act 2004 provides that a charitable company may *become* a CIC, with the written consent of the Charity Commission.[27] A CIC may also convert to a charity, provided the shareholders, the Charity Commission and the CIC Regulator agree.[28] However, a company may not simultaneously have the status of a CIC and a charity in the UK, regardless of whether its purposes are exclusively charitable.[29] This rule was criticized during the legislative debates as confusing and as contradicting the long-standing principle that charitable status is a function of substance rather than form.[30] However, it serves the purpose of clarifying that CICs are in no circumstances 'subject to the benefits or obligations of charitable status, nor ... subject to regulation by the Charity Commission or the charitable jurisdiction of the High Court'.[31]

Once a company is registered as a CIC, its directors assume regulatory burdens in addition to those already imposed on all UK companies. In particular, CICs are required to prepare an annual 'CIC Report', which is delivered to the Registrar of Companies and placed on the public record.[32] Among other things, the CIC Report must contain a fair and accurate description of the manner in which the company's activities during the financial year have benefited the community.[33] The CIC Report must also contain specified financial information regarding the company's asset distribution activities.[34]

Apart from the community interest test, the most defining feature of the UK's social enterprise regime is the regulatory restrictions on the distribution of a CIC's assets. The starting point of the regime is that CICs are subject to an 'asset lock': while a CIC may use its assets for normal trading and business activities, in general it cannot transfer any assets out of the company other than for full consideration.[35] The statutory provisions related to terminating CIC status reinforce this general

[25] ibid ss 33, 36A(2)(b) and (c), 38(2)(b) and (c). Political parties, political campaigning organizations and their subsidiaries are 'excluded companies': Community Interest Company Regulations 2005, SI 2005/1788 (CIC Regulations 2005) reg 6.

[26] Companies (AICE) Act 2004, ss 32, 36A(2)(a), 38(2)(a); CIC Regulations 2005, pts 2 and 3.

[27] Companies (AICE) Act 2004, s 39. However, a Northern Ireland charity may not become a CIC: s 40A.

[28] Companies (AICE) Act 2004, ss 54, 54A–C, 55A–B.

[29] ibid s 26(3) ('A CIC established for charitable purposes is to be treated as not being so established, and accordingly is not a charity').

[30] HL Deb 8 January 2004, vol 657, col 277.

[31] Explanatory Notes to the Companies (AICE) Act 2004 [196].

[32] Companies (AICE) Act 2004, s 34(1).

[33] CIC Regulations 2005, reg 26(1).

[34] ibid, regs 26–28.

[35] Companies (AICE) Act 2004, s 30(1); CIC Regulations 2005, para 1(1) of schs 1–3.

asset-lock rule. The Act provides that a CIC may only cease to be a CIC by dissolution, or by following the statutory procedure to become a charity or a (not-for-profit) industrial and provident society.[36] And where a solvent CIC is dissolved, its remaining residual assets must be transferred to another asset-locked body—a CIC, charity or permitted industrial and provident society—'in such proportions or amounts as the CIC Regulator shall direct'.[37]

While the asset lock is an important feature of the CIC regime, it is subject to significant exceptions. The first and best known of these exceptions allows a CIC with share capital to pay dividends to its members and pay interest on performance-based debentures issued by the company within the limits set by the CIC Regulator.[38] A CIC may also transfer assets out of the company for less than full consideration where the transfer is to another asset-locked body,[39] or the transfer is 'for the benefit of the community'.[40] A CIC with share capital is entitled to return paid-up capital to its members on dissolution, after satisfaction of the company's liabilities.[41] Finally, while the CIC Regulator takes the position that the 'full consideration' principle applies equally to payments for services,[42] the legislation itself does not place any direct limits on the remuneration of staff or directors. During second reading debates, Lord Phillips of Sudbury argued that this absence of control over remuneration would 'drive a coach and horses through [the] attempt at controlling the distribution of the assets of a CIC'.[43]

B. The Community Contribution Company (British Columbia)

The parallel move towards a new 'social enterprise era' in British Columbia began in October 2010 when the Ministry of Finance announced that it was considering the creation of a new 'hybrid' company, which would be modelled on the UK's CIC. In the weeks and months that followed, the government announced the creation of Canada's first Parliamentary Secretary for Social Entrepreneurship, a

[36] Companies (AICE) Act 2004, ss 53, 54; Community Interest Company (Amendment) Regulations 2009, SI 2009/1942, reg 5.

[37] CIC Regulations 2005, regs 2 ('asset-locked body'), 23. The definition of asset-locked body also includes equivalent bodies established outside the UK.

[38] Companies (AICE) Act 2004, s 30. These limits have changed several times, but as at January 2016, there was in effect an aggregate dividend cap of 35% of a company's distributable profits. There are also rules regarding the distribution of assets on winding up, the redemption of shares, and the reduction of share capital: see CIC Regulations 2005; Community Interest Company (Amendment) Regulations 2009, SI 2014/2483.

[39] ibid, schs 1–3, para 1(2)(a).

[40] ibid, schs 1–3, para 1(2)(b). The CIC Regulator's guidance on the asset lock does not specify what type of transfers it considers to be for the benefit of the community: CIC Regulator, *Chapter 6: The Asset Lock* (October 2014).

[41] CIC Regulations 2005, reg 23.

[42] CIC Regulator, *Chapter 6: The Asset Lock* (October 2014) s 6.1.5 ('payments to staff and directors must not be disproportionately high in relation to their abilities and the services they perform').

[43] HL Deb 8 January 2004, vol 657, col 277 (Lord Phillips of Sudbury).

'Social Innovation Council' with participants from the government, business and community sectors, and an associated governmental committee. Consultations were carried out on the proposed CIC model, and in March 2012 the Social Innovation Council published its final report, setting out a series of recommendations 'on how best to maximise social innovation in British Columbia'.[44]

The legislature had set the wheels in motion for the establishment of a new social enterprise vehicle even before the publication of the Council's report. On 5 March 2012 the government introduced a series of amendments to the British Columbia Business Corporations Act (BCBCA), which, like the Companies (AICE) Act 2004, would establish a new type of corporation to carry out social enterprise activities. 'CIC' was already a moniker used by the government of BC, so the government named the new corporate vehicle the community contribution company (or 'C3'). Bill 23, which contained the relevant amendments, was supported by both sides of the Legislative Assembly. Consequently, it passed third reading on 25 April 2012 with very little substantive debate.[45] In February 2013 an associated regulation was signed into law, fleshing out further details of the C3 regime.[46] The C3 has been available as a corporate vehicle in British Columbia since 29 July 2013, the date the legislation came into effect.

On the surface, British Columbia's new social enterprise model is very similar to the UK model on which it is based. Like the CIC, the C3 is subject to the general corporate law of its jurisdiction, but is distinguished from other companies by its obligation to carry out community purposes.[47] Like the CIC, the C3 is required to publicize its social enterprise status in its corporate name.[48] It must also produce a supplemental annual report, containing a fair and accurate description of the manner in which the company's activities have benefited society.[49] Finally, like the CIC, the C3 is subject to regulatory restrictions on the distribution of its assets. The BCBCA prohibits a C3 from transferring assets out of the company for less than fair market value, unless the transfer is to a charity or other 'qualified entity', is in furtherance of the company's community purposes, or is in accordance with the regulations.[50] At present, those regulations set an aggregate dividend cap of 40 per cent of the C3's profit for a financial year.[51] They also provide that where a C3 is dissolved, 60 per cent of the company's distributable assets must go to another asset-locked entity.[52]

[44] BC Social Innovation Council, 'Action Plan Recommendations to Maximize Social Innovation in British Columbia' (March 2012).

[45] British Columbia, Official Report of Debates of the Legislative Assembly, *Hansard*, 39th Parl, 4th Sess, No 34:2 (16 April 2012) 10656.

[46] Community Contribution Company Regulation (BC), Reg 63/2013 (C3 Regulation).

[47] BCBCA, s 51.92.

[48] ibid s 51.921.

[49] ibid s 51.96.

[50] ibid s 51.931.

[51] C3 Regulation, s 4(1)(a). A C3 may also bring forward any unused dividend amount for any previous financial year: s 4(1)(b).

[52] C3 Regulation, s 8.

However, the touted similarities between the CIC and C3 models may be less significant than the differences between them. These differences will become apparent in the ensuing sections, as we consider how doctrinal and procedural features of each model measure up against comparable features of the law of charities. A crucial distinction between the CIC and C3 regimes must be flagged at the outset: unlike the Companies (AICE) Act 2004, the BCBCA does not establish a C3 Regulator, nor does it assign to an existing regulator special responsibility for the supervision of C3s. We shall see in Section IV how this regulatory void affects the remedies that are available for a misuse of social enterprise property, and the range of persons with standing to invoke them. First, however, we shall examine the particular 'community benefit' standards that are incorporated into the CIC and C3 regimes, and consider what a comparison of these standards and the public benefit doctrine may reveal about the public–private equilibrium set by each jurisdiction's social enterprise law.

III. 'Community Benefit' and the Substantive Public Law–Private Law Divide

Charities, CICs and C3s are all subject to a general requirement that they benefit a section of the community. However, the parameters of each regime's requirement differ in significant ways. We have already seen that in order to be eligible for registration as a CIC, a company must satisfy the CIC Regulator that it will meet the community interest test set out in the Companies (AICE) Act 2004. A company satisfies the statutory test if 'a reasonable person might consider that its activities are being carried on for the benefit of the community or a section of the community'.[53] However, the Secretary of State is authorized to adjust this broad test by making regulations that treat certain activities as falling within or beyond its parameters.[54] To date, two rules have emerged from the exercise of this rule-making authority. First, political activities are not to be treated as activities carried on for the benefit of the community, unless they can reasonably be regarded as incidental to activities that otherwise meet the community interest test.[55] Second, activities are not to be treated as activities carried on for the benefit of the community if a reasonable person might consider the activities to benefit 'only the members of a particular body or the employees of a particular employer'.[56]

British Columbia's social enterprise regime imposes a different community benefit standard on companies that wish to be C3s. Pursuant to the amended BCBCA,

[53] Companies (AICE) Act 2004, s 35(2), (5).

[54] ibid s 35(4). Regulations relating to CICs must be approved by resolution of each House of Parliament: s 62(4).

[55] CIC Regulations 2005, reg 3.

[56] ibid reg 4.

at least one of the primary purposes of a C3 must be 'a community purpose'.[57] The Act defines a community purpose as 'a purpose beneficial to (a) society at large, or (b) a segment of society that is broader than the group of persons who are related to the C3', and specifies that the term 'includes, without limitation, a purpose of providing health, social, environmental, cultural, education or other services'.[58] The persons who are 'related' to a C3 are defined as its directors, officers, shareholders, associates and affiliates.[59] Like the Companies (AICE) Act 2004, the BCBCA also authorizes the Lieutenant Governor in Council to exclude identified purposes from the definition of community purpose by regulation.[60] As of March 2016, this regulatory authority had not been exercised.

How are we to evaluate these differing community benefit standards? I would suggest that we begin by situating them on the doctrinal map this book has begun to construct. The particular public law-private law composition of a hybrid legal rule, I have already suggested, is sometimes best discerned by comparing it to another legal rule, whose public or private nature is more readily identifiable. In Chapter 3 I applied this methodology to the public benefit doctrine, contrasting the rule that charities must be for the public benefit with the quintessentially public law principle that governments must act in the public interest. The two concepts were compared according to three criteria: the parameters of the community each rule required its subject to benefit, the identity of each rule's arbiter, and the nature of the interests that each concept allowed its subject to have and pursue. Applying these criteria to the CIC community interest test and the C3 community purpose standard is somewhat more difficult, both because the standards are in a nascent stage of development, and because the public benefit doctrine to which they are being compared is itself a hybrid rule. Nevertheless, by attempting to analyse the emerging community benefit standards according to these criteria, we may gain some preliminary insights into where each concept might 'sit' on a map oriented around the public law–private law divide.

A. The Parameters of the Benefiting Community

A first way we can compare the particular 'community benefit' rules that apply to charities, CICs and C3s is to consider the parameters of the community that each rule requires its subject to take into account. Unlike government, we saw in Chapter 3, charities are not generally required to consider the interests or needs of the whole political community; the 'public' that they must benefit is an amorphous group of persons, bounded by a number of negative criteria or rules. These rules stipulate, in the main, that the benefiting community must be a

[57] BCBCA, s 51.92.
[58] BCBCA, s 51.91(1) 'community purpose'.
[59] ibid s 51.91(2).
[60] ibid s 51.91(1) 'community purpose'; s 432(9.1).

human community, and that it must not be defined by a relational nexus with any particular person or employer. In England and Wales, they also stipulate that the benefiting community must not be defined in a manner inconsistent with modern equality norms, and that it must not explicitly exclude the poor.

The CIC community interest test is very similar to the public benefit doctrine in this respect. The Companies (AICE) Act 2004 broadly tracks the language of the common law of charities in its stipulation that a CIC must benefit 'the community or a section of the community', while the regulations specify that the benefiting community must not be defined according to a relational nexus with a particular body or employer.[61] Given that 'community benefit' is a statutory concept that is subject to the ECHR, it is also safe to assume that charities and CICs are subject to similar restrictions with regard to defining their benefiting communities according to a protected personal characteristic. Unlike English charities, CICs are not prohibited from excluding the poor by the terms of their governing instruments. Apart from the absence of any reference to the poor, however, the 'community' that CICs must benefit looks very much like the 'public' that charities must benefit; each doctrine limits the autonomy of individuals to define their benevolent projects in a substantially similar manner.

If the CIC community interest rule largely mirrors the public benefit doctrine in its definition of the benefiting community, British Columbia's community purpose standard moves in quite a different direction. The BCBCA does not invoke the language of the law of charities in defining the community that C3s must benefit; instead, it specifies that a community purpose may benefit *any* segment of society 'that is broader than the group of persons who are related to the C3'.[62] Based on this definition and the broader statutory environment in which C3s will operate, there appear to be only two limitations on the ability of a C3 to define its own benefiting community. First, under the British Columbia Human Rights Code, it will be impermissible in most cases for a C3 to define its community of beneficiaries according to their race, sex or creed.[63] Second, C3s, like charities and CICs, are subject to a 'relational nexus' prohibition. However, the ambit of British Columbia's relational nexus prohibition is far narrower than that of its counterparts: its only effect is to prohibit a C3 from providing benefits *solely* to its directors, officers, shareholders, associates and affiliates.

Unlike a charity or a CIC, then, a C3 *may* benefit the employees of a particular employer, or the family members of its directors and officers. It may also benefit its own officers and associates without breaching the community purpose rule. The community purpose concept, in sum, places great value on the autonomy of individuals to define what type of benefit their social enterprise will provide and what community will benefit from their project. By contrast, it displays little

[61] CIC Regulations 2005, reg 4.
[62] BCBCA, s 51.91(1) ('community purpose').
[63] Human Rights Code, RSBC 1996, c 210, s 8.

commitment *either* to ensuring that social enterprise meets the needs of the whole community *or* to protecting the social enterprise sector from self-regarding acts. In relation to both the continuum between altruistic and self-regarding projects, and the continuum between public-welfare-compliant and public-welfare-deviant projects, the C3 community purpose standard inclines markedly towards private law thought.

B. The Nature of the Arbiter

The CIC and C3 community benefit concepts can also be compared to the public benefit doctrine in terms of the identity of each concept's arbiter. We have already seen that the issue of 'who decides' what is in the interests of a community is an important issue, which has ramifications for the substance of the concept itself. The fact that the courts, rather than the political authorities, determine what is 'for the public benefit' within the law of charities, for example, means that the public benefit concept is more stable and less tied to public consensus than the concept of the public interest that government must pursue.

Who, then, are the arbiters of community benefit under the CIC and C3 regimes, and what nature of community benefit concepts are they likely to produce? Under the Companies (AICE) Act 2004, the CIC Regulator is the primary arbiter of the statutory 'community interest' test. The CIC Regulator assesses community benefit at the registration stage on the basis of a company's objects[64] and a prescribed community interest statement, which declares that the activities of the company will benefit the community, and explains how they will do so.[65] According to the regulator's published guidance, it is not necessary that each activity carried on by a CIC be directly beneficial to the community, but 'everything that a CIC does should in some sense contribute towards achieving a purpose that is beneficial to the community'.[66] If the CIC Regulator decides a company does not meet the community interest test (and the office has, to date, rejected a number of applications for CIC status)[67] the company may appeal that decision to an Appeal Officer also appointed by the Secretary of State.[68] As of March 2016, however, no company had exercised that right.[69]

The CIC Regulator is developing an institutional approach to the community interest test by applying statutory criteria to the individual cases before her. Given the similarities between these criteria and the public benefit doctrine, it seems

[64] An object stated in a company's articles is a community interest object if 'a reasonable person might consider that the carrying on of activities by the company in furtherance of the object is for the benefit of the community': Companies (AICE) Act 2004, s 35(3).

[65] CIC Regulations 2005, regs 11, 12, and 2 ('community interest statement').

[66] CIC Regulator, *Chapter 4: Creating a CIC* (April 2013) [4.6].

[67] Email from cicregulator@companieshouse.gov.uk to author (9 November 2012).

[68] Companies (AICE) Act 2004, ss 36B(3), 38A(5).

[69] Email from cicregulator@companieshouse.gov.uk to author (1 March 2016).

likely that the manner in which the CIC Regulator assesses community benefit is, and will remain, similar to the manner in which the Charity Commission assesses public benefit. Certain procedural features of the CIC regime are nonetheless likely to distinguish the community interest concept from its public benefit cousin. First, unlike the Charity Commission, which has a policy of publishing its decisions to accept or reject an application for charitable status where the decision is novel or significant,[70] the CIC Regulator does not publish its reasons for granting or refusing to grant a company CIC status.[71] This makes it impossible for the public to discern exactly how the community interest test is being applied. Second, unlike the Charities Act 2011, the Companies (AICE) Act 2004 does not provide for an appeal from the decisions of the CIC Appeal Officer to the courts. It seems inevitable, in these circumstances, that the CIC community interest concept will continue to be somewhat less predictable and less transparent than its English charity law counterpart.

While the distinctions between the designated community benefit arbiters under English charity law and social enterprise law are significant, they pale in the face of the very different adjudication mechanism envisioned for British Columbia's C3 regime. We have seen that the BCBCA does not establish a C3 Regulator, nor does it assign to any statutory officer the responsibility of determining whether a company's objects meet the community purpose test. Instead, the BCBCA allows C3s to 'self-select', defining a C3 as any company that declares in its notice of articles that it 'is a community contribution company and, as such, has purposes beneficial to society'.[72] Significantly, this provision allows companies to fashion *themselves* the primary arbiters of what purposes and activities are beneficial to the community within the meaning of the statute. We shall examine who can contest or seek a remedy of such a decision in the next section. On its face, however, the policy of making applicant companies the sole arbiters of the community purpose concept supports the view that the C3 regime maximizes the individual autonomy of property owners, but does little to recognize or protect competing public interests in the use of social enterprise property.

C. The Nature of the Company's Interests

A final way to compare the CIC and C3 community benefit concepts with the public benefit doctrine is by considering the kinds of interests that each concept allows its subject to have and pursue. In Chapter 3 we identified three kinds

[70] Charity Commission, 'Charity Commission reports, decisions, alerts and statements' (3 September 2013), www.gov.uk/government/collections/charity-commission-reports-decisions-alerts-and-statements.

[71] Email from cicregulator@companieshouse.gov.uk to author (9 November 2012).

[72] BCBCA, s 51.911. The Act also anticipates that future regulations may authorize a C3 to delete its declaration of C3 status under certain conditions: see BCBCA, s 51.911(2).

of interests that may be distinguished in discussions of the public law duties of government: the public interest, individual self-regarding interests and individual other-regarding interests. The rule that government must act in the public interest, the chapter concluded, precludes government from having or pursuing *any* individual interests. The public benefit doctrine, on the other hand, only precludes charities from having *individual self-regarding* interests; charities can and do have *individual other-regarding* interests, although the public benefit rule imposes certain constraints on their ability to define and pursue them.

It has always been a premise of the CIC regime that CICs should be allowed to pursue certain 'self-regarding' activities, to the extent of issuing shares and debt instruments to investors with a limited nominal return.[73] However, the Companies (AICE) Act 2004 requires CICs to carry out these activities within a generally other-regarding framework. As applied by the CIC Regulator, the community interest test requires that all of a CIC's activities 'in some sense benefit the community'.[74] While the standard may be less stringent than that applicable to charities, it would appear, at the least, to preclude CICs from having individual self-regarding objects. British Columbia's social enterprise regime, on the other hand, permits C3s to have and pursue a wide range of self-regarding objects. The BCBCA requires only that *one* of the principal purposes of a C3 be a community purpose, and that community purpose may benefit the company's directors, officers and shareholders, provided it does not benefit them *exclusively*.[75] The shift away from the protection of altruism in British Columbia's social enterprise legislation is striking, and distinguishes the C3 sharply from its counterpart in the UK. It allows us to conclude that while the CIC community interest rule is only a slightly less public-leaning hybrid than the public benefit doctrine, the C3 community purpose standard is primarily a manifestation of the values and impulses of private law.

IV. Social Enterprise Standing Rules and the Procedural Public Law–Private Law Divide

A second point of comparison between the law of charities and the emergent social enterprise regimes arises from a consideration of the remedies available for the misuse of property held by a CIC or C3, and the standing rules limiting entitlement to those remedies. As we saw in Chapter 4, the common law's historical approach to standing in the charities context, despite exhibiting certain private law-leaning tendencies, generally aligned with the common law's historical

[73] *Private Action, Public Benefit*, 54.
[74] CIC Regulator, *Chapter 4: Creating a CIC* (April 2013) [4.6].
[75] BCBCA, s 51.92.

approach to standing in paradigmatic public law contexts. The effect of this alignment was to suggest that misuses of charity property were first and foremost a matter of collective concern. This alignment has decreased somewhat over time; the contemporary Charity Commission regime has increasingly focused on personal and associational standing, while the core disciplines of public law have shifted towards the expansion of rights to sue in the public interest. The result, as Chapter 4 argued, is that the standing rules governing relief for misuses of charity property continue to be marked by a public–private *hybridity*, which communicates mixed messages about whether the proper administration of charity property is a matter of collective or individual concern. The purpose of the present inquiry is to consider whether the CIC and C3 regimes approach the question of who should be entitled to sue for a misuse of social enterprise property in a similar way.

A. Standing Under the CIC Regime

There are three principal categories of remedial procedures available to address misuses of CIC property in the UK. The first of these categories consists of corporate remedies of general application. The Companies Act 2006 (UK), which sets out the general corporate law regime governing CICs, establishes two principal procedures through which persons can seek relief for a misuse of corporate property. The first, the derivative action, entitles an authorized complainant to bring a claim on behalf of a company, seeking relief in respect of a cause of action involving negligence, default, breach of duty or breach of trust by a director of the company.[76] The second, the unfair prejudice action, entitles an authorized complainant to seek a remedial order from the court on the ground that a company's affairs are being or have been conducted in a manner that is unfairly prejudicial to the interests of the members.[77] Together, these corporate actions would seem to open the door to a wide range of judicial remedies for the misuse of property by a CIC.[78] However, each action is limited by its rules of standing: only a member or shareholder of a CIC (or, in special cases, the Secretary of State)[79] may seek relief for a misuse of corporate property under the relevant provisions of the Companies Act 2006.

In addition to these general corporate remedies, the Companies (AICE) Act 2004 establishes both regulatory and judicial remedies that are specific to the CIC. With regard to the former category, the Act authorizes the CIC Regulator to

[76] Companies Act 2006 (UK) s 260.

[77] ibid s 994.

[78] See, for example, Companies Act 2006, s 996 (If the court believes the petition is well founded, it may make such order as it thinks fit, including an order regulating the conduct of the companies affairs in the future).

[79] Companies Act 2006, s 995.

exercise a variety of supervisory and remedial powers in cases where the 'company default condition' is met. This condition is satisfied, according to section 41, where the CIC Regulator believes it is necessary to exercise a power because there has been 'misconduct or mismanagement in the administration of a CIC', or there is a need to 'secure the proper application of [CIC] property'.[80] In such circumstances, the CIC Regulator may investigate the affairs of a CIC, or appoint a third party to carry out the investigation on her behalf.[81] She may order the audit of a CIC's annual accounts,[82] appoint, suspend or remove CIC directors,[83] or appoint a manager to take temporary control of a CIC's property and affairs.[84] Where the company default condition is met, the CIC Regulator is also authorized to vest CIC property in an Official Property Holder that she has appointed, and to restrict the transactions and payments that a CIC may complete.[85] Arguably, these powers are only slightly less extensive than the Charity Commission's powers to act for the protection of charities.[86]

However, at least two points differentiate the CIC regime of regulatory remedies from that of the Charities Act 2011. First, despite the extensive remedial powers that the officer enjoys, the CIC Regulator was always intended to be a 'lighter-touch' regulator than the Charity Commission.[87] This intention is manifested in section 41(1) of the Companies (AICE) Act 2004, which provides that in deciding whether and how to exercise her supervisory powers, the CIC Regulator 'must adopt an approach which is based on the principle that those powers should be exercised only to the extent necessary to maintain confidence in CICs'.[88] The CIC Regulators that have been appointed to date appear to have taken this 'light-touch' mandate seriously: as of March 2016, the CIC Regulator had instructed the Companies Investigations Team to carry out certain investigations on her behalf, but had not directly exercised her extensive enforcement powers.[89]

Second, different rules of standing apply to exercises of the CIC Regulator's remedial powers. As we have seen, under the Charities Act 2011, either the Attorney General, a majority of a charity's trustees, or, in the case of a small charity, 'any person interested in a charity' may apply for an exercise of the Commission's jurisdiction to establish a scheme, appoint or remove trustees, or transfer

80 Companies (AICE) Act 2004, s 41(3).
81 ibid, s 42.
82 ibid, s 43(1).
83 ibid, ss 45, 46.
84 ibid s 47.
85 ibid ss 29, 48.
86 Charities Act 2011, ss 69–87. While the CIC Regulator does not officially have 'scheme-making' powers, she is authorized to 'give directions' in circumstances where CIC property has been vested in the Official Property Holder: see Companies (AICE) Act 2004, s 48(7).
87 HL Deb 8 January 2004, vol 657, col 262 (Lord Sainsbury of Turnville).
88 Companies (AICE) Act 2004, s 41(1). See also s 27(4), stating that the CIC Regulator must adopt an approach to its functions that has regard to, among other things, the outcome of consultations with CICs.
89 Email from cicregulator@companieshouse.gov.uk to author (1 March 2016).

charity property.[90] Under the Companies (AICE) Act 2004, however, no person has a legal entitlement to request that the CIC Regulator address misconduct or mismanagement in the administration of a CIC. If the CIC Regulator continues to take her 'light-touch' mandate seriously, in other words, there does not appear to be another person who could compel her to intervene.

The Companies (AICE) Act 2004 establishes a final, CIC-specific judicial remedy for the misuse of CIC property by authorizing the CIC Regulator to bring civil proceedings 'in the name and on behalf of a CIC'.[91] According to the Explanatory Notes to this provision, Parliament intended that the CIC Regulator would exercise this power to bring a 'derivative action' on behalf of a CIC in situations where it would be 'in the interests of the CIC or the community' to do so.[92] To date, the CIC Regulator has not invoked this power.[93] Nevertheless, it is evident that the designation of a public official with responsibility for initiating litigation on behalf of the community in respect of the misuse of CIC property aligns the CIC regime to some extent with the regime for the protection of charity property by the Attorney General. Moreover, like the common law charities tradition, the CIC regime applies special rules to proceedings by its representative officer. Unlike an ordinary litigant in a derivative action, the CIC Regulator is not required to establish a prima facie case in order to continue her claim against a CIC's directors.[94] And she is subject to special rules on costs: the CIC Regulator must indemnify a CIC against any expenses it incurs as a result of a section 44 action, but in return any costs awarded to the company are to be paid to the CIC Regulator.[95] In other words, section 44 does more than simply extend the standing rules generally applicable to derivative actions; it creates a procedure for the protection of CIC property in which the CIC Regulator is the unique and privileged litigant. In so doing, it suggests that the proper administration of social enterprise property is at least partially a matter of general concern.

B. Standing Under the C3 Regime

We have seen that in contrast to the Companies (AICE) Act 2004, the BCBCA does not establish a C3 Regulator. The Act also does not create any specific judicial remedies for the misuse of property held by a C3. Where a person wishes to seek relief for a misuse of non-charitable social enterprise property in British Columbia, therefore, he or she must have resort to the general remedial procedures available to all corporations in the province.

[90] CA 2011, s 70(2), (3).

[91] Companies (AICE) Act 2004, s 44.

[92] Explanatory Notes to the Companies (AICE) Act 2004, 244.

[93] Email from cicregulator@companieshouse.gov.uk to author (1 March 2016).

[94] cf Companies Act 2006 (UK) s 261. Instead, s 44 places the onus on the directors to apply for an order that the proceedings be discontinued: Companies (AICE) Act 2004, s 44(3).

[95] Companies (AICE) Act 2004, s 44(6), (7).

The substance of the two most common of these procedures—the derivative action[96] and the oppression action[97]—largely emulates the substance of the derivative action and the unfair prejudice action established under the Companies Act 2006 (UK). However, the rules of standing applicable to the British Columbia actions are notably broader. Under the BCBCA, the 'complainants' that have standing to bring a derivative action include any one of a company's directors, and any other person whom the court considers an 'appropriate person' to make the application.[98] The BCBCA also authorizes a court to grant discretionary standing in the context of an oppression action, extending a right of *locus standi* to 'any … person whom the court considers to be an appropriate person to [bring an oppression claim]'.[99] It is therefore at least theoretically possible that an 'unrelated' person could seek relief for the misuse of property held by a C3 on the basis of a public interest in the proper use of that property.

The short list of remedies available to address the misuse of C3 property, together with the absence of cases applying those remedies in a social enterprise context, provide a rather thin foundation for assessing the relationship between the C3 rules of standing and the procedural public law–private law divide. Two observations may nonetheless be made. The first is that a wide range of persons might *potentially* be granted personal, associational or public interest standing to seek relief for misuses of social enterprise property in British Columbia. This would be contingent on a compelling argument being made for the creative use of the court's discretion to grant standing to appropriate persons under the province's general corporate law regime. The second is that the C3 regime itself creates no specific remedies for the misuse of social enterprise property. Each of these observations admittedly communicates a somewhat different message about the 'public law-leaning' or 'private law-leaning' tendency of the C3's procedural regime. However, both observations clearly demonstrate that the BCBCA regime treats the property of C3s in precisely the same way as other corporate property in British Columbia. To this extent, at least, the standing rules applicable to actions for the misuse of C3 property suggest that British Columbia does not consider the protection of non-charitable social enterprise property to be a matter of general concern.

V. Conclusion

In light of the increasing number of public law pressures being exerted on the charitable sector, and the manner in which these pressures are limiting the ability

96 BCBCA, s 232(2).

97 ibid s 227(2). Unlike the Saskatchewan Non-Profit Corporations Act that was discussed in Ch 4, the BCBCA's oppression remedy is not specifically designed to address acts 'that are oppressive to or unfairly disregard the interests of the public generally'.

98 BCBCA, s 232(1).

99 ibid s 227(1).

of charity founders and managers to improve the world as they please, it is unsurprising to be witnessing a search for *new* hybrid vehicles, which place heightened value on the ability of individuals to change the world in accordance with their own particular vision. To the extent that benevolent property-owners view the law of charities as providing insufficient protection to their autonomy interests, it is likely that they will continue to shift their attention—and their resources—from charities to post-charitable legal forms that strike a different balance between individual and collective project pursuit.

The social enterprise vehicles that I have examined in this chapter represent but two of these post-charitable forms. I have argued that the CIC and the C3, together with their associated regulatory regimes, can be understood as alternative hybrid compositions of public law and private law elements for the pursuit of benevolent projects. I have also sought to highlight that each of these hybrid compositions departs to a very different extent from the particular public law–private law equilibrium established by the law of charities. Part two of the Companies (AICE) Act 2004 reflects the basic structure and commitments of English charity law, altering the balance between its various public and private elements only in degree. While the regime is premised on CICs being allowed to distribute a limited percentage of their assets to investors, the statute's community interest test requires CICs to pursue other-regarding interests. Further, it grants them only slightly more autonomy than charities to define what benefit they will provide, and what community will receive that benefit. And while the demonstrated impulse of the CIC Regulator is to implement a much lighter-touch regulatory regime than the Charity Commission, the remedies available for a misuse of CIC property—and the standing rights that are attached to those remedies—suggest that the British public does have an interest in non-charitable social enterprise property.

Considered from this standpoint, British Columbia's new C3 regime reflects a strikingly different vision of how the equilibrium between individual and collective project pursuit should be set in the social enterprise sphere. Like CICs and charities, C3s are being marketed as institutions that will benefit the community. Indeed, at a certain level they are required to do so. However, the BCBCA only requires a C3 to be other-regarding to *one* of its primary purposes, and even in respect of this 'community purpose' the C3 is only required to benefit a group that is broader than its own owners, managers and affiliates. What types of purposes are beneficial to society under the C3 regime? That is for the companies themselves to decide. The BCBCA neither establishes a social enterprise regulator, nor assigns to an existing officer the function of monitoring the creation or administration of C3s. The absence of any specific remedies for the misapplication of C3 property only reinforces the message that the British Columbia public has no special interest in 'social enterprise' property. If the CIC regime has made 'adjustments' to the functional equilibrium set by the law of charities, the C3 regime is situated firmly towards the private law pole.

The principal object of this chapter has been to bring my central claims regarding the public law–private law hybridity of the law of charities into sharper focus by comparing and contrasting key features of two newly emergent social enterprise regimes with 'parallel' features of charity law. I have suggested that there are indeed significant (if varying) contrasts between the legal regulation of charities and that of social enterprise with regard to the various public law–private law continuums that have been envisaged in this work. This conclusion places us in a favourable position to resume the book's central arguments, and to draw together some concluding reflections on this work as a whole.

8

Conclusion

This book has sought to describe and analyse various aspects of the law of charities in terms of their relationship with the public law–private law divide. The primary goal has been to improve our doctrinal 'map' of the law of charities by plotting the particular ways in which the common law charities tradition, and two modern regimes of charity regulation, partake of the contested spheres of public law and private law. In constructing this doctrinal map, the book has also sought to contribute to the development of a useful normative discourse about the manner in which charities are regulated, and the merit of specific charity law rules.

People mean different things when they talk about the distinction between public law and private law. As a result, it has been necessary to adopt a working account of the public law–private law divide to be applied in service of the book's mapping and evaluative goals. The principal tenets of this project-based account, which were set out in the introductory chapter, may be briefly restated as follows. There is an operational distinction between public law and private law, which, despite its limited descriptive capacity, is integral to law's self-understanding in much of the common law world. This operational distinction is underlain by a *normative* public law–private law divide, which is based on the value that private law and public law respectively accord to the pursuit of individual and collective projects. Private law is the law of *individual* project pursuit; it is concerned to protect the autonomy of individuals to formulate their own projects without regard to the value or disvalue that others place on those projects. Public law is the law of *collective* project pursuit; it is concerned to protect the ability of the political community to determine the overall character of our society. There is a deep tension between these two legal realms, which is mirrored in the tension that the law of charities experiences between the goal of enabling property owners to improve the world in accordance with their individual vision, and the goal of limiting that ability to ensure conformity with a collective ideal of the good.

Generally speaking, the law treats individual and collective projects in a manner that reflects the respective normative commitments of private law and public law. The law's impulse is to regulate individual projects minimally, so as to maximize the individual project pursuer's autonomy and his or her capacity for creativity and innovation. The law's impulse is to regulate collective projects more intensively, with a dual view to protecting whatever *specific* public interest the collective project is understood to raise, and to protecting a perceived *general* public interest in having certain entities model 'public virtues' for the benefit of the collectivity. This spectrum of public law and private law impulses exists in multiple legal dimensions, and can be explored in (at least) institutional, substantive, procedural and functional terms. The public law–private law hybrid occurs at a point on any of these spectrums where the two sets of regulatory impulses bear down with comparable force on a set of rules or institutional arrangements.

The question of charity law's relationship with the public law–private law divide may therefore be broadly reframed as a question about the extent to which the law treats charitable projects as individual projects, and the extent to which it treats them as collective ones. Once we begin mapping in more detail, however, it becomes evident that there are in fact multiple 'public–private' continuums along which the equilibrium of the law of charities is continuously set. This book has identified four. The first is a continuum between wholly altruistic projects and wholly self-regarding projects. The second is a continuum between projects that have no cognizable owner and projects that do. The third is a continuum between projects that are a matter of general concern and projects that are a matter of individual concern. The fourth is a continuum between projects which are fully aligned to the public welfare goals of the state or polity in question, and projects which, although altruistic, are nevertheless at variance with those public welfare goals—what I have called public-welfare-compliant projects and public-welfare-deviant projects.

In applying this project-based account of the public law–private law divide to the common law charities tradition and two modern regimes of charity regulation, the book has made a number of analytical claims. The first is that despite the common association of the law of charitable trusts with the private law sphere, it is appropriate to regard the common law charities tradition, in a general or categorical sense, as a true *hybrid* of public law and private law. The charitable trust is a public law–private law hybrid in the general sense that it represents the adaptation of a private law institution to a variant that is more of a public law nature. While the trust was specifically designed to enhance the autonomy of property-owning individuals to formulate and carry out their own projects, the *charitable* trust was an adaptation of this institution, whose development reflected the perceived public interest in the devotion of property to charitable purposes. The charitable corporation, an entity whose role in the common law tradition has historically been underplayed, was a very different type of hybrid, whose public element stemmed in large part from the use of the Royal Prerogative to constitute such corporations. Nevertheless, each of these charitable forms partook in significant ways of the traditions of public law and private law. The common law of charities thus became infused with a number of public law characteristics, chief among which was the 'constitutional' role that the Crown and the Court of Chancery played in ensuring the proper administration of these institutions. The Crown and the courts took their responsibility as the public guardians of charity seriously, while also seeking to protect the interests of donors in controlling and directing their own wealth. In this sense, the common law of charities can be seen to have accorded comparable importance to the autonomy interests of benevolent property owners, and to the public interest in properly and effectively administered charity property.

My second analytical claim has been that within this framework of general hybridity, charities also function and are regulated as public law–private law hybrids in a *context-specific* or *functional* sense. By this I mean that within particular regulatory contexts, both the conditions for obtaining charitable status, and the regulation of the conduct of charities and their trustees, are continually being adjusted in such a way as to maintain in a broad sense a functional equilibrium between individual and collective project pursuit. These equilibrium adjustments occur within the law's substantive dimension, manifesting themselves in the detailed working out of the definition of charity, the laws regulating the conduct of charity trustees, and particularly the public benefit doctrine. They also occur within the very regulatory institutions and procedures that carry these substantive equilibrium adjustments out. Every regime of charity regulation embodies a unique constellation of public and private interests. However, I have claimed that it is possible and useful to identify a general dichotomy between 'civil' and 'tax-based' regimes of charity regulation, based on the fundamental public interest that each regulator is mandated to protect. A civil regime of charity regulation, in my account, is one in which decisions about the status and regulation of charities are made independently of the tax consequences that attach to that status. A tax-based regime of charity regulation is one in which decisions about the status and regulation of charities are embedded within a general framework of tax administration.

The balance of the book has been concerned to map some of the context-specific ways in which the 'civil' English Charity Commission regime and the 'tax-based' Canadian registered charity regime have balanced competing public and private interests related to the administration of charitable resources. I have sought to identify both the particular public interests that each regime seeks to promote, and the particular 'equilibrium' that each has achieved. I have not attempted to comprehensively analyse either regulatory regime. Rather, I have pursued these goals by applying the public law–private law 'lens' to an eclectic set of charity law issues, which (it is hoped) have shed some light on my analytical and comparative claims.

The principal conclusions of this exercise are these. In developing a statutory regime for the regulation of charities in the nineteenth century, English law maintained the common law's duality of focus on the autonomy interests of benevolent property-owners, and the public interest in properly and effectively administered charity property. These interests were in constant tension: the charity law reformers sought to protect the public's interest better than the Court of Chancery had done, while powerful charitable institutions and philanthropists pushed back. The contemporary Charity Commission regime continues to balance these two values. However, successive iterations of the Charities Act have increasingly oriented the Charity Commission towards intervening to protect the public interest in charity property, even if the funding of the regulator has not kept pace. As a result, the civil model of charity regulation that is enshrined in the Charities Act 2011 may broadly be characterized as a 'public law-leaning hybrid' model, which seeks to protect the public's interest in charity property more effectively than was accomplished in Chancery, but nonetheless remains modelled in the image of the common law.

Turning from this high-level overview of the Charity Commission regime to our selection of illustrative charity law features, we have examined one of the central hinges upon which turns the whole notion of charity law's public law–private law hybridity. The common law rule that a charity must be 'for the public benefit' is a prime example of a hybrid legal doctrine, I argued in Chapter 3, in the sense that it does not have a single or even primary site of belonging within either the public law or private law sphere. The common law public benefit doctrine has always required charities to be mostly other-regarding, and embodies public law thinking to this extent. However, it provides benevolent property owners with considerable autonomy to define what type of benefit their project will provide, and what public will receive that benefit. It treats charitable projects as *altruistic* but largely *public-welfare-neutral* projects, and is a public law–private law hybrid in that sense.

The well-known conflict that has surrounded the operation of the English public benefit criterion since the enactment of the Charities Act 2006 has provided us with a unique opportunity to study the tensions inherent in a legal doctrine that occupies the border zone between public law and private law. The UK Parliament introduced somewhat ambiguous public benefit provisions into the Charities Act 2006, and then assigned to the Charity Commission the task of elucidating and operationalizing these provisions. The Commission responded to this challenge by shifting the traditional equilibrium of the public benefit doctrine, restricting the autonomy of benevolent property owners to define the terms of their charitable projects in two significant ways. The first shift, which limited the autonomy of charities whose projects were targeted at persons sharing a protected personal characteristic under human rights law, was affirmed by Parliament and by the courts. However, the second shift, which limited the autonomy of charities whose projects were targeted at the 'well-off', met a more equivocal judicial response. *Independent Schools Council* can itself be regarded as a hybrid legal decision, which seeks, somewhat unsuccessfully, to reconcile competing public law and private law values that are not entirely reciprocal. In operation, however, *Independent Schools Council* has led to a significant pulling back of the Commission's public law-oriented position, and a readjustment of public benefit's functional equilibrium towards the private law pole.

The substantive doctrines of the law of charities are of little value without attendant remedies, and competent persons to enforce them. Thus, Chapter 4 sought to apply the book's public law–private law lens to a *procedural* element of the law of charities: the rules of *locus standi* that determine who can seek relief for the misadministration of charity property. The quintessential 'private law' and 'public law' approaches to the question of who can sue, I have claimed, can be distinguished on two grounds: private law integrates the question into its causes of action and grants standing on the basis of the plaintiff's rights and interests, while public law considers the question separately and grants standing as a matter of discretion on the basis of a variety of factors. The common law's historical approach to standing in charity matters exhibited certain private law-leaning tendencies, but substantially aligned charity law with the historical approach to standing in judicial review. While the courts occasionally permitted individuals to bring charity proceedings where they had an ownership interest related to charity property, it was the chief law officer of the Crown who was entitled and expected to initiate charity proceedings on behalf of the public. Because the Attorney General rarely proceeded without a relator who assumed responsibility for the costs, the practical effect of this procedure was to restrict in great measure the notionally 'unlimited' charities jurisdiction of the superior courts. Nevertheless, the Crown's historical role as the constitutional defender of charity property communicated a powerful symbolic message that charity property was *valuable* property, and its administration a matter of general concern.

The Crown's effective monopoly over charity proceedings in England and Wales has long since come to an end. The Charities Act 2011 establishes a number of different remedies for misuses of charity property, some of which the Charity Commission can invoke of its own motion, and some of which can be invoked by trustees or persons with a 'greater-than-public' interest in the charity. Stepping back from this picture, we have identified both public law-leaning and private law-leaning adjustments being made to the common law approach. On the one hand, the question of who can sue a charity in England and Wales continues to be decided separately from the merits of the claim, with the courts increasingly treating standing as a 'practical rule of justice' affording the court discretion in each case. On the other hand, the categories of personal and associational standing have been expanded, while the Act continues to deny standing to persons with a merely public interest in a charity. This departure from the general public law trend towards granting individuals public interest standing is a *private law-leaning* departure, which the courts have specifically defended as a way of protecting charity trustees from the taxing procedures of judicial review. The combination of these public law-leaning and private law-leaning tendencies has allowed us to conclude that the rules of *locus standi* in English charity law remain marked by a public law–private law hybridity.

The institutional, substantive and procedural features of English charity law that have been examined in this book are paralleled, to varying extents, in other civil regulatory regimes. However, I have argued that a very different type of public law–private law hybridity inheres in a tax-based regime of charity regulation. Chapter 5 explored this claim by reference to Canada's primary regime of charity regulation, the 'registered charity regime' that is administered by the Charities Directorate of the CRA. Unlike the Charity Commission regime, Canada's primary regime of charity regulation was not designed to improve the protection of charity property, but rather to prevent charities and donors from abusing the fiscal privileges of charitable status to the detriment of other Canadian taxpayers. Embedded in Canada's federal system of tax administration, and limited by the fact that primary legislative authority over charities lies with the provinces, the registered charity regime incorporates some of the doctrines of the common law charities tradition, but few if any of its procedures and institutions. I have argued that like the Charity Commission, the Directorate has increasingly become oriented towards intervening in the affairs of charities to protect a public interest, and may broadly be characterized as a 'public-leaning hybrid' in this sense. However, the public interest that the Directorate aims to protect is not a public interest in properly and effectively administered charity property. Rather, it is a public interest in the integrity of the tax base.

The defining features of Canada's tax-based charity regulator—its orientation towards protecting the fisc, its lack of a charity-specific mandate, and its status as the agent of an elected Cabinet Minister—reverberate throughout the substantive and procedural dimensions of Canadian charity law. Substantively, we have seen that in a context where the regulator's primary public concern is to protect the integrity of the tax base, public benefit plays a subsidiary role, and legal tools with more direct fiscal consequences tend to be relied upon to monitor the altruistic quality of charitable projects. At the registration stage, where public benefit arguably plays a more prominent role, there is evidence of a regulatory effort to use the criterion to align the projects of registered charities more closely with the public welfare goals of the state. The tax-based nature of Canada's regulatory regime also has procedural repercussions: no private individual has standing to seek relief for the misadministration of charity property under the registered charity regime, while opportunities to seek relief outside the regime are limited. These and other differences between English and Canadian charity law support the book's claim that the public law–private law hybridity that inheres in any modern regime of charity regulation must be regarded as context specific. They also highlight the extent to which the law of charities is no longer 'common' to the common law world.

Despite their major differences and their public-leaning tendencies, I have claimed that the Charity Commission and registered charity regimes, and their associated public benefit doctrines and rules of *locus standi*, are generally consistent with the claim that charity law has achieved a long-term, functional equilibrium between the protection of the autonomy of property-owning individuals to control and direct their own wealth, and the furtherance of competing public interests. However, this characterization of the law of charities as a 'hybrid' legal discipline, perfectly suspended between the competing domains of public and private law, is jarringly discordant with the current swell of opinion lamenting the increasing use of charities as instruments of government welfare policy, and warning of the dangers associated with this trend. In response to this growing consensus, I have sought in Chapter 6 to advance a theoretical contrast between 'independent' and 'co-opted' charities, and to identify certain legal and institutional mechanisms in England and Wales and Canada that may either encourage or limit the governmental co-optation of charitable resources.

This exploration of modern mechanisms of co-optation in the charitable sector has yielded a number of interesting comparative conclusions. With regard to the first identified co-optative mechanism—the exertion of government influence over the legal definition of charity—we have seen that the common law definition was anchored to a specific legislative agenda at a very early stage, ensuring that there would always be a good deal of alignment between charitable and governmental visions of the good. The precise degree of this alignment has vacillated over time, with courts, then charity regulators, continually adjusting the precise level of separation between charitable and government functions. With the enactment of a statutory definition of charity in the Charities Act 2006, the UK Parliament has reasserted its perennial power to direct charitable resources to objects of its own choosing. However, it is the Canadian government that has the greatest capacity for ongoing political influence over the definition of charity, since its charity regulator, a ministerial government agency, interprets and applies the common law concept of charity with very little in the way of oversight, guidelines or constraints.

There are other mechanisms through which government can bring charitable resources under its effective direction and control. One of these is the creation of statutory charities, with legislated charitable objects and governance rules. Historically, the sovereign could effectively place these charities outside of the supervisory authority of the courts, and thus maintain a high level of control over their charitable resources. While statutory charities still play an important role in the charitable sector, the Charity Commission regime limits the UK government's ability to control them, both by operationalizing the common law's prohibition of pro-government political purposes, and by requiring that *all* charities be subject to the controlling power of the courts. The Canadian registered charity regime is silent on this issue, by contrast, and includes on its register institutions that the Supreme Court of Canada has described as 'part of the apparatus of the government both in form and in fact'.

This book has explored a final mechanism of governmental co-optation of charitable resources, which is particularly relevant in the present day. Charities, I have suggested, are today experiencing unprecedented levels of government influence through the negotiation and implementation of service delivery agreements, and the appointment of government authority trustees. The considerable pressures that charities face within this 'contract culture' to align themselves with the policies and preferences of the incumbent government are, in theory, largely addressed by the duty of adherence to the charitable instrument, and the fiduciary duties of charity trustees. However, the virtual absence of case law in this area suggests that these legal protections against third party influence are less robust than the co-optative trends. Against this background of government *dominium*, the Charity Commission has demonstrated its commitment to an independent charitable sector, publicizing guidance on government contracts, and warning against the use of government authority trustees. It is unclear to what extent these measures will protect English charities from the strong co-optative pressures that exist in the current economic climate. However, the protections are much greater than in Canada, where the issue of co-optation has gone largely unaddressed and the registered charity provisions suggest that government is entitled to control registered charities that it funds.

The law of charities has always sought to balance the interests of property owners in formulating their own benevolent projects with competing public interests in projects that promote a collective vision of the good. While the law of charities has, by and large, historically achieved this functional equilibrium, the story that has emerged from this book is a story of increasing public law pressures coming to bear on charity law in different jurisdictions, and altering this delicate balance. Canada's tax-based regime of charity regulation evidences a far greater tendency than the Charity Commission regime to treat charitable projects as *both* altruistic and significantly public-welfare-compliant, In both jurisdictions, however, we have witnessed the ascendance of this hybrid legal discipline's public elements, and a corresponding reduction in the autonomy of individuals to pursue benevolent projects in the charitable sphere.

This book has not, by and large, taken a normative position on this shifting equilibrium, other than to suggest that we should guard against 'co-optative' activity that strongly orients charities towards conformity with the incumbent government's agenda, and away from independent agency and dissent. Nevertheless, in casting the emerging social enterprise movement as a quest for alternative hybrid models for benevolent action, I have sought to demonstrate that shifts in the balance between charity law's public and private elements are not without effects. As Lord Beveridge so acutely noted back in 1948, the philanthropic motive is in practice almost always a *specialist* motive. Unless and until our conceptions of private property change, therefore, property-owning individuals (and particularly the very wealthy) are likely to feel that they are entitled to dictate how, to whom, and for what purpose they will give their property away. If the law of charities fails to accord sufficient value to that interest in individual project pursuit, it is likely that benevolent individuals will increasingly turn their energies and resources towards CICs, C3s and other post-charitable forms, which will allow them to 'improve the world' with a greater degree of autonomy.

The strength of these competing pressures is unlikely to decrease over time. The financial crisis of 2007–08, and the austerity climate that it has ushered in, have heightened the concern of governments that charities not be used as mechanisms for the wealthy to avoid the payment of tax. Austerity measures have shrunk the pool of public capital that is available to fund charitable projects, and made it likely that condition-heavy, performance-based contracts will continue to be the chosen instruments for the transfer of public funds to the sector. Tough economic times have also shrunk the public's appetite for charitable projects that are overly idiosyncratic, or do not reflect prevailing public views. As in all times of economic downturn, however, the economic crisis has also increased the reliance of governments on private philanthropy, and increased the desire of governments to direct the energies and resources of charities to pressing social needs. The quest for equilibrium is therefore likely to continue with increased urgency. This book has not sought to resolve this quest. If it has improved our understanding of the doctrinal background against which the discussion takes place, and contributed to the creation of a useful normative discourse about the manner in which charities are regulated under a civil or tax-based regime, it will have accomplished its goals.

INDEX

www.ingramcontent.com/pod-product-compliance
Ingram Content Group UK Ltd.
Pitfield, Milton Keynes, MK11 3LW, UK
UKHW020141290926
15471UKWH00004B/634

9 781509 927968